Praise for
Science Unit Studies for Homescho[...]

You make learning science fun!
-Brianna, homeschooler, age 10-

My two boys absolutely love Sue's unit studies. Their favorite activity has been building molecules out of colored marshmallows and toothpicks. That project really helped them to grasp the concept of atoms and molecules, and gave them a terrific introduction to the Periodic Table. The lesson plans in "Science Unit Studies for Homeschoolers & Teachers" provide step-by-step instruction to parents to guide them simply and easily through each day's science activities. It makes science fun for students and parents.
-Claire Brouwer, homeschooling mother of two boys, ages 9 and 11-

We used "Science Unit Studies for Homeschoolers and Teachers" at home as part of our homeschooling science lessons. The directions were easy to follow and I loved that they used materials that could be purchased from the grocery store. My children, ages 5, 7 and 9 became excited about learning science, actually jumping up and down when it was time to start Science lessons!
-Ilya Perry, homeschooling mother of three with a degree in elementary education-

Excellent age-appropriate activities and effective assessment tools with which to measure authentic learning
-Frank Hustace, Masters in Education, Stanford University and former Headmaster of Waimea Country School-

Sue's science units made learning fun and introduced key scientific concepts that will serve as building blocks for our daughter's ongoing science education.
-Mia King, national bestselling author of *Good Things* and homeschooling mother of three-

The best part is seeing how proud they feel when they really understand what they are learning, and they realize it is fun. This is not just a science curriculum with a bunch of reading and answering questions. "Science Unit Studies for Homeschoolers & Teachers" introduces children to even the more difficult concepts in a way that has their interest and holds their interest all the way through to the next lesson. I definitely recommend this book for any family wanting to nurture the innate love of learning about the world around them.
-Rachel, homeschooling mother of three-

It's obvious Ms. Kilbride's units of study were developed using both her extensive knowledge of the scientific realm, and how children learn best. Her activities are well though out, age-appropriate, and easy to follow. I thoroughly enjoyed our well-guided exploration of weather!
-Christine Hustace, Homeschooling mom and resource teacher for over fifteen years-

"What I liked best about Sue's science class is learning about atoms and molecules, and weather. I enjoyed the experiment we did on cookies--and we got to eat them! What I liked about Sue as a teacher is that she gave us fun tests. I learned a lot and want to take another class from her.
-Maya Gee, homeschooler, age 8-

I'm impressed with the weather lesson. It's very thorough and easy to follow. You do a really good job of writing this down.
-Susan L., homeschooling mother of three and science educator for 33 years-

If you are looking for quality science units, but simply don't have the time to put a unit together, Susan's book is perfect for you. If you want to supplement your existing science program, I definitely recommend taking a close look at the book. Those of you who might be a little scared of trying to put together your own science lessons for fear you might get something wrong, fear no more....
-Jackie from Quaint Scribblers-

....the conversational style and logical, easy-to-follow instructions certainly make this a recommended and useful tool for any parent; especially those that may be uncomfortable or unfamiliar with teaching science. –
-Jeanie Frias of California Homeschooler-

Susan's book is full of so many activities that one would have a very full study of general science over the course of a school year if every activity was completed. I teach a General Science class at a local homeschool co-op and I am implementing a lot of the activities in this book into my class this year. There are even short quizzes (complete with answer keys) provided for the older student unit studies. The quizzes are multiple choice in format and cover the main points students should glean from each unit. I highly recommend this book for any science teacher or student. It really makes the teaching of science quite simple and fun. Overall I give Susan's book 5+ stars.

--Heart of the Matter Online--

Science Unit Studies
for Homeschoolers and Teachers

Susan Kilbride

Funtastic Unit Studies
USA

www.funtasticunitstudies.com

Science Unit Studies for Homeschoolers and Teachers

Copyright © 2010 by Susan Kilbride

ISBN-13: 978-1463549152

ISBN-10: 1463549156

To My Family;
I love you all so very much!

Acknowledgements

I would like to thank the students in my homeschool science class who allowed me to use them as "guinea pigs" for many of the activities in this book: Aidan, Brianna, Dylan, Cougar, Elijah, Eric, Jacob, Kaialuna, Kainalu, Koa, Luke, Makana, Maya, Mckenzie, Morgan, Myla, Naomi, Rowan, Sammy, Sean, Shanti, Tiger, and Zack. I hope you had as much fun in the classes as I had teaching them! I would also like to thank Ilya, Riley, Quinn, Xander, and Lena, who tested some of the lessons at home for me, and Rachel who opened up her home to my science classes. Also, I would like to thank my friend Tina for being my homeschooling buddy for all of these years, and all of my other homeschooling friends whose support and friendship have enriched my homeschooling experience. I never could have done it without you!

A special thanks to my son Dylan, who was my original "guinea pig," and without whom I never would have written this book, and to my wonderful husband Jim whose love and support made this all possible. I would also like to thank my parents for encouraging me to love science and my sister who has always been a great cheerleader for my endeavors.

Susan Kilbride May 2010

Note to the Reader

This book was written by a homeschooling parent for other homeschooling parents. However, it can also easily be used by elementary school teachers since most of the units have been tested in a classroom setting. Homeschoolers vary greatly in ability, so the suggested ages are just listed as a general guideline. The units build upon each other, so it is recommended that you teach them in the same order as the table of contents, though since homeschooling parents are inclined to want to go their own way in teaching, it is not necessary that you do so! Please, however, do not go your own way when it comes to any of the safety precautions mentioned in the book, especially those regarding checking for food allergies. This book was written for homeschooling parents and teachers, not for students to do on their own. Some of the activities, such as those using a stove, should have adult supervision, and some of the activities use small items which could be a choking hazard for young children, so make sure that the younger siblings of your students don't get hold of them (or that your students themselves don't put them in their mouths!)

There is a materials list in the beginning of each chapter. The amounts listed on these materials lists are based on one student, so if you have more than one student, you will need to increase the quantities of some of the items. Check the individual activities within the chapter to determine the amounts you will need for more students. Most of the materials needed for these units are either common household items or are easily obtained from grocery, hardware, drug, discount stores, the local library, or pet stores. However, there is one chapter (Microscopes and Invisible Creatures) that requires the use of a microscope for some of the activities. A number of the activities in that chapter can be completed without a microscope, but if you can find access to one, the experience will be much more fun for your students.

"Fun" is the key word here, the goal in writing this book was to give homeschooling parents and teachers some ideas for how to teach science in a way that will capture students' interest, and open their eyes to the fun in the world of science.

Table of Contents

Chapter 1: Our Senses
Ages 4-7

<u>Materials Needed for this Unit</u>

One large-sized potato for each student
Toothpicks
Various vegetables
The story "Goldilocks and the Three Bears"
Two jars the same size with lids
Salt
Sugar
Small cups
Various food samples
Lemon juice
Tonic water
Chicken nuggets
Sweet and sour sauce
Two inch square piece of corrugated cardboard
Three pins with small heads
White construction paper
Stapler or brass fasteners
Ice
Three bowls
Tape recorder
Empty prescription bottles
Small items to put in prescription bottles
Colored construction paper
An empty oatmeal container (cylinder-shaped)
Crayons or markers
A twelve inch or larger diameter balloon
Rubber band
Rice
Packing bubbles
Eight empty soda-type bottles
Food coloring
Cinnamon
Various liquids or spices with different scents
Samples of items with various textures such as sandpaper, fabrics, etc...
A large brown grocery bag
Various small objects that will fit in the above grocery bag
A large piece of chocolate with a gooey center

Fine-grade sandpaper
One Cinnamon stick
Cotton balls
Vanilla extract
Drawing paper
Scissors
Perfume
Strawberry extract
Almond extract
Baby food jars
Tape
Peppermint extract
Ginger
Spoon
Some type of music player
Masking tape
Hammer and nail
Crayons
Glue
Blindfold

Part 1: Introduction

Before doing some of the activities in this unit, make sure that your students don't have any food allergies!

Tell your students that you are going to say some sentences and that you when you stop, you want them to guess what the next word is. Then say the following:

"I see with my_____(point to your eyes)."
"I hear with my_____(point to your ears)."
"I touch with my_____(point to your fingers)."
"I smell with my_____(point to your nose)."
"I taste with my_____(point to your mouth)."

Now tell your students that we call all of these things; seeing, hearing, touching, smelling, and tasting our *senses*, and that we have five of them. Our senses tell us about the world around us.

Activity:
Give each of your students a good-sized potato and some toothpicks. Provide a selection of vegetables that they can use for the eyes, ears, nose, mouth, and hands. Using toothpicks that have been cut in half, have them attach the vegetables to their potato to give it a vegetable face. For example, cut a piece of red pepper for the mouth, a cherry tomato for a nose, etc.... Let the children choose what vegetables they'd like to use for each part of the face. Remind them as they do this activity what the five senses are (for example as they put the eyes on the potato, remind them that eyes are for seeing, etc...).

Activity:
*Read your students "Goldilocks and the Three Bears," and have your students call out when one of the five senses is used. Goldilocks **tastes** the food, **touches** the chairs, the bears **see** Goldilocks and they **hear** her scream when she **sees** them, etc...*

Part 2: Taste

Activity:
Show your students two closed glass jars, one with sugar in it and one with salt in it. Have them use their five senses to describe what is in the jars, starting with what they look like, what they sound like (leave the lids on the jars and shake them), what they smell like, what they feel like, and what they taste like. Be sure and do taste last since that will give them the answer. Point out to your students that while we rely on our eyes to tell us things a lot of the time, in this case it was taste that finally told us for sure what was in the jars.

Activity:

Tell your students that there are five types of tastes; sweet, salty, bitter, sour, and savory (also called unami). They just tasted salty and sweet in the last experiment. Now have them take little tastes of something bitter and sour (for example, tonic water for bitter and lemon juice for sour). Tell them that savory relates to the taste of meats and cheeses.

Activity:

Put a sample of foods in small cups and have your students taste them and say whether the food tastes sweet, salty, bitter, or sour. You could use things like strawberries, pickles, pretzels, etc...

Activity:

Tell your students that we all have taste buds on our tongues that we taste our food with. Stick out your tongues and look for the little bumps on them. These bumps are called papillae and many of them contain taste buds that help us taste our food.

Activity:

Make some chicken nuggets, or something similar, and give your students sweet and sour sauce to dip them in. Point out to them that this sauce tastes both sweet and sour!

Part 3: Touch

Tell your students that our sense of touch comes from our skin; not just the skin on our fingers, but on all of our skin. Some parts of our skin are more sensitive than others, so those parts of our skin can sense what it's touching better.

Activity:

Before you start this activity, take a piece of corrugated cardboard that is about 2 inches square and poke three pins with small heads into it in a triangle shape. It is important that all three pins are at the same height. The pins should be no more than ¾ of an inch apart from each other. Do not let your students see how many pins are on the cardboard.

Blindfold a student and have him or her hold out an arm, palm up. Gently touch the heads of the pins to the arm and ask the student how many pins can he or she feel. Start on the upper arm, farthest away from the hand, and keep testing, gradually moving closer to the hand. The part of the arm farthest from the hand is the least sensitive, so it is likely that he or she won't be able to feel all three pin heads in that area. As you move closer to the hand, the student should eventually be able to feel all three pins.

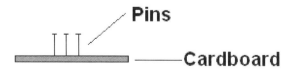

Activity:

Have your students make a "Sense of Touch Book." Take some pieces of white construction paper and cut them in quarters. Decide how many pages you want the book to be, and using staples or brass fasteners, bind them in a book form. Write "My Sense of Touch Book" on the front page. If your students can write, have them write this themselves. On the bottom of the next pages write the following types of words, one to each page: Rough, Smooth, Bumpy, Silky, Slippery, Soft, or whatever other words you can think of. Provide a number of items that your students can glue to the pages, such as sandpaper, felt, fake fur, silk, the corrugated part of cardboard, or netting. Make sure they match the texture of the item with the word on the page.

Activity:

Take either a large brown grocery bag, and fill it with various items of different textures and shapes. Have your students reach a hand into the bag without looking inside and describe the first thing they touch. Have them guess what it is. Then let them pull it out of the bag and see if they guessed correctly! Remind them that they used their sense of touch to figure out what was in the bag.

Tell your students that our sense of touch tells us more things than just how rough or smooth something is; it can also tell us how hard we are gripping something. Hold up a large piece of chocolate with a gooey center between two fingers (a chocolate egg with a filling would be perfect) and say that your sense of touch is telling you how hard you are holding on to the chocolate. Then say something like "Let's pretend that I don't have a sense of touch, and I can't tell how hard I'm holding this chocolate. I might end up holding it too hard… (increase your hold on the chocolate and squish it so the gooey center comes out) and squish it!"

Activity:

Tell your students that another important thing that our sense of touch tells us is whether things are hot or cold.

Take three bowls and fill one with water and ice, one with hot water (not too hot, a child will be putting his or her finger in it!) and one with lukewarm water. Line the bowls up so that the lukewarm bowl is in the middle. Have your students put one finger in the hot bowl and one finger in the cold bowl for one minute. After one minute is up, have them put both fingers in the bowl of lukewarm water. One finger will be tricked into feeling that the lukewarm water is hot and the other will be tricked into feeling that it is cold, even though the water is just lukewarm! This is because our sense of touch tells us if things are hot or cold by comparing them to how hot or cold the skin is already. The skin on the finger that was in the hot water felt hot, so when that finger was put in lukewarm water, it felt that the water was cold. The skin on the finger that was in the cold water felt cold, so when that finger was put in the lukewarm water; it felt that the water was hot.

If you have more than one student, you can do a variation of this experiment where one child has a finger in the hot water, and one child has a finger in the cold water and when they both put their fingers in the lukewarm water, one will say it feels hot and the other will say it feels cold!

Activity:

    Read the story below to your students. It is a version of "The Parable of the Blind Men and the Elephant," a tale from India. At the end of the story, ask them which of the men was correct about what an elephant was like (they all were partly right). Point out how in this case the sense of touch didn't give the three men enough information to really see what an elephant was like, and that sometimes we need information from more of our senses before we can decide about something.

The Story of the Blind Men and the Elephant

    Once upon a time there were three blind men *(at this point make sure your students know what the word "blind" means)*. One day they were sitting in front of a house talking when a man leading an elephant walked by. One of the blind men called out "what is that large tromping noise that I hear?" The man leading the elephant answered "It is an elephant that I am leading to the market." The three blind men did not know what an elephant was, so they asked the man if they could touch the elephant to see what it was like, and the elephant man agreed.

    The first blind man went up to the elephant and touched its tail. He said "An elephant is like a piece of rope, long and skinny."

    The second blind man went up to the elephant and touched the side of its body. He said "No it is not; an elephant is big and broad like a house."

    The third blind man went up to the elephant and touched its ear. He said, "You are both wrong, an elephant is flat and thin, like a pancake."

    The three men started arguing with each other about what an elephant was like until they all stomped home in disgust, each sure that the others didn't know what they were talking about!

Part 4: Sight

    Remind your students that we use our eyes to see. Have them look at their eyes in a mirror (or look at someone else's eyes) and see if they can find the parts of an eye shown below.

Parts of the Eye

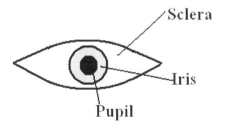

    Tell them that the *pupil* is actually a hole that lets light into your eye and the *iris* is a ring of muscles that opens and closes the pupil.

Activity:

Remind your students about the story of the three blind men and the elephant and ask them what they think it would be like to not be able to see anything. Have them put a blindfold on and see what it is like. Play a game of blind man's bluff, where one child is blindfolded and the rest of the children (or even just you!) stand in one spot while the blindfolded child tries to find them.

Activity:

Play a game of "I Spy." Look around the room, find an object, and say "I spy something green." Have your students guess what it is you found. Whoever guesses correctly is the person who does the spying next. Remind your students that they are using their sense of sight to find things in this game.

Part 5: Sound

Tell your students that inside their ears is a tiny structure called an **eardrum** that works a lot like a drum that you make music with. This little drum senses the vibrations (movements) in the air that make sound and sends signals to the brain about them. The brain decodes the signals to tell you what the sound is.

Activity:

Take a cylinder-shaped oatmeal container and tape construction paper around it. Have your students color designs on the construction paper. Next take a 12-inch round balloon and blow it up as far as you can, then let the air out (it is important to blow it up first to stretch it out a little). Using a pair of scissors, cut the neck end of the balloon off at the point right before the balloon starts to get widest and discard the neck end. Stretch the rest of the balloon over the top of the oatmeal container and secure it tightly with a rubber band. You have now made a drum! Now take a few grains of rice and scatter them over the top of the drum. Have your students tap on the drum and watch the rice bounce as it vibrates. Tell them that an eardrum vibrates like this drum does and that those vibrations are what the brain decodes to figure out what sound a person is hearing.

Activity:

Before the class, take a tape recorder and record various sounds, both outside and in. Play each sound to your students and have them try and guess what the sound is. Remind them that they are using their ears to hear the sounds.

Activity:

Ask your local pharmacy for some empty prescription bottles. Before the class, cover each bottle with construction paper so that you cannot see what is inside it. Put various items in each bottle, such as coins, rice, paperclips, etc… Pass them out to your students and have them shake the bottles and try and guess what is in each bottle by the shaking sound.

Activity:

    Ask your students if they can guess why we have two ears (to help us figure out what direction a sound is coming from). Blindfold your students and have them cover one ear so that they can't hear out of it. Walk around them (not too close) and make a quiet clap. Have them point in the direction that the clap is coming from. Do this from different parts of the room. You will find that they will often point in the wrong direction. Next, have them uncover their ear and try the experiment with both ears open. Now they will point correctly every time! This is because we need both ears to help us tell what direction a sound is coming from.

Activity:

    Take a sound walk. Go for a walk outside and see how many different sounds you can hear!

Activity:

    Take eight glass soda-type bottles of the same size (you can also use jars or drinking glasses, but they all need to be identical), and fill them with different amounts of water. Add food coloring to each bottle so that you can see the water easily. Take a spoon and gently tap each bottle to make a sound. Point out to your students that the bottles with more water in them have a lower-pitched sound than the bottles with less water.

Activity:

    Get a bunch of packing bubbles and put them all over the floor. Put on some music and have your students stomp on the packing bubbles and listen to them burst. See if they can do it to the beat of the music.

Part 6: Smell

Activity:

    Before you start this activity, take six baby food jars and, using a hammer and nail, punch holes in the tops. Put masking tape on the outside of each jar and label one "Cinnamon," one "Ginger," one "Peppermint," one "Strawberry," one "Vanilla," and one "Almond." Place two cotton balls inside each jar and sprinkle some cinnamon in the jar labeled "Cinnamon" and close the lid. Sprinkle some ginger in the jar labeled "Ginger," put drops of peppermint extract in the one labeled "Peppermint," and close their lids also. Do the same thing with the strawberry, vanilla, and almond extracts. Now sit down with your students and tell them the story on the following page. As you mention each of the smells, pass the corresponding jar around so that they can sniff the smell you are talking about (be sure to tell them to keep the lids on the jars!)

The Cookie People

One day I was walking down the road when I smelled a wonderful smell *(pass out the cinnamon jar)*. Where was it coming from? I followed my nose to the source until I saw something that made me blink. What was it? It looked like a walking, talking cookie, shaped like a little man! I asked "Who are you?" and he replied "I'm the Cinnamon Man." I stared in astonishment. It was like a seeing a storybook character come to life.

"Where did you come from?" I asked.

"I don't know," he replied, "The first thing I remember is a boy picking me up, and his mouth was open. He was about to take a huge bite out of me! I screamed and that scared him so much that he dropped me, and I ran away."

"How awful" I said. Then I asked "Have you ever heard of the Gingerbread Man?"

"Of course; he lives next door to me. Would you like to meet him?"

The Cinnamon Man took me to visit his neighbor the Gingerbread Man. As we came up to the Gingerbread Man's house, I started smelling a different smell; it was the smell of ginger *(pass out the ginger jar)*.

When I was introduced to the Gingerbread Man I said, "I am so pleased to meet you, I've read the story about you, but I had no idea it was real!"

The Gingerbread Man said "Of course I'm real, and so are the Peppermint Man *(pass out the peppermint jar)*, and the Strawberry Woman *(pass the strawberry jar)*, Vanilla Man *(pass out the vanilla jar)* and Almond Boy *(pass out the almond jar)*."

I spent the rest of the afternoon meeting the cookie people. We all became very good friends.

Activity:

Give each of your students a piece of fine-grade sandpaper and have them draw a cookie man or woman shape on it. You might want to have one drawn beforehand so that they have some idea of the shape they need to draw. Have them cut out their cookie person and give them a cinnamon stick to rub on it. This will make the project smell like cinnamon. They can also use crayons to draw in a face or other features.

Activity:

Before this activity starts, take some baby food jars and using a hammer and nail, punch holes in the lids. Put two cotton balls in each jar and put liquids or spices with different scents in each jar. For example you could use lemon juice, vinegar, pickle juice, basil, etc... Do not tell your students what is in each jar. Then let them smell the jars and guess what is in them. You might want to put paper around the outsides of some of the jars to hide the contents. Remind your students not to open the lids!

Activity:

Have your students draw a picture of some flowers. Tell them that the flowers need to be bigger than a cotton ball, because each flower will have a cotton ball in its center. When they have finished their pictures, glue a cotton ball to the center of each of their flowers. Give the flowers scents using the various extracts from the previous activities by placing a few drops of extract on the cotton balls. You can also use perfume if you would like.

Part 7: Review of the Senses

Activity:

    Below is a story which needs some blanks filled in. Before reading the story to your students, tell them that you need help finding some words for a story. Below each blank in the story is a description of the type of word that you need to fill in the blank. Without telling your students what the story is about, ask them for words to put in the blanks. For example, if the blank needs a smell, ask them for a word that describes a smell and fill it in the blank. When the story is complete, read it to them to see what they've helped create.

    One morning Amy woke up and saw a _____ . She screamed in surprise and ran out
                         (something you see)

of her room. Her mother came running over and said "Are you o.k.? I thought I heard a _____."
                                                              (a sound)

Amy said "Mom there's a _____in my room!" They both ran back into Amy's room, but
                    (repeat first blank)

there was nothing there. However, now there was a strong smell in her room of _____ .
                                                           (a smell)

    "Phew, what's that smell?" Amy's mother asked as she went to open a window. "I don't

know," said Amy, "but come check out my chair, it feels _____ ." Amy's mother felt the
                                             (a touch word)

chair and said, "You're right, why don't you clean that off and then come down for breakfast; I've

made your favorite, French toast."

    After cleaning the chair, Amy hurried downstairs and sat down at the table. "Boy this looks

_____ ," she said. She opened her mouth and took a big bite. "Yuck," she cried, "This tastes like
(a sight word)

_____ !" Her mother stared at her. "What are you talking about; it tastes perfectly fine, I've
(a taste word)

had some myself."

    Amy said "Well, I'm not eating it; I'll just have an orange." As she started peeling the orange,

Amy asked, "Mom, where did you get this orange, its skin feels_____ ." Her mother said "I
                                                           (a touch word)

just don't know what's gotten into you today; there is nothing wrong with that orange!

    As Amy stared at the orange, it turned into a _____ . She said "Oh how cute!" and
                                      (something you see)

gave the _____ a hug.
        (repeat previous line)

    Suddenly, Amy found herself back in bed. It had all been a silly dream!

Chapter 2: The Human Body
Ages 4-7

Materials Needed for this Unit

Ice
Funnel
Food coloring
One quart re-closable plastic bag
Apple cider vinegar
Soda crackers
Measuring tape
Markers or crayons
Pink or purple construction paper
Blue construction paper
Red construction paper
Clear tape
Small balloon
Drinking straw
Small rubber band
Rubber band
Modeling clay
Drinking glass
Brass fasteners
Hole punch
Scissors
Tray
Cotton balls
Twenty small objects for a memory game
Pencil and paper
Modeling clay
Access to a copy machine
White copy paper, cardstock, or construction paper
A plastic bottle that is at least 1.4 liters that you can see through and is made of stiff plastic. A plastic soda bottle would be a good choice, except that most soda bottles these days are not made of stiff enough plastic.
Sturdy clear plastic bag (one quart or one gallon-size)
A twenty-two foot long, 1-1 ½ inch diameter rope
A very large piece of newsprint or butcher paper
A balloon that is at least twelve inches in diameter when blown up
Recommended Magic School Bus movies, published by Scholastic, are listed at the end of this unit in Part 6.

Rubber band
Plain white paper
Blue marker or crayon
Red marker or crayon

Part 1: The Digestive System

Tell your students that the parts of their body that deal with the food they eat are called the **digestive system.** Ask them what is the first thing that they do when they eat (put their food in their mouth and chew it). The mouth is the first part of our digestive system. We use the teeth in our mouth to chew our food into small pieces and the saliva in our mouth helps break the food down even more. After the food leaves our mouths, it travels down a long tube called the **esophagus.**

Activity:

Give your students a glass of ice-water and have them take a <u>small</u> swallow. Tell them to pay attention to how the water feels going down their throat. Can they feel it go down their esophagus?

Next, tell your students that after the food goes in their mouths and down their esophagus, it goes into their stomachs.

Activity:

Take a funnel and attach a sturdy clear plastic bag to it with a rubber band. Tell your students that the mouth of the funnel is like their mouth (you can even tape some paper "teeth" around the edges if you like), the neck of the funnel is like their esophagus, and the plastic bag is like their stomach. Take some water and add some food-coloring to it. Pour the colored water into the funnel and tell your students that you are pouring the water into the mouth and show them how it goes down the esophagus, and into the stomach.

Now tell your students that inside the stomach, the food gets mixed with different liquids that break the food up into even smaller pieces.

Activity:

Take a quart-sized, re-closable bag and put some broken up soda crackers in it. Pour in some water and apple cider vinegar and close the bag. Tell your students that the soda crackers are like the food they eat and that the liquid you poured in is like the stomach liquids that break the food down. Mix the crackers around in the bag a bit to break them up more.

Tell your students that after the food leaves the stomach, it goes into something called the **small intestine**. The small intestine is anything but small; it is a long, soft tube that in adults is about twenty-two feet long. In the small intestine, the food is broken down even further, until it is so small that it can go through the walls of the small intestine and into the blood which takes it to the parts of the body that need it.

Activity:

Take a twenty-two foot long piece of rope that is 1 to 1 ½ inches in diameter and stretch it out for your students to see. Tell them that this is about the size of the small intestine of an adult. How do they think this fits in an adult's body? Show them that when the rope is all looped up, it can fit into a smaller size.

Now tell your students that some of the things that we eat can't be used by our body. After the parts of the food that we use are moved out of the small intestine, the rest of the food, what we call "waste," (or "poop"), goes into the large intestine. It is called the large intestine because it is wider than the small intestine, not because it is longer. As the waste moves through the large intestine, the remaining water is taken out of it. The waste leaves the large intestine and our bodies through a hole called the anus.

Activity:

Make a pretend digestive system that your students can crawl through. Have the opening be the mouth, which you can surround with paper "teeth." The mouth should lead into a tunnel that represents the esophagus. You can make the tunnel with chairs covered with blankets, or perhaps with boxes. The esophagus should lead into a larger covered area that is the stomach which should have another tunnel that they leave the stomach through to represent the small intestine (you could even have this tunnel wind around a little to represent how the small intestine winds through the body). Have this tunnel open into a slightly wider tunnel for the large intestine which opens back out into the room. As your students go through each part of the digestive system, have them call out the name of each section.* Have them go through it more than once, until they have memorized the parts of the digestive system.

Activity:

Give each student a piece of newsprint or butcher paper and trace their body on it. Have them draw a picture of their digestive system inside the outline of their body. Save the drawing for the next activity.

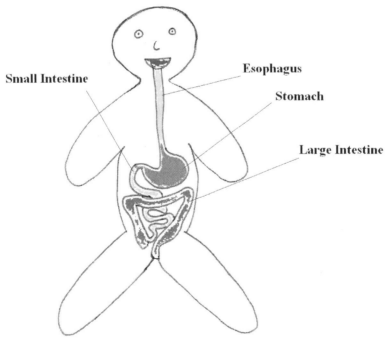

**Author's note:* I will never forget my 4 year-old son coming out of the end of our crawl-through digestive system excitedly calling out "and now I'm poop!" He wanted to go through it again and again.

Part 2: The Respiratory System

Ask your students if they can think of something else that goes in their mouths besides food (air or oxygen). Tell them that when they breathe in air, it does not go down their esophagus, like their food does. There is another tube called the windpipe, or **trachea** that the air they breathe goes down. The trachea is located in the neck like the esophagus, but it lies on top of the esophagus. When the trachea reaches the chest, it splits into two separate tubes called **bronchi** *(singular is bronchus).* The bronchi lead into the lungs, one on each side of the chest. The lungs take in oxygen from the air and pass it on to the parts of the body that need it.

Activity:

Have your students take some pink or purple construction paper and draw two lungs that will fit on the drawing they made of their digestive system in the previous activity. Cut the lungs out and set them aside. Now take some blue construction paper and have them draw a trachea and two bronchi to go with the lungs (have them do this in one piece, so that the trachea and bronchi are connected). Cut them out also. Tape the trachea and bronchi in place on the digestive system drawing by taping it down only at the top of the trachea with a tape "hinge" so that you can lift it up and look underneath at the esophagus. Next, tape the two lungs in place, again making a hinge of tape on only one side of each lung, so that they can be lifted open. Save the drawing for the next activity.

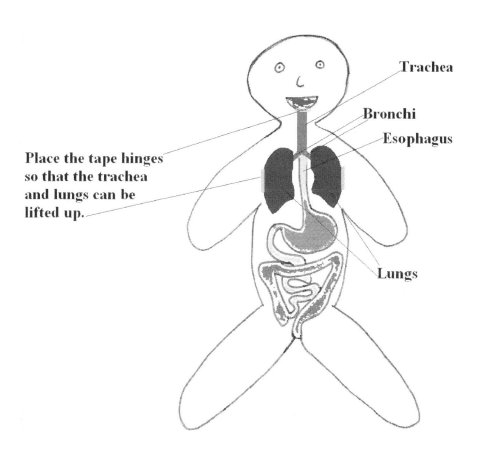

Trachea

Bronchi

Esophagus

Place the tape hinges so that the trachea and lungs can be lifted up.

Lungs

Tell your students that the place where the lungs are located is called the **chest cavity.** When they breathe, the chest cavity gets larger and that draws air into the lungs.

Activity:

You will need to set this experiment up ahead of time. First, find a 1.4 - 2 liter plastic bottle that you can see through and that is made of stiff plastic. A plastic soda bottle would be the perfect size, but most of them these days aren't made of stiff enough plastic. Unscrew the bottle top and cut off the bottom of the bottle. Next, take a straw and, using a small rubber band, attach a balloon to one end of it. Push the straw through the neck of the bottle so that the balloon is inside of the bottle and hold the straw in place with modeling clay. Make sure that you have made a good seal with the modeling clay so that no air can escape through the neck of the bottle, except through the straw.

Now, take a twelve-inch diameter (or more) balloon, blow it up, deflate it, and then cut the end off that is <u>opposite</u> to the neck (it is important to blow it up first to stretch the rubber). Tie the neck of the balloon shut with a knot. Stretch the open end of the balloon over the open end of the bottle and secure it with a rubber band. You are now ready to show your students your model of how a lung works!

Tell your students that underneath the lungs is a muscle called the diaphragm. When the diaphragm moves up, it decreases the space in the chest cavity, and when it moves down, it increases the chest cavity space. Show them the balloon at the bottom of the bottle and tell them that it is like the diaphragm in their bodies and that the balloon on the straw is like one of their lungs. The space in the bottle itself is like their chest cavity. Push up on the balloon on the bottom or "diaphragm" and show them that pushing up on the diaphragm makes the chest cavity smaller, and that as this happens, the "lung" also gets smaller. Using the tied neck of the balloon-diaphragm, pull down on it and show them that the chest cavity gets larger when you do this and that the "lung" in the bottle also gets larger. The diaphragm is one of the things that make the chest cavity larger when they breathe.

Contract the chest cavity by pushing up on the diaphragm:

Expand the chest cavity by pulling down on the diaphragm:

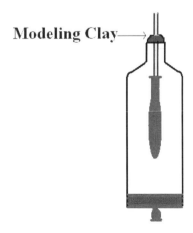

Modeling Clay——→

Activity:

Have your students go back to their large picture and draw in the diaphragm. It should go under the lungs and above the stomach. Save the picture for the next section.

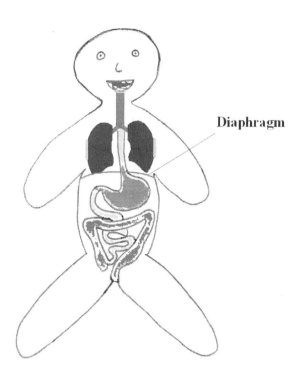

Diaphragm

Part 3: Circulatory System

Tell your students that the circulatory system is the transportation system of the body. It moves all kinds of things around the body like oxygen, nutrients, waste products, etc... One of the most important parts of the circulatory system is the heart. The heart is a big pump that pushes the blood around the body.

Activity:

Have your students take a drinking glass and listen to someone's heart with it by placing the open end over the heart and the closed end up to their ear. Tell them that the noise they hear is the heart pumping blood. If for some reason, their glass doesn't transmit the sound, they can also do this with a funnel by placing the wide end over the heart and the narrow end up to, <u>but not inside</u>, their ear (tell them that they should never put things in their ears).

Activity:

Have your students take their large human body drawing and lift up the lungs and trachea. Next, have them cut and draw a red heart out of construction paper and using a hinge-tape (so they can lift up the heart and see the esophagus if they want), tape the heart in the middle of the area where the lungs go, so that the lungs will fold back down and cover most of it. Now, have them take blue and red crayons or markers and draw in the veins and arteries. Have them use blue for the arteries and red for the veins. Tell them that the arteries take the blood away from the heart (they can remember this because arteries starts with "a" like "away") and the veins take the blood back to the heart. Fold the parts of the respiratory system back down when they are finished.

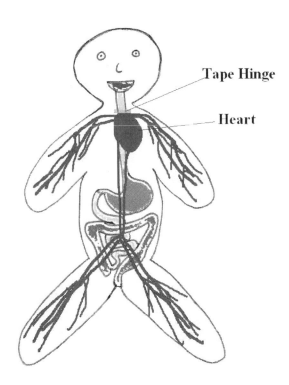

Tape Hinge

Heart

Part 4: Skeletal System

Ask your students what holds up our bodies (our bones or skeletons). Tell them to think about what our bodies would be like without skeletons--all floppy and uncoordinated (you can show them visually by flopping your arm or body around). Another important thing that bones do for us is to make our blood cells. Inside our bones is something called bone marrow, which is where our blood is made.

Activity:

On the following page is a skeleton for your students to cut out and put together with brass fasteners. If you can, copy it onto card stock or construction paper to make it stronger, but you can also just make it out of plain white paper. Use a hole-punch to make holes where the black circles are marked, and hook the various pieces together with brass fasteners, so the joints can move. After the students have made their skeletons, recite the following version of "Dem Bones" to them as you point the parts of the skeleton out. Save the skeleton for the next activity.

Dem Bones

The foot bone's connected to the Tibia
The Tibia's connected to the knee bone
The knee bone's connected to the Femur
The Femur's connected to the hip bone
The hip bone's connected to the spine bone
The spine bone's connected to the rib bones
The rib bone's connected to the collar bone
The collar bone's connected to the neck bones
The neck bone's connected to the head bone
And the head bone sits on top!

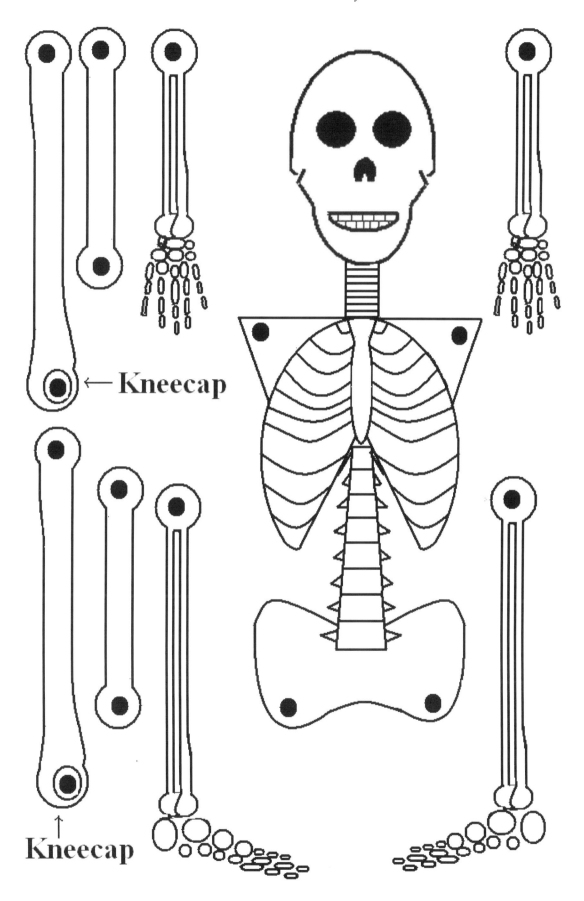

← **Kneecap**

↑
Kneecap

Part 5: Nervous System

Tell your students that there is one part of our body that controls the rest. Do they know what it is? (the brain). The brain is the control center of our bodies. It takes in all of the information from our senses and tells our bodies how to react to this information. The brain is part of something called the nervous system. The main parts of the nervous system are the brain, the spinal cord, and the nerves. The brain is located in our heads, the spinal cord is located inside the vertebrae (show them the vertebrae in the skeleton from the previous project), and the nerves branch out from our spinal cord to the rest of our body. When we touch a hot pan, it is our nerves that transmit the information to the brain to let us know we've touched something hot. Without our nervous system, we would burn ourselves when we touched a hot pan because we would have no way of knowing that it was hot.

Activity:

Tell your students that our brains are also responsible for our memories. Everything we have ever done is recorded inside our brains. Take a tray and place about twenty small objects on it. Have your students look at the tray for one minute and then either cover it or take it away. Give them a pencil and paper and have them write down as many objects as they can think of that were on the tray (or they can tell you the names of the objects and have you write them down). Try it again a second time and see how many more objects they remember after seeing them twice.

Activity:

Tell your students that our reflexes allow us to act quickly without thinking about something. Have one person stand behind a glass window or door, with their face right up to the glass (don't tell them what you are about to do). Have another person throw a cotton ball (be sure to only use a cotton ball, you don't want to break the window) at their face. Did the person behind the window blink? Try it again and see if they can keep from blinking if they try really hard. When something comes quickly at our face, we blink to protect our eyes. That is our reflexes in action. If we had to think about it and tell ourselves to blink, it would take too long and our eyes could get damaged. Our reflexes are controlled by our nervous system.

Part 6: Recommended Movies

The "Magic School Bus" series has movies on the digestive system and the circulatory system. You can usually get them at your local or school library. They are listed below:

* *The Magic School Bus For Lunch*
* *The Magic School Bus Inside Ralphie*

*The DVD *The Magic School Bus: Human Body* contains both of these and another one called *The Magic School Bus Flexes Its Muscles*.

Chapter 3: Dinosaurs and Prehistoric Life
Ages 4-7

<u>Materials Needed for this Unit</u>

Books from the library with pictures of dinosaurs. Try to find ones that have pictures of the following dinosaurs: Supersaurus, Tyrannosaurus rex, and Stegosaurus. You could also try the internet.

Books from the library that have pictures of Saber-toothed cats and Indricotherium (also called Paraceratherium). One book that has both in it is National Geographic's "Prehistoric Mammals" by Alan Turner.

Tape measure
String or yarn
Masking tape
Copy paper and access to a copying machine
Butcher paper
Two colors of index cards
A variety of small plastic dinosaurs
White glue
Sandbox or dirt pile
Newspaper or newsprint
Paint and brushes
Disposable bowl
Clay that dries
Plaster of Paris
Cooking oil spray or cooking oil
Round stones that are about ½ to 1 inch wide
Styrofoam meat tray
Safety goggles
Small hammer
Paint brush
Plastic knife
Three different colored dog treats shaped like bones
Dirt or sand
Sour cream
Various herbs and spices
Misc. vegetables
Cheese grater
A cheap dinosaur skeleton that comes in pieces, made of wood or plastic
Recommended movie, published by Scholastic: *The Magic School Bus: The Busasaurus*
A Webster's Dictionary that has at least eight hundred and forty-three pages in it

Apple
Bagel
Cream cheese
Carrot
Broccoli
Drawing paper
Crayons or markers
Paint brushes
Magnifying glass
Bar soap
Mirror

Part 1: Dinosaurs

Ask your students if they know what a **dinosaur** is (a large lizard-like creature that lived over 65 million years ago). Younger children might not understand how long ago 65 million years was, so you can just tell them dinosaurs lived a long time ago, long before humans lived on the earth. Tell them that the word "dinosaur" means "terrible lizard." Why do they think scientists called dinosaurs "terrible?"

Activity:

Take some bar soap and grate it with a cheese grater. Mix it with water to make a dough-like substance. Give your students a plastic dinosaur and some of the soap dough and have them form the soap around the dinosaur to make a "dinosaur egg." To hatch the dinosaur from the egg, they need to wash their hands a lot!

Activity:

Before you start this activity, take two colors of index cards and write the prefixes below on the cards of one color and the suffixes on the cards of the other color. Write the definition of the prefix or suffix underneath each one.

Prefixes	Suffixes
Tri (three)	dactyl (finger, toe)
Aqua (water)	saurus (lizard)
Compo (pretty)	raptor (thief)
Crypto (hidden)	rex (king)
Pseudo (false)	odon (tooth)
Velocis (swift, fast)	ichthys (fish)
Paleo (old)	derma (skin)
Iso (equal)	gnathus (jaw)
Dino (terrible)	derm (skin)
Multi (many)	cephalic (head)
Micro (small)	pteryx (wing)
Hetero (different)	mimus (imitator)
Coelo (hollow)	spinax (spine, thorn)
Cerato (horn)	morph (shape)
Sapro (rotten)	

*Show the cards to your students and explain that dinosaur names are often made up of two parts, the **prefix**, or the beginning part, and the **suffix**, or the ending part. Remind them that the word "Dinosaur" means "Terrible Lizard," and show them the prefix card for "Dino" (which means terrible) and the suffix card for "saurus" (which means lizard), and how they go together to make the word "Dinosaur." Now take all of the cards and place them face-down on the floor or a table in two piles, one pile of prefixes and one pile of suffixes. Have your students randomly chose one prefix card and one suffix card. Put them together to see what type of dinosaur they have named. After you have done this for awhile, have them chose their favorite dinosaur from the ones they just created and draw what they think it would look like.*

Activity:

Tell your students that a "Supersaurus" was a type of dinosaur that was about 138 feet long. Show them a picture of a Supersaurus from a library book or the internet. Take a tape measure and go outside. Measure off 138 feet to get a feel for just how long a Supersaurus was.

Activity:

Take some butcher paper, or some other large type of paper and have each of your students lay down on it. Draw a very rough outline of each of your students on the paper, without the arms and legs defined. Next have your students turn their outline into a dinosaur by adding teeth, arms, legs, and a tail. Name their dinosaurs after them, such as a "Sammyasaurus."

Activity:

Show your students a picture of a Stegosaurus and tell them that they are going to make a Stegosaurus that they can eat. Take a bagel and cut it in half so that you have two half-circles. Open up one of the half-circles and spread it with cream cheese. Take an apple and slice it in thin sections to look like the plates that go across a Stegosaurus's back. Place the plates on top of the bagel you just spread with cream cheese. Now take a carrot and cut it so that it is shaped like the Stegosaurus's tail and put it in place. Cut another piece of carrot for the neck and head. Close the bagel with the other half and enjoy!

Bagel Stegosaurus

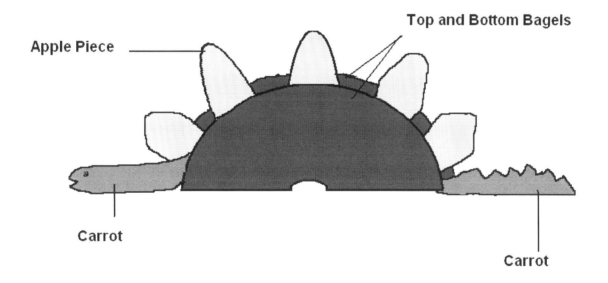

Part 2: Herbivores and Carnivores

Activity:

Take some small plastic dinosaurs and have your students sort them using different categories, such as by color, or by shape. Next tell them that people who study animals have special ways that they sort animals, and that one of these ways is by what they eat. Animals that eat meat are called **carnivores** and animals that eat plants are called **herbivores**. Show your students a picture of a Tyrannosaurus rex, which was a carnivore and then show them a picture of a Supersaurus, which was an herbivore. Point out the differences between the two dinosaurs. If a dinosaur was shaped like Tyrannosaurus rex, it was probably a carnivore and if it was shaped like Supersaurus, it was probably an herbivore. Have them sort their plastic dinosaurs into "herbivores" and "carnivores."

Activity:

Tell your students that carnivores have sharp, pointy teeth that are good for biting prey while herbivores have flat teeth, like our back molars, good for chewing plants. Have them look at their molars in a mirror to see what chewing teeth look like (only do this if you are sure your dog or cat won't bite you). If you have a dog or cat, look at their teeth to see what a carnivore's teeth look like. If you have a chance, look at the teeth of other animals, such as a horse or cow.

Activity:

Before you start this activity, copy the template on the following page ten times to make forty Tyrannosaurus rex teeth (you can make more or less if you want). Cut out the teeth and hide them around your house. Show your students one of the paper teeth and ask them if they think this is a tooth from a carnivore or an herbivore (carnivore). Show them a picture from a library book of a Tyrannosaurus rex, or "T-Rex" and tell them that this is what a T-Rex's teeth look like. Tell them that the T-Rex could open its mouth about four feet high!

Now cut a piece of string or yarn eleven feet long. Form it into an oval on the ground about four feet tall, taping it down with masking tape. Tell your students that this is a T-Rex's mouth, but it has lost its teeth. Now tell them that they are going to be like **paleontologists** (scientists who study dinosaurs) and go search for the teeth. As your students find the teeth, tape them into the T-Rex's mouth. When you are finished, see how many of you can fit inside the T-Rex's mouth!

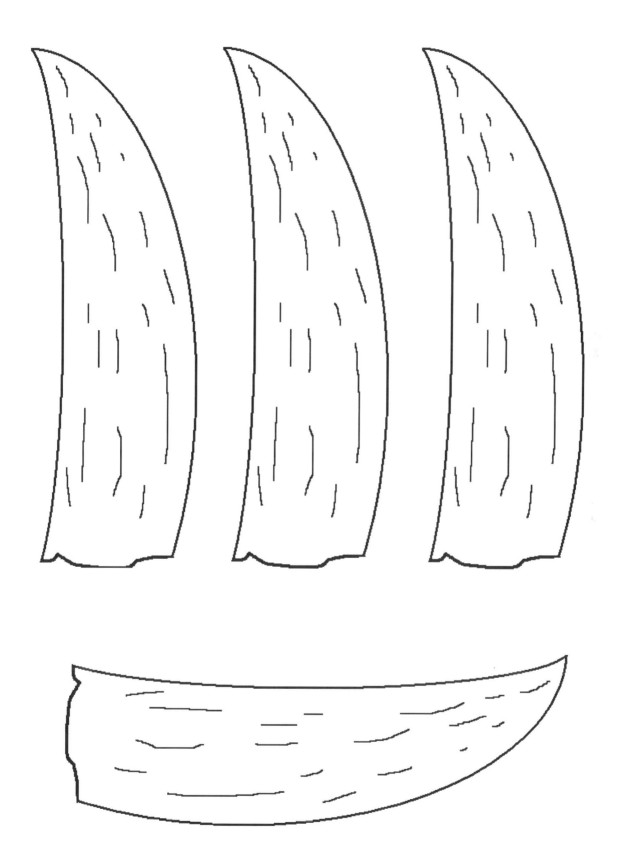

Part 3: Fossils

Ask your students "How do we know that dinosaurs once lived on Earth?" Tell them that we know because paleontologists have found old dinosaur bones buried in the earth. These old bones are called "**fossils**."

Activity:

Before you start this activity, take a cheap put-together dinosaur skeleton (one that comes with a number of pieces) and bury the pieces in a sandbox or dirt pile. You could also just fill a box with sand or dirt and put them in that. Tell your students that one of the jobs of a paleontologist is to hunt for dinosaur bones that are buried in the earth and that today they are going to pretend they are paleontologists looking for bones. You can supply paint brushes and magnifying glasses to help them with their search if you would like.

Once your students have found all of the bones, tell them that the next thing a paleontologist does is to try and figure out how the bones go together to make a skeleton. Help them to put the bones they found together to make the skeleton.

Finally, tell your students that paleontologists have to use the clues they find in the dinosaur skeleton to see what the dinosaur would look like with skin on it. Make a paper mache paste by pouring a bottle of white glue in a bowl and mixing in about the same amount of water to it. Cut an old newspaper or newsprint into one inch by two inch strips. Dip the strips in the glue mixture and cover the dinosaur skeleton with them until the dinosaur takes shape. Let it dry and paint it.

Activity:

*Tell your students that fossils of bones or shells are called **body fossils**. There is another type of fossils called **trace fossils**. Trace fossils are things like animal tracks, animal poop, trails, or burrows, things that tell us an animal was there but are not part of its body. Ask your students to try and think of some things you could tell about an animal by its tracks (if it has claws, how heavy it is, if it is running or walking, if it is young or old, if it walks on two legs or four, how big it was, if it traveled alone or in herds, if its young traveled with it).*

Go outside and have your students experiment with their own tracks. They can do this in the snow, at a beach, in a sand box, or even a muddy lane! Have them both walk and run, and compare the two different tracks. Compare your track to theirs to show how a heavier person's tracks will be deeper. Try and find some animal tracks to see what you can tell about the animal that made them.

Activity:

Tell your students that fossils are made in a number of different ways. A fossil of an animal track is called an **imprint**. It is made when an animal steps in soft mud that dries out and becomes hard. A fossil called a **mold** is made when a plant or animal is buried in mud that hardens into rock. Over time the plant or animal dissolves, leaving a hole that is shaped like their body in the rock.

Take a disposable bowl and fill it with clay (use a type that dries). Smooth out the top. Now press an object into the clay, such as a shell, plastic dinosaur toy, or anything that you think would make an interestingly-shaped "fossil." Take the object out of the clay. You have now made a "mold" of your object, just like a fossil mold.

Sometimes a mold of an animal gets filled up with mud or other materials that eventually hardens. This forms a type of fossil called a **cast**.

Take another disposable bowl and fill it with clay just like the first one. Press your object into the clay and make another mold of it, exactly like you did with the first bowl. Spray the new mold with cooking oil spray or lightly grease it with oil. Mix up enough Plaster of Paris to fill in the mold (making sure you follow any safety precautions on the label). Pour the Plaster of Paris into the mold and let it dry. Once the Plaster of Paris has dried, carefully break the clay around the Plaster of Paris. You have now made a "cast" of your object, just like a fossil cast.

Activity:

Before your students start this activity, take some round stones about ½ to 1 inch wide and place them on a styrofoam meat tray. Mix up some Plaster of Paris (making sure you follow any safety precautions on the label), and pour it over the stones. Let it dry. Now tell your students that you have some "dinosaur eggs" buried in plaster that you would like them to excavate like a paleontologist would. Give them a small hammer, a plastic knife, and a paint brush to remove the Plaster of Paris from around the stones. Have them wear safety goggles as they work and don't give them any items to work with that might be too sharp.

Part 4: Extinction

Ask your students if they know what the word **extinction** means (an animal is **extinct** when there are no more of that type of animal left on earth). Tell them that dinosaurs are extinct, there are no more dinosaurs left on earth. Dinosaurs went extinct about sixty-five million years ago. No one knows for sure why, but some scientists think it happened when a giant asteroid hit the earth which caused a lot of dust and debris to go up into the air and block the sunlight for months. Many animals besides the dinosaurs went extinct at this time.

Activity:

   Take a Webster's Dictionary and show your students the first page. Tell them to imagine that each word in the book stands for thirty years of life (every word in the book, not just the words that are being defined), and that the first word stands for this year, the second word for thirty years ago, etc…See how many words are in the first paragraph and talk about how many years back that was, perhaps mentioning things that were happening in the world back then (you might want to count this up ahead of time so that you have some ideas of what to say ready). Now go to the end of page 843, showing them all of the words in between page 1 and page 843. Show them the last word on page 843 and tell them that this word stands for the year that the dinosaurs went extinct. Stress how many words (years) away from now that was. Tell them that during all those years, other animals besides dinosaurs lived on earth. The calculations in this activity are just approximations and are made to help the children visualize how long ago the dinosaurs lived on earth.

Part 5: After the Dinosaurs

   Tell your students that all kinds of interesting creatures have lived on Earth between when the dinosaurs died and now. Some of them looked a lot different from the animals we see today. Show them a book from the library that has prehistoric animals in it. Be sure to point out the Indricotherium (also called Paraceratherium) and the Saber-toothed cats.

Activity:

   Ask your students if they can guess how paleontologists know if an animal whose fossil they have dug up lived before or after the dinosaurs. Hold up a colored dog biscuit that is shaped like a bone (you don't have to use a dog biscuit; you could use a plastic dinosaur or anything else you choose). Tell them to pretend it is a dinosaur bone and place it in the bottom of a cake pan. Now take some dirt or sand and tell them that over time dirt starts accumulating on top of the dinosaur bone until it is buried. Sprinkle enough dirt on top of the bone to cover it completely up. Now take another colored dog bone and tell them that this is the bone of an Indricotherium (sometimes called Paraceratherium), and place it on top of the dirt. Again, tell them that over time this bone will get covered up also. Now take a third colored bone and place it on top of the dirt and tell them that it is the bone of a Saber-toothed cat. Place it on the very top and cover it with dirt, telling them that the dirt on the very top is the dirt that was just blown onto the bone today.

   Next, give them brushes and tell them to pretend they are paleontologists digging for bones. Have them very carefully brush the dirt off of the first bone (the Saber-toothed cat). Since this bone is the closest to the top of the dirt, it was alive the most recently. Now have them brush down to the next bone and tell them that since this bone is the next closest to the top, it is the next oldest bone. When you get to the dinosaur bone, tell them that since it is on the bottom, it is the oldest bone; it is the farthest from the surface of the "Earth."

Activity:

The *Indricotherium* was a prehistoric herbivore that lived in Asia 23 to 29 million years ago. Have your students show you Asia on a map. Next get out the Webster's Dictionary and remind them how the last word on page 843 represented 65 million years ago when the dinosaurs went extinct. Show them the last word on page 337 and tell them this word represents when *Indricotherium* was living on Earth.

Have your students create their own vegetable dip by taking one cup of sour cream and adding various herbs and spices to it. They can also add dried chopped onions, garlic salt, or small pieces of diced vegetables. Cut up some broccoli and have your students pretend they are *Indricotheriums* eating parts of trees as they dip the broccoli into their new recipe. You can also provide other vegetables to dip and tell them that they are eating parts of plants, just like herbivores.

Part 6: Recommended Movie

The "Magic School Bus" series has a fun dinosaur movie titled "*Magic School Bus: The Busasaurus.*" You can usually order it at your local or school library. It might be a bit scary for very young children, so you should probably look at it yourself first to make sure you want to show it.

Chapter 4: Animals
Ages 4-7

<u>Materials Needed For This Unit</u>

One cup whipping cream
Salt
Four cups ice
Large metal or plastic coffee can
Medical thermometer
Construction paper
Spray bottle
Colored drinking straws
Small cloth
Fan
Shortening
Two sandwich bags
Large mixing bowl
Ice
Newsprint
Crayons
Access to a bicycle tire
English muffins
Tomato sauce
Thin cheese slices
Plastic knife
Coffee grounds
A plastic lizard or snake
Ruler
Newsprint

Clear Tape
Soda crackers
Cream cheese
Fish crackers
Glue
Old socks
Play dough
Markers
Rubber bands
Shoelace
Cheerios®
Salt
Milk carton
Lettuce
Yeast
Pinecone
String
Pins
Stale bread
Cookie cutters
Pipe cleaners
Dried beans
Basil or other spices
Tape measure
Spray bottle

Sugar
Vanilla
Chocolate syrup (optional)
Party blower
Self-sticking Velcro®
Plastic insects
Paper lunch bag
Blue food-coloring
Five shoebox-sized boxes
Small fish net
Flour
Fabric paint
Plain tee-shirt
Parsley
Aquarium with a lid
Wide paint brush
Peanut butter or shortening
Modeling clay
Different types of birdseed
Oatmeal or cornmeal
Green construction paper
Dried pea soup
Rocks
Newspapers
Duct tape

Two identical outdoor thermometers
Dead fish complete with head, tail, and fins
Photos of reptiles from books or the internet that show their scales
Photos of frogs from books or the internet that shows the stages from tadpole to frog
A non-glass container with a lid that fits inside a large coffee can

Tadpoles; if you do not have access to tadpoles you may, depending on where you live, be able to purchase them at:

Nasco
(800)558-9595
(920)563-2446
www.eNasco.com/science
901 Janesville Ave.
Fort Atkinson, WI 53538

Part 1: Mammals

Ask your students if they have ever heard of the word **mammal.** A *mammal* is a type of animal that feeds its babies milk. Ask them if they can think of any animals that feed their babies milk. Did they include humans in this list? Tell them that, yes, humans are mammals too, because we feed our babies milk, as do dolphins and whales.

Activity:

Remind your students that the milk we buy from the store is usually cow's milk. The mother cow produces this milk to feed her babies, but she makes so much that we can use it too. Ask them to list all of the things they can think of that we make from cow's milk (cheese, ice-cream, yogurt, butter, etc...). Now tell them that they are going to make ice-cream!

Mix 1 C whipping cream, 1/8 C sugar, and 1 t vanilla and pour it into a container that will fit inside a large coffee can. If you would like to make chocolate ice-cream, add 2 T chocolate syrup. The container should not be made out of glass and should have a lid that closes tightly. Run a piece of duct tape around the lid to give it an extra seal after it is closed.

Place the container inside a large coffee can that is made of either metal or plastic and surround it with alternating layers of salt and ice. You should use about one quarter cup of salt for every four cups of ice. Close the coffee can lid tightly and run a piece of duct tape around the lid to seal it.

Now, take the coffee can outside and have your students play with it for about one half hour. One good way to do this is to have them roll it back and forth to each other, or they could play "Duck, Duck, Goose," but instead of having the child who was running sit down to participate in the next round of the game, have them take a turn standing in the middle of the circle shaking the can. You might want to have a towel on hand to wrap around the can when you shake it, as it can get fairly cold. It is important to keep the can moving constantly. If the half-hour is not yet up, and you can tell when you shake the can that the ice has melted, remove the tape from the coffee can (leaving the inner container closed), pour out the water, and add some more ice and salt. After the half hour is up, carefully open the coffee can and its inner container, making sure not to let any salt or salty water get into the inner container. The inner container should now be full of ice-cream!

This recipe makes about two servings of ice-cream. If you would like to make more, just double or triple the batch. If you increase the batch size, it may take a bit longer for the ice-cream to set.

Activity:

Tell your students that another characteristic of mammals is that they are warm-blooded. This means that their body temperature will remain pretty much the same even when the temperature outside changes.

Take your students' temperatures and compare them to each other (or to yours). Point out how our body temperatures stay pretty much the same, unless we are sick or exposed to extremes of hot or cold for too long.

Tell your students that the bodies of warm-blooded animals have lots of ways to keep their body temperatures from getting too hot or too cold. When their bodies get too cold, they change the food that they eat into energy to help heat their bodies. When their bodies get too warm, they do things like sweat to cool them off.

When your body temperature starts getting hotter than 98.6, your brain sends messages to the sweat glands to start making sweat. The sweat will start leaving your skin through tiny holes called pores.

Activity:

Tell your students that you are going to have them make two small fans. Give them each a piece of construction paper and have them fold it in half so that the two short sides touch each other. Cut the paper along the fold. Now tell them they can draw a picture on each piece if they would like their fans to be decorated. To complete the fan, tell them to take one of the pieces of paper and hold it so that a short side is on top. Take that side and fold the top of it down about ½ inch. Now turn the paper over, keeping that same side on top. Again, fold the top of the paper down about ½ inch. Turn the paper over again and repeat. Keep doing this until you reach the bottom of the page. They should now have a pleated piece of paper. Form it into a fan shape by pinching the pleats together on one of the long sides of the paper. You can hold it in place with a piece of tape across the bottom.

Repeat this process with the second piece of paper. Now, tell your students that you are going to do an experiment with the two fans. Have your students hold out both arms. Spray a bit of water on one arm and using both fans, fan the arm with the water on it while you are also fanning the arm without the water on it. Ask your students which spot feels cooler, the one on the arm with the water on it, or the one on the arm without the water. The arm with the water on it should feel cooler because when water evaporates, or goes up into the air, it cools the air around it. Sweat is mostly made of water, so when it evaporates on your skin, it helps cool it.

The following experiment will help prove that evaporating water cools the air.

Activity:

Take two identical outdoor thermometers and place a small piece of wet cloth around the bulb of one of the thermometers. Blow a fan on both thermometers for two minutes and then read the temperatures. The one with the wet cloth on it should have a cooler temperature than the one without the cloth.

Activity:

Tell your students that besides turning their food into energy, mammals have a number of other ways to help keep their body temperature warm. One way they do this is to have fur or hair on their bodies. Another way is by shivering when they are cold. Shivering produces heat which helps keep the body warm. Some mammals like seals or whales have blubber or fat to help them stay warm.

Take a plastic sandwich bag and put a one-inch layer of shortening in the bottom of it. Now place another plastic sandwich bag inside of the first one, so that it is sitting on top of the shortening. Fill the space between the two bags with shortening, so that the layer of shortening is at least one inch thick and completely surrounding the inner bag. Now take some duct tape and tape the tops of the two bags to each other so that there is no opening to the shortening layer. You have now made a shortening "mitten!" Next, take a large mixing bowl and fill it three quarters full with ice and water. Have each of your students put one hand inside the inner bag of the plastic mitten and place the hand with the plastic mitten on it into the ice water. Make sure that they don't place it so far in that the water flows into the mitten. Now, have them place their other hand in the bowl of water. Can they feel a difference? The hand in the shortening mitten should feel warmer than the other hand. That is because the shortening acts like blubber to insulate and keep the body warm.

Part 2: Reptiles

Ask your students if they can list some animals that are reptiles (lizards, snakes, turtles, alligators, tortoises, crocodiles). Can they think of anything that reptiles have in common with each other (they have scales, they lay eggs, they are cold-blooded). One thing that all reptiles have in common is that, unlike mammals, they are cold-blooded. This means that their body temperature changes with the outside temperature more than mammals. This also means that reptiles can't stand being in cold climates as much as mammals can, because they can't get warm as easily as mammals. Another thing different between reptiles and mammals is that reptile's bodies have scales on them. Their scales help to protect them and keep them moist. Below is a close-up picture of a Garter Snake's scales:

Show your students some other photos of reptiles, pointing out the scales to them.

Activity:
Take a piece of newsprint and have your students use it to make a rubbing of a bicycle tire. Place the paper on the tire and take the wrapper off a crayon. Using the long side of the crayon, rub it on the paper that is covering the tire. Now, take your rubbings and cut them out to look like snakes! You can also add more color to them if you like. Be sure to point out that the rubbings look like a snake's scales.

Activity:

Give your students one side of an English muffin. Tell them they are going to make turtle shell pizzas! First, have them spread a thin layer of tomato sauce on the English muffin. Next, cut out some thin pieces of cheese into small hexagons and give them to your students so that they can place them on the English muffin to resemble the pattern of a turtle's shell. If you want, you could give them plastic knives to cut the hexagons themselves. This might be a good time to get a little math in and explain what a hexagon is! You can toast the muffins in a toaster oven or bake them at 350 degrees in a regular oven. Before baking, you can add some basil or other spices to the top.

Tell your students that most reptiles lay eggs like birds do. Their eggs can either be hard and brittle (like bird eggs) or leather-like.

Activity:

You will need to set-up this activity a few days ahead of time. Make some "lizard eggs" for your students to hatch. A few days before your class, mix together 1 C of coffee grounds, 1 C of flour, ½ C of salt, and 1 C of water. It should be the consistency of a stiff bread dough. If it is too runny, add some extra flour. Take a small plastic lizard or snake and form a ball of the dough around it, so that it looks like an egg. Let it air dry for about three days until it is hard. Give the eggs to your students and tell them that it is a special kind of lizard egg that they can help hatch with a plastic knife. You can also use small plastic snakes instead of lizards for this.

Activity:

Take some different colors of drinking straws and cut them into 1 inch pieces. Now, take a shoelace that is at least one foot long and tie a knot in one end. Have your students string the straw pieces onto the shoelace. Once the shoelace is completely full of straw pieces, tie off the other end. They have now made the body of a snake! Take a piece of colored construction paper and have your students draw a snake head on it. Tape the snake head to one end of the straw body, so that it covers the knot. Make a snake tail from the construction paper and use it to cover the knot at the other end of the body.

Activity:

Tell your students that snakes come in many different sizes. One of the smallest snakes, called a Thread Snake, is only about 4 inches long (show them on a ruler how long that is). One of the largest snakes, The Asiatic Reticulated Python, can grow to be about 33 feet long. Take a tape measure and measure out 33 feet to show your students.

Part 3: Amphibians

Tell your students that many folks mix reptiles and amphibians up. Though they are both cold-blooded, they are not the same. Ask them if they can name any animals that are amphibians (frogs, toads, salamanders, newts). One of the main differences between reptiles and amphibians is that when amphibians are young, they live in water, and when they are adults, they live on land. Their don't have shells like reptile or bird eggs, so they have to lay them in water or they will dry out. Find some photos of the stages in a frog's life from tadpole to frog to show your students.

Activity:

If you live near a pond or stream that has tadpoles, you can bring some home to raise, so that you can watch them grow into frogs. Collect some tadpoles using a small fish net and collect enough of the pond water with them so that you can put them in a small aquarium with about 2 inches of water. Place some rocks in the aquarium so that the little frogs have something to climb up on once they grow legs, making sure that the slope of the rocks isn't too steep for them to climb out of the water on. If your aquarium is not very tall, you should have a lid on hand for when the tadpoles turn into frogs; you don't want them to jump out! Make sure the lid has holes to let air in. You can feed your tadpoles lettuce that has been boiled for ten minutes and cooled. Any extra lettuce that you make can be frozen for future use. Do not over-feed the tadpoles, just give them a small pinch of food at least two days a week. The amount you feed them will really depend on how many tadpoles you have, so just make sure that there is not a lot of food left floating around when they are done eating. If the food is always completely gone after a feeding, you might want to feed them a little more often. Different species of tadpoles like different types of food. If your tadpoles don't seem to like the lettuce (or even if they do), try feeding them a few grains of dried yeast to see if they like that. Another thing that your tadpoles might like is dried pea soup.

After the front legs appear, the frogs won't need to be fed. They will be living off of the energy they get from re-absorbing their tails. This is a good time to get ready to release them back into the wild. As-soon-as the tadpoles have turned into frogs, release them back into the pond that you found them in, or they will starve.

If the water in the tank gets too cloudy, you should change it. It would be best if you could replace it with more pond water, but you can also use tap water that has been "aged" by letting it sit in an open jar or bucket for a few days to let the chlorine or other additives dissipate.

<u>*Be sure that you and your students always wash your hands after touching the frogs. Most frogs carry salmonella on their skin!*</u> *You should also make sure that there are no poisonous frogs or toads where you live.*

If you do not have easy access to tadpoles, there is a source for them listed on the materials page. You may not be able to purchase them, depending on where you live. If possible, it is really best to find them locally, so that you can release them back into the wild. If you do decide to purchase tadpoles, you need to decide what to do with them once they turn into frogs. Perhaps a local pet store would be interested in them, or you could keep one as a pet.

Activity:

Tell your students that frogs catch insects to eat with their tongues! Take a party blower and put a small piece of self-sticking Velcro® on the very end of it. Put a corresponding piece of Velcro® on a plastic insect and have your students try to "catch" the insect by blowing the party blower at it. Point out how much harder it would be to catch a real insect.

Activity:

Cut out some lily pad shapes from green construction paper and write numbers on them from one to ten. You can repeat numbers if needed; you want to make sure that there are enough lily pads to play the game comfortably (the amount of pads will depend on the amount of children you have playing). Place the pads on the floor and have each student stand on a number. Now tell them to jump like frogs to the next higher number. Keep giving them instructions like "jump to an even number," or "place your right hand on an odd number," etc....

Part 4: Birds

Ask your students to list everything that they can tell you about birds. Now look at the list and see if they can come up with some things that <u>all</u> birds have in common (they lay eggs, are warm-blooded, have feathers).

Activity:

Ask your students why they think so many birds make their nests in trees (to keep away from predators). Give each of your students a paper lunch bag and take them outside to collect materials to put in it such as sticks, grass, and leaves that they think a bird might use to make a nest. You can make it even more fun by having them pretend that they are birds collecting items for their nest. Once they have filled their bags, empty them out and roll the sides down to make a nest-like shape. Glue the items that the students found to the bag to make it look like a real bird's nest. Take some play dough and have them make "eggs" to put in their nests.

Activity:

Have your students make some bird feeders. A few different types are listed below. Put them outside and see which type attracts the most birds. Do some birds prefer one feeder over another? Try using different types of bird seed to see what types of seeds different birds prefer.

Bird Feeder 1:

Take a milk carton and cut out a window on one side that is about one inch from the bottom. Poke holes in the top and run a string through it to hang it from a tree.   Fill the bottom with bird seed.

Bird Feeder 2:

Give each of your students a pipe cleaner; have them bend it like a candy can, and string Cheerios® on it. Hang it outside from the branch of a tree.

Bird Feeder 3:

Take some stale bread (or toast some bread lightly) and cut it into shapes with cookie cutters. If your cookie cutters aren't sharp enough, you may need to cut the shapes out with a knife by cutting around the cookie cutters. Poke a hole in the top and string a piece of yarn or string through it. Spread peanut butter (if any of your students has a peanut allergy, use vegetable shortening) on both sides of the bread and roll it in either oatmeal or cornmeal.

Bird Feeder 4:

Take a pinecone and tie a loop of string or yarn to the top of it. Spread peanut butter (if any of your students has a peanut allergy, use vegetable shortening) on the outside. Roll it in birdseed and hang it outside from a tree.

Part 5: Fish

Tell your students that amphibians and fish have some things in common. They are both cold-blooded, and they both live in the water for at least part of their lives. Amphibians live in water when they are young (remind them of tadpoles), and fish live in water their whole lives. Both amphibians and fish need oxygen to live, just like we do. We get our oxygen by breathing air. Fish and young amphibians that live in water get their oxygen from the water itself using their gills. Their gills absorb oxygen from the water, just like our lungs absorb oxygen from the air.

Activity:

Take some old socks and have your students decorate them like fish using colored markers. Fill them up with beans and tie the ends with rubber bands. Take five boxes that are about shoebox size and put large numbers on them from one to five. Tell your students that the boxes represent the ocean and that they need to toss the fish they made back into the ocean so that their gills can work and they can breathe. Have them throw the fish into the boxes, with fish that landing in the box with a "one" on it getting one point, fish that land in the box with a "two" on it getting two points, etc... If your students know how to add, use this as a way to practice their addition by having them add up their points.

Ask your students what parts of their bodies they use to get information about the world around them (eyes, ears, nose, mouth, skin). Remind them that they use their eyes for seeing, their nose for smelling, their mouth for tasting, and their skin for touching. Fish get information about the world around them in similar ways. They usually have eyes, ears, a nose, a mouth, and skin. However, they also have another sense organ that we don't have. It is called a lateral line and it looks like a faint line on the side of a fish, from its gills to its tail. Fish use their lateral lines to detect movement and vibrations in the water. Have your students imagine that they are underwater, and then have them imagine that they can feel the water against their skin. Do they think they could feel changes in water movement? Tell them that because of the lateral line, fish are even more sensitive to water movements than we are.

Activity:

Tell your students that the Japanese have been making fish prints on paper for over one hundred years as a way to record the fish they catch. But you can also make fish prints on tee-shirts!

Take a whole, dead fish and wash and dry the outside of it. Place the fish on a table covered with newspapers. Spread out the fins of the fish and hold them in place by pushing a pin through them into a bit of modeling clay. Next, take some fabric paint and brush a thin layer of paint over one side of the fish, including the fins. Before you make your fish print on a tee-shirt, test it out on a piece of paper first. Take a piece of newsprint and gently press it over the surface of the fish, making sure that it touches all of the parts of the fish. Remove the newsprint by slowly peeling it up from one end. If you like how your print turned out, make the next one on a tee-shirt.

While you are doing this project, point out some of the parts of a fish to your students. The dorsal fin is on the top of the fish, the pectoral fins are on each side of the body, close to the head. The caudal fin is the tail. Lift up the gill cover, which is on the head between the eye and the pectoral fin, and you will see a reddish area that looks a bit like uncooked liver, these are the gills. See if you can see the lateral line running along the side of the fish (you can't always see it).

Activity:

 This is a fun game to play if you have a group of students, so if you only have one homeschooler, wait until your student is playing with his or her friends and try it out. Ask your students if they know what a group of fish are called (a school). Tell them that one reason fish swim in schools is to help them escape from predators (make sure that they know what a predator is). Predators find it harder to catch a fish if it is in a group of fish because it is hard to pick just one out of a whole group.

 Now tell your students that you are going to have them pretend that they are a school of fish and that you are the predator. They can only get away from you by walking fast, not by running, and they can't touch each other as they move. The only fish that you can catch are ones that have split off from the group, so as long as they are with the group they are safe. Any fish that you catch become predators with you and can help you catch more fish. Tell them that you will be calling out directions to them such as "go left" or "go right" as you play the game.

Activity:

 Make a little edible ocean scene by taking some cream cheese and put a small amount of blue food coloring in it. Give your students a soda cracker and have them spread the blue cream cheese on it. Then give them a couple of fish crackers to press into the cream cheese, so that it looks like fish swimming in the water. Take some parsley and add it to the cracker to look like seaweed.

Chapter 5: Insects and Their Kin
Ages 4-7

Most of the materials needed for this unit are either common household items, or are easily obtained from grocery, hardware, drug, or discount stores. However, there are two activities that require the purchase of kits. These are not necessary for the unit, just fun additions to it for those who would like to do these activities.

Materials Needed For This Unit

String or yarn
A Styrofoam ball about 1 ½ inches across
A Styrofoam ball about ¾ inches across
Pipe cleaners
Small wiggle eyes
Peanut butter
Powdered milk
Raisins
Brown sugar
Coconut
Granola
Pretzels (the thin stick kind)
Sugar cube
Toilet paper
Colored markers
Paper lunch bag
Glue
Tempera paint
Fifteen paper drinking cups
Large open-topped container, such as a cake pan, old aquarium, etc.
Fine wire mesh to cover the above container
Black and yellow pom-poms about 1 inch across
Black pom-poms that are about ½ inch across
Petroleum jelly
Clothespins
Empty coffee can with lid
Flat stones
Small pieces of decaying wood
Half a potato
A picture from the library or internet of some honeycomb
Spray bottle of perfume
Brown construction paper or a large grocery bag
Optional Ant Farm Kit, see the activity in Part 3 of this chapter for details
Optional Butterfly Kit, see the activity in Part 5 of this chapter for details

Funnel
Colored construction paper
Celery
Fruit juice
Scissors
Paperclips
Green construction paper
Ruler
Drinking straws
Drawing paper
Paper drinking cup
Black construction paper
Soil
Egg carton
Map of the world (or a globe)

Part 1: Introduction

Tell your students that you are going to be studying small creatures like insects and spiders. Have them list some things that they don't like about insects and spiders. Next have them list some good things that insects and spiders do for us (make honey, catch mosquitoes and other harmful insects, make silk, animals like frogs and birds need them to eat, etc…).

Activity:

Go on a small creatures activity hunt. Take your students outside and see how many signs of insect or spider activities you can see. Make a list of what you find. Look for things such as holes in leaves, ant nests, spider webs, insect egg cases, tunnels in logs, etc… You could also do a variation of this by making a list beforehand and going on a small creatures scavenger hunt, trying to find all of the signs of insect and spider activity that you listed.

Part 2: Spiders

Ask your students to tell you everything they can think of about spiders. Do they know how many legs a spider has? (eight). Do they know that if some spiders lose a leg, they can grow a new one? There are lots of different kinds of spiders and they have many different ways of catching insects. The trap-door spider digs a burrow and makes a door for it out of plants and dirt. It even has a hinge made of silk! The spider waits under the door for an insect to walk by and jumps out to catch it. Other spiders hide in flowers to catch insects as they search for nectar. Jumping spiders pounce on their prey. There is even a spider in South America that eats mice! But what spiders are best known for are their webs made of sticky silk to catch insects.

Activity:

Take some yarn or string and tie it to pieces of furniture to make a web. Play a game pretending that one of you is the spider and the rest are insects caught in the web. Spiders can feel the web vibrate when an insect is caught in it, so have the insects wiggle the web to let the spider know they are there.

Tell the students that when spiders are afraid they can jump down from their web trailing a piece of silk called a "dragline" behind them. Then when it is safe, they can climb back to the web on their dragline. Tie a piece of yarn or sting around the waist of the student who is the spider and have him or her go hide, trailing the dragline behind. Then, when it is "safe," the spider can move back along the dragline to the web.

Activity:

*Spiders move from place to place by **ballooning**. They jump into the air and trail a line of silk out behind them, letting the wind blow them along like a balloon. Tie a piece of yarn or string around your students' waists and have them jump into the wind, pretending that they are spiders being carried along. Make up a story about where the spiders are going and what they will find in their new home.*

Activity:

Tell your students that before spiders eat an insect, they wound it with their fangs, and inject a poison into the insect's body. This poison dissolves the insect's body so that the spider can suck it up like a milkshake! Since spiders don't have teeth, this is how they eat their food. Give each of your students a sugar cube in a cup. Have them pour a few drops of water on the sugar cube and watch it dissolve. Tell them that the sugar cube is like the insect's body and the water is like the poison that the spider uses to dissolve its food. The students can now use a straw and suck the sugar water into their mouths like a spider.

Activity:

Make a spider snack by mixing ½ C peanut butter (**always make sure that none of your students has a peanut allergy before giving them peanut butter**), 2 ½ T powdered milk, 2 T granola, 2 T brown sugar, and ¼ C coconut in a bowl. Take some of the dough and form it into two balls, one larger than the other. Stick the two balls together to make a spider's head and body. If you have problems sticking them together, you can skewer them together on a pretzel (see the diagram for the next activity, only use a pretzel instead of a pipe cleaner). Add raisins for eyes and push four pretzels into each side of the larger dough ball for legs (just have the pretzels stick straight out of the sides, don't try to have the spider stand up on them). Place it in the refrigerator for about an hour and you will have a tasty spider that you can eat!

Activity:

Take a Styrofoam ball that is about 1 ½ inches across and another one that is about ¾ inch across. Attach them together by pushing a pipe cleaner that is about 2 inches long through the middle of the large ball, leaving some of the pipe cleaner sticking out of the end of the ball. Push the smaller ball on to the exposed end of the pipe cleaner. You can add a little glue between the two balls for extra strength. Cut 8 more pieces of pipe cleaner so they are about 2 inches long. Push them into the larger ball to form the spider's legs. Curl the ends of the pipe cleaners back so they are not sharp. Glue two wiggle eyes onto the smaller ball and you have a spider!

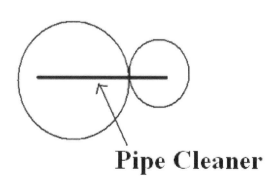

Pipe Cleaner

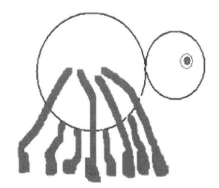

Part 3: Butterflies

Ask your students to tell you everything they know about butterflies. Did they know that some Monarch Butterflies fly from the Great Lakes to the Gulf of Mexico (about 2000 miles) every year? Point out on a map where they fly. There are some butterflies that are only one-eighth of an inch across, and some that are twelve inches across. Show them how small and large that is using a ruler. Can they guess which continent is the only one without butterflies or moths on it? (Antarctica). Of course, what people remember the most about butterflies is that they start off life as caterpillars and change into butterflies.

Activity:

Tell your students that butterflies have a long straw-like mouth called a "proboscis" that they use to drink nectar from flowers with. In the next activity they will be using their own type of proboscis to drink some "nectar."

Have your students draw some flower shapes on colored construction paper. The flowers need to be large enough so that they can be glued to the top of a paper drinking cup. Cut the flowers out and then cut a hole in the middle of each one that is large enough to fit the neck of a funnel through. Glue each flower flat across the top of a paper drinking cup so that the hole is in the middle. Let your flowers dry. In the meantime, cut some drinking straws into one inch lengths.

Using a funnel, pour about one inch of fruit juice into the bottom of your paper cup flowers. Give your students the one inch straws and tell them that each straw is like a proboscis. Now have your students try drinking "nectar" out of the flowers. Point out that if their proboscis isn't long enough, they can't get to the nectar inside the flower. Tell them that there is a moth called the Morgan's Sphinx Moth from Madagascar (show them Madagascar on a map or globe) that has a proboscis that is 12 to 14 inches long! It uses it to get to the nectar of a 12- inch deep orchid! Now let them drink the nectar with a longer straw.

Take good care of your cup flowers; you'll need them for another activity in the next section on bees.

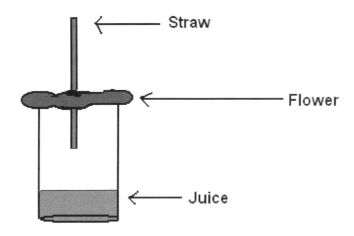

Activity:

Tell your students that when many moth caterpillars are born they eat, and eat, and eat until they get big and fat. Then they make a cocoon, which is like a little tent that they hide in until they turn into moths.

Have your students pretend that they are moth caterpillars. Start by having them crawl around the room looking for food. Next tell them that it is time to make a cocoon and wrap toilet paper all around them, so that when you are done, they are wrapped up like a mummy. Have them sit quietly in the toilet paper until you say it is time for them to come out, and then they can break out of their toilet-paper "cocoon" to become moths!

Activity:

Cut a section of an egg carton about three or four egg-cups long. Have the students color them with colored markers and glue wiggle eyes on the front. You now have a little caterpillar. Tell the students that it is time for the caterpillars to turn into a chrysalis. Point out to them that a chrysalis is not the same thing as a cocoon, though many people think it is. A cocoon is a covering, often made of silk, over the pupa stage of an insect (usually a moth) and a chrysalis is the pupa stage of a butterfly. Put the caterpillars inside paper lunch bags, tie them shut and tell your students that now their caterpillars are chrysalises. That night, while your students are asleep, draw some butterfly wings and glue them to the caterpillars. Put the caterpillars/butterflies back in the lunch bags and tie them shut again. In the morning, tell your students that the caterpillars are ready to come out of their chrysalis skin and have them open the lunch bags to find that their caterpillars have changed into butterflies!

Activity:

Take a piece of paper and fold it in half width-wise. Open the paper back up and place a large thick blob of tempera paint on one side of the paper near the fold. Fold the paper back together and press it down flat. When you open the paper, you should see a butterfly-like pattern. Have your students add eyes and antenna to make it into a beautiful butterfly!

Activity:

There is a company called "Insect Lore" that sells a butterfly kit complete with live caterpillars so that you can watch a real caterpillar turn into a chrysalis and change into a butterfly. You can find them online by doing a search titled "Insect Lore." Please note that they only ship butterflies to the Continental US.

Part 4: Bees

Ask your students if they can think of two good things that bees do for us (give us honey and pollinate flowers). Ask them if they can think of one bad thing about bees (they sting). Why do they think that bees sting? (to protect themselves and their hive).

Activity:

Have your students take a yellow pom-pom that is about one inch across and glue it to a black pom-pom that is about one inch across. Glue a smaller black pom-pom to the other side of the yellow pom-pom. Cut out some wing shapes out of white paper and glue them to the top of the yellow pom-pom. They should now have a little bee. Glue wiggle eyes on the head and glue the whole thing to the top of a clothespin so that your students can open the clothespin and attach their bees all over the house!

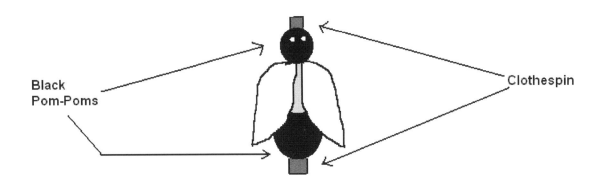

Black
Pom-Poms

Clothespin

Activity:

Tell your students that bees store their honey in little wax containers that they make in their hive called honeycombs. Show them a picture from the library or online of some honeycomb.

Next, tell your students that they are going to make their own beehive. Take five paper drinking cups and, <u>leaving them standing upright</u>, hook them together in a row using paperclips. Then, take four more drinking cups and hook them into a row and paperclip it in place next to the row of five cups. Take three cups and hook them into a row next to the row of four cups, and so on until you have one cup on top. Once you are finished you should be looking down at a pyramid of cups that looks like this:

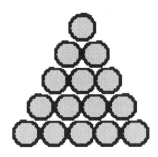

Tell the students that bees fill the honeycomb cups with nectar and fan them with their wings to help the water that is in the nectar evaporate into the air. Once the water is gone from the nectar, it becomes honey! You will be using your hive in the next activity, so take good care of it.

Activity:

  Tell your students that bees "talk" to each other using a special bee dance and that they are going to play a game using the bee dance to find flowers. Choose a place to put the bee hive that you made in the previous activity. Tell your students that when a scout bee finds flowers, it flies back to the hive and starts doing a dance where it wiggles and makes a buzzing sound. The longer the bee wiggles in one direction, the farther from the hive the flowers are. The direction the bee dances in tells the bees where the flowers are located. If a bee can see the sun while it is doing its dance, and the flowers are toward the sun, it will wiggle in the direction of the sun. If the flowers are opposite to the sun, it will wiggle in that direction. Here is the pattern of the dance:

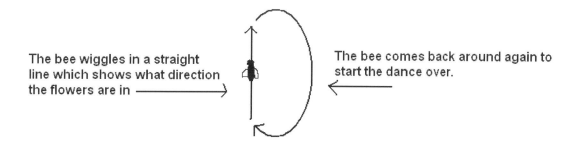

The bee wiggles in a straight line which shows what direction the flowers are in ———————→

The bee comes back around again to start the dance over.

  Have your students practice doing the "bee dance" until you feel that they understand it. Remind them that if they wiggle longer when they do the straight line part of the dance, it means that the flowers are farther away. Choose a child (or yourself!) to be the "scout bee." The rest of the students will be the "worker bees." Have the scout bee hide the flowers that you made in the previous section on butterflies, and then go back to the worker bees to do the wiggle dance. The worker bees have to find the flowers using the information the scout bee has given them in the dance.

  You can expand the game by giving each student a straw. Show them how they can carry water in the straw by putting it in a cup of water and holding a finger over one end. Put some water in the flower cups and when the worker bees find the flowers, have them get water out of the cups using straws, and carry it back to the hive. Let the water out of the straws into the cups of the hive. The students can then pretend they are fanning the nectar with their wings to turn it into honey.

Part 5: Ants

  Ask your students to tell you everything they can think of about ants. Did they know that there are Leaf Cutter Ants in South America that are farmers? They cut leaves from plants and bring them back to their nest. Next they chew the leaves into a mushy substance that they grow fungus on! There are other ants that act like dairy farmers and "milk" aphids for honeydew. There are ants that eat seeds, ants that eat insects, ants that eat meat, and ants that eat sugar. Whatever you can think of, it seems like there is an ant that can eat it!

Activity:

  Make an old favorite ant snack, "Ants on a Log," by cutting pieces of celery into sticks, spreading peanut butter on them, and placing raisins (the ants) on top of the peanut butter. **Always make sure that none of your students has a peanut allergy before giving them peanut butter.**

Activity:

Ask your students if they know how ants tell each other where food is. The scout ants leave the nest to hunt for food. Once they find a food source, they go back to their nest to tell the other ants where the food is located. They do this by laying down a chemical trail down that the other ants can follow back to the food.

Take your students outside and go on an ant hunt. See if you can find a trail of ants leading to a food source. Once you find an ant trail, spray some perfume across it (making sure not to spray any ants) and watch what happens. The ants should become confused and unable to follow their trail. You have disrupted their trail by laying down a different chemical over it.

If you can't find an ant trail, make one by putting food out for the ants to find. You could try sugar or bread crumbs. Once the ants find the food, they will make a trail back to their nest.

Activity:

Ants, like all true insects, have six legs. Make some pretend pairs of ant legs out of brown construction paper (or a large grocery bag) and attach them to your students' waists so that when they go down on all fours it looks like they have six legs. Pretend that they are Leaf-Cutter Ants who need to build a nest and start growing fungus for food. Have a "scout" ant go outside with a ball of string or yarn and find some leaves (make sure the leaves your student chooses aren't poison ivy or something equally bad!) to cut. You could also make pretend leaves out of green construction paper if you would rather not have them cut live plants. Once the scout has located the leaves, he or she can lay a trail of string (to represent a chemical trail) back to the nest for the other ants to follow. Have them bring the leaves back to the nest and mash them up to grow their fungus on.

Activity:

A great ant activity is to have an ant farm. We've tried making our own, but haven't had much luck. There is a company named "Uncle Milton" that has been selling ant farms for years at a reasonable cost. You purchase the kit from them, and they send you the ants. You can find them online by doing a search titled "Uncle Milton Ant Farm." Please note that they only ship the ants to the Continental US and Canada.

Part 6: Woodlice, Sow Bugs, Pill Bugs

Ask your students if they have heard any of the following names: Sow Bug, Armadillo Bug, Wood Bug, Pill Bug, Roly-Poly, Cheese Log, Doodlebug, Potato Bug, Woodlouse, Roll up Bug, or Slater. All of these are names for some closely related creatures that look very much alike, are about one inch long, and live under old logs, leaves, or in other damp places. Some species roll up into a little ball when they are touched, hence the names Roly-Poly or Pill Bug.

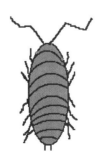

Activity:

Go on a Sow Bug hunt. Look under old logs, rocks, or leaves. If you live in an area with poisonous bugs or snakes, never stick your fingers under a rock or log to lift it up. Know the dangerous creatures in your area and be aware of them. If you move a rock or log, always keep the rock or log between you and the ground you are exposing. Use your own judgment to decide if this is a safe activity to do in your area. Collect some Sow Bugs to use in the following activity.

Activity:

Test to see if Sow Bugs prefer light or dark areas. Take an empty coffee can and cut the lid in half. Spread a band of petroleum jelly around the can, about 2 inches from the top. If your coffee can lets any light through the sides, take a piece of black construction paper and tape it on the outside of the half of the coffee can that is covered by the half-lid. You are trying to make one half of the coffee can dark and one half light. Place a few Sow Bugs in the bottom of the can, right in the center. Put the half-lid back on the top and place the can in a well-lit area, such as in a room with bright lights overhead. Do not put them in direct sunlight; you don't want them to get too hot!

Wait one half-hour and then every five minutes for the next hour check the sow bugs and keep a tally of how many are in the dark side of the coffee can and how many are in the light side of the coffee can. Did you count them more often in the light side or more in the dark side? They should prefer the dark side of the can because Sow Bugs like dark, damp places. Be sure to let the Sow Bugs go once you are finished with the experiment.

Chapter 6: Fun with Magnets
Ages 4-7

<u>Materials Needed for this Unit</u>

String
Stick or dowel to use as a "fishing pole"
Clear tape
Small magnet that is about 1" x 1"
Tongue depressors
Markers
Stick-on magnet tape
Wiggly-eyes
Strong magnet
Cotton balls
Drinking glass
Paint stir stick
Two small magnets
Aluminum foil
Monofilament or white thread
A piece of Styrofoam that is at least 1 inch thick and about 2 x 2 inches around
Two bar magnets with the poles clearly marked
Large rectangular plastic container, about the size of a cake pan
Two pieces of 1" x 2" wood that are the length of an adult-sized shoebox lid
An adult-sized shoebox lid
A box or basket that is about 9" x 9"
Construction paper
Corrugated cardboard
Colored pom-poms, about one-half to one inch in diameter

At least three boxes of salt
Pencil
Four ring magnets
Crayons or colored pencils
Small jewelry box
Poster board
Masking tape
Drawing paper
Glue
One box of small metal paperclips

If you have a hard time finding the types of magnets needed in this unit, one good source for them is:

Nasco
(800)558-9595
modesto@eNasco.com
4825 Stoddard Rd.
Modesto, CA 95356-9318

Part 1: Introduction

Tell your students that long ago people discovered that there were special rocks in the world that would attract (pull) a metal called iron toward it. Some people say that the first person who discovered this special rock was a shepherd who had a shepherd's crook with an iron tip on it. When he placed his crook down on a rock, the rock stuck to it! No one knows if this story is true, but it could have happened that way. This special kind of rock is called **lodestone** (if you have access to a piece of lodestone now, this would be a good time to show it). Eventually, scientists figured out how to make their own lodestones, which we call magnets.

Activity:

Have your students draw some pictures of fish that are about three to four inches long and cut them out. Write a number from one to three on the back of each fish. Then, take a metal paperclip and clip it on the mouth area of each fish. Make a fishing pole by taking a small piece of dowel and attaching a string on one end. Tie a small magnet to the other end of the string. Put up some type of barrier so that your students can't see over it and scatter the fish behind it. Have the students toss the fishing line with the magnet on the end over the barrier and try to catch a fish. You can use the numbers on the back of the fish in various ways, such as playing a game to see who catches the most "points," or passing out prizes based on the number caught. Be sure to remind your students that they are using magnets to catch the fish!

Part 2: Attraction

Activity:

Give each of your students a tongue depressor and have them decorate one side of it with markers. Take some stick-on magnet tape and stick it to the other side of the tongue depressor. Now have your students go around the room looking for things that the magnet sticks to (do not let them test their magnets on a computer, this could potentially damage it). Make a list of these items and see if your students can figure out what all of these things have in common (they are metals). Tell them that magnets are only attracted to certain kinds of metals, the main ones being iron, nickel, and cobalt. Have them test the magnet on something that is aluminum or copper to see that they don't stick to the magnet.

Activity:

Give each of your students another tongue depressor and some pom-poms to decorate it with. Have them glue the pom-poms onto the tongue depressor to make little creatures. Two possibilities are caterpillars or snowmen. You can also add wiggly-eyes to the creatures. Stick some magnetic tape on the back of the tongue depressor and you've now made a refrigerator-magnet! Be sure to point out to your students that refrigerator doors have iron in them, or the magnet would not stick!

Activity:

Take a large rectangular plastic container (the size of a cake pan) and fill the bottom with about one inch of salt. Mix a box of small metal paperclips into the salt so that you can't see the paperclips. Have your students stir magnets (the tongue depressor magnets they made probably won't be strong enough) through the salt and watch the paperclips stick to the magnets. Tell your students that since paperclips have iron in them, the magnets will pull them out of the salt, which is not made of iron.

Part 3: The Power of Magnets

Activity:

      Take a piece of corrugated cardboard and place a paperclip on top of it. Ask your students if they can think of a way to make the paperclip move without ever touching it or putting a magnet above it. After you have discussed this, show them how you can move the paperclip by placing a magnet <u>under</u> the cardboard and moving it around. Point out to them that the force of the magnet was so strong that it worked through the cardboard! Show them that the magnet is not attracted to the cardboard itself.

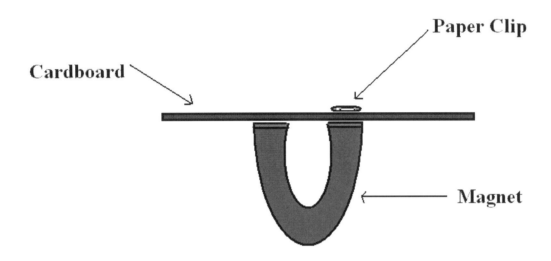

Activity:

      Have your students take the paperclip from the previous experiment and try putting it on some other objects to see if the magnet works through them. You could try a thin book, a table top, etc…. Try different sizes of books, or see how many pages in one book it can move the paperclip through. Next, try and see if the magnet works through glass. Place the paperclip in a drinking glass and see if they can move it up the side of the glass by putting the magnet on the outside of the glass and moving it upward.

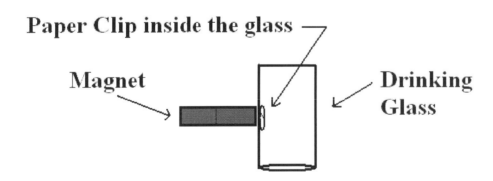

Activity:

     Tell your students that you can use magnets to make a toy. Two possibilities are described below, but your students can use the same idea and come up with their own if they like. Make sure you read through all of the directions before you start this activity.

Toy #1: The Moving Figure Skater

     Take a piece of wood that is about 1" by 2" and cut it into two pieces so that they are the same length as the long sides of the top to a shoebox. Glue them to the sides of a shoebox lid so that they look like this:

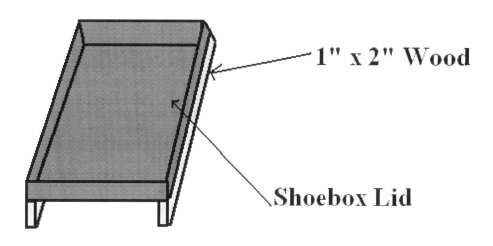

     Next, take some aluminum foil and glue it to the bottom of the inside of the lid. This will be your figure skater's lake. Take some cotton balls and glue them around the edges to look like snow.

     Now take a piece of poster board that is 1 ½ inches by 6 inches and mark two lines across it, one at 2 ½ inches and one at 3 ½ inches. Fold it on the two lines so that when you look at it from the side, it looks like a "U" with two sides and a bottom:

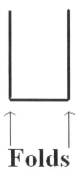

Folds

Now, unfold the poster board and fold it again right down the middle. Have your students draw a picture of a figure-skater on one side of the poster board, making sure not to put any part of the drawing below the marks of the previous folds:

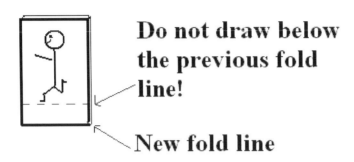

Do not draw below the previous fold line!

New fold line

Next, cut out the figure without cutting below the previous fold lines or cutting through the fold on the bottom of the paper. Cut through both sides of the poster board:

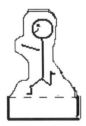

Now, unfold the figure at the bottom and re-fold it on the original two folds. Tape the top together with clear tape so that the whole thing is shaped like a triangle if you look at it from the side. Finally, tape a small magnet (about 1" x 1") on the bottom, between the two sides of the figure.

Tape Here

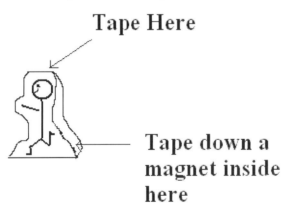

Tape down a magnet inside here

To finish this toy, take a paint stir-stick and, using masking tape, tape another magnet to it. **Make sure that the side of the magnet that faces up is attracted to the magnet on the bottom of the skater.** *Place the figure skater on the lake and move it around the lake by moving the magnet underneath the shoebox.*

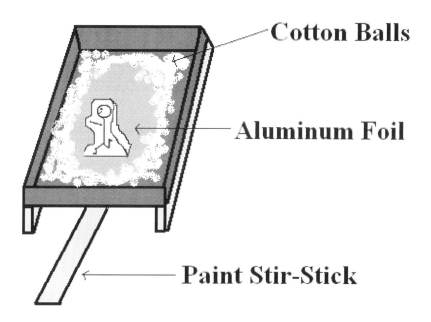

Cotton Balls

Aluminum Foil

Paint Stir-Stick

Toy #2: Race Car Track

   You make this toy in the same way as the previous toy, but instead of putting aluminum foil in the shoebox lid, draw a race-car track there instead. You can make a race-car to run on the track in the same way as you made the figure skater, or you could take a small matchbox-type car and hot glue a small magnet to the bottom of it.

Part 4: Push and Pull

Activity:

   Take two bar magnets that have the north and south poles marked on them (instead of saying "north" or "south," one side might be blue and one red). Ask your students to try and push the two magnets together so that the matching ends touch each other (i.e. blue to blue or north to north). Ask them if they can feel that the magnets "don't want" to go together. Now, have them hold them together on a table so that the <u>matching</u> ends are touching and then let go of one magnet. The one they let go of should move away from the other. Show them how they can move one magnet around by getting close to it with the matching side of the other magnet. Have them try and "chase" one magnet around with the other. Next, show them that it works the same way with the "south" ends of the magnets.

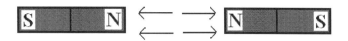

   Finally, show them that the ends that are different (i.e. "north" to "south" or blue to red) are attracted to each other. Tell them that sometimes people say "opposites attract," when they are talking about people, but that's exactly how it works with magnets! The sides that are opposite are attracted to each other and the sides that are the same push away from each other.

Activity:

     Take a pencil and poke the sharpened end into a piece of Styrofoam that is at least one inch thick and approximately two by two inches around. Now slide a ring magnet over the pencil so that it lands on the Styrofoam. Slide another ring magnet on the pencil <u>so that the bottom side of the new magnet repels the top side of the magnet that is already on the pencil</u>. Add two more magnets to the pencil in the same way, so that you end up with all of the ring magnets "levitating" on top of each other. Show the students how they can actually feel the force of the magnets pushing away from each other when they try to push them together. Tell them that there are levitating trains that use magnets to keep them from touching the track as they move. This helps the train to move faster than trains on other types of tracks.

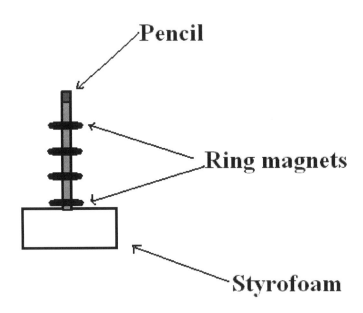

Part 5: Magnetic Fields

Activity:

     Have your students put a paperclip on a table and then slowly lower a magnet closer to the paperclip. At some point, the paperclip will "jump" up to the magnet. That point is where the magnet's magnetic field starts. If it is an inch above the table, than the magnetic field of that magnet spreads out at least an inch away from the magnet itself.

     Tell your students that the space around a magnet that a magnet has attraction through is called a magnetic field.

Activity:

     Give each of your students a paper clip and have them tie a piece of thread to it that is about seven inches long. Tape the other end of the thread to a table top. Now give each of them a magnet and have them put it up to the paper clip so that it sticks to it. Then, have them slowly raise the magnet and paper clip away from the table until the thread is pulled tight. Next they should very, very slowly pull the magnet away from the paper clip until the paper clip and the magnet are separated. If they do this slowly enough, the paper clip will be hanging in mid-air just below the magnet. Point out to your students that this works because the magnetic field of the magnet extends out past the magnet itself.

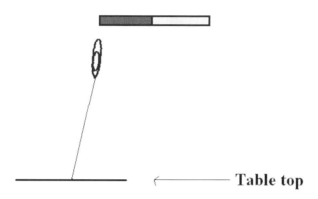

← **Table top**

Part 6: Induced Magnetism

Activity:

     *Show your students a metal paperclip. Ask them if they think it is magnetic (no). Show them that it is not magnetic by seeing if another metal paperclip will stick to it. Now, take a magnet and stick a metal paperclip to it. Next, stick another metal paperclip to the first one. Keep attaching paperclips to each other until they won't stick anymore. Explain to your students that magnets can make other iron objects that are close to them temporarily magnetic. If you take the paperclips off of the magnet, they may still stick together (sometimes they won't), but once you pull them apart, they won't be magnetic anymore. Tell your students that you are going to teach them a new word; "induced." **Induced** means "to make something happen." We say that these paperclips are sticking together because of **induced magnetism**. They aren't magnets themselves, but the magnet is "inducing" them to act like magnets.*

     Have your students try this with different magnets and see how many paperclips they can pick-up. Different magnets will have different strengths. Stronger magnets will be able to pick up more paperclips than weaker magnets.

Activity:

Take a small jewelry box (or similar-sized box) and cut a number of pieces of corrugated cardboard to fit inside the box. Place enough of the pieces of cardboard in the box to fill it to about ¼ inch from the top. Place at least three ring magnets on top of the cardboard in the box so that the same pole is facing up in all three magnets (you can test this by taking a fourth ring magnet and making sure that one side of it repulses all three ring magnets in the box as they face up). Close the lid of the box, tape it shut, and place a number of small metal paperclips on top of it. Show the students how they can make "sculptures" using magnetic force and the paperclips on top of the box.

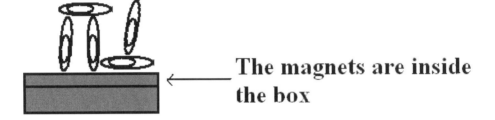

The magnets are inside the box

Chapter 7: Stars and Planets
Ages 4-7

Materials Needed for this Unit

Aluminum foil
A dowel that is about ¼ inch in diameter
Black poster board
Large marshmallows
Graham crackers
Chocolate squares
Plastic oven-cooking bag (from a grocery store)
Duct tape
Globe
Stick
Needle and thread
Crayons or paints
Good quality binoculars
Shoebox
Flour
Baking soda
Cinnamon
Marble
Irregularly-shaped pebble
Movie of the Apollo 11 moon landing from the library
A large box or plastic garbage can
Silver spray paint
A large paper grocery bag
Freeze-dried food or dried soup, etc…
Utility knife
Pencil
Clear tape
Toilet paper tube
Black construction paper
Pictures from the library or internet of the various planets
A small piece of white poster board
A large piece of white poster board
Powdered juice drink
A pizza box that is the type that pizza would be delivered in
A bright flashlight that has only one bulb in it
A clothes hanger or a large piece of corrugated cardboard or foam board

White paper
Soup ladle
Pins
Rocks
Scissors

Part 1: Our Closest Star

Ask your students if they have ever gone outside at night and tried to count the stars. There are billions of stars in the sky, most of which we can't even see. Do your students know what the closest star to the earth is? (the sun). The sun is a huge ball of fiery gases that is incredibly hot and bright. It is so hot and bright that its light and heat travel 93 million miles to our earth to give us heat and light. To get an idea of how far 93 million miles is, if you drove to the sun in your car at 55 miles per hour (highway speed), it would take you a little over one hundred and ninety-three years of straight driving to get to the sun.

Now think about how big the sun looks in the sky and compare it to when you watch a car drive off until it gets so small that you can't see it. The sun still looks big in the sky, even though it is 93 million miles away! Think about how big it has to be for us to be able to see it. The sun is so big that about one million earths would fit inside it!

Activity:

Tell your students that you are going to use heat from the sun to cook marshmallows to make s'mores with. Take a pizza box (the kind that pizza is delivered in) open it up, line the bottom of it with aluminum foil, then cover the aluminum foil with a piece of black poster board:

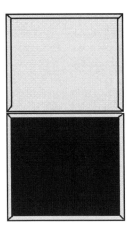

Close the lid of the pizza box and place a plastic oven cooking bag (you can find them in your local grocery store) on top in the middle of the lid. You may need to trim some of the sides of the bag if it is too large. Using a pencil, trace around the bag and then remove it. Take a ruler and draw lines to make a window in the box lid that is about one inch <u>smaller</u> all around than the plastic bag. You can erase the pencil marks where the bag was once the window is done. Cut out three sides of the window, but do not cut along the edge where the lid is hinged:

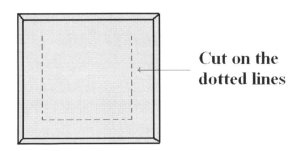

Cut on the dotted lines

Next, open the window you just made in the lid and fold it back so that it will open and close easily:

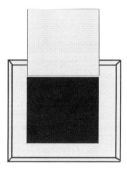

Tape the plastic oven cooking bag on top of the hole in the lid with duct tape, making sure that the edges are sealed tightly:

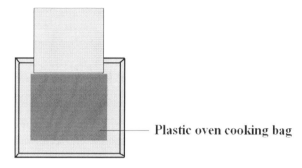

Glue or tape aluminum foil to the cover of the window you made so that the foil is on the side facing the window. Make sure that you smooth as many of the wrinkles in the foil out as possible before you glue it:

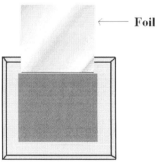

Your completed solar cooker should look something like the picture below. Use a stick to prop up the reflective flap.

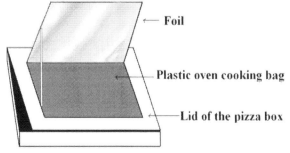

You are now ready to make s'mores. Place some graham crackers with marshmallows on them in the middle of the bottom of the solar cooker (on top of the black poster board) and close the lid. Prop up the aluminum flap so that it catches the sunlight and reflects it into the bottom of the cooker. Be patient, it could take three to five hours for the cooker to heat up the marshmallows. Once they are soft, take them out, put a square of chocolate on top of each marshmallow and place another graham cracker on top of the chocolate. You have now used heat from the sun to make s'mores! This cooker may not get hot enough to cook some foods safely, so it is best to just use it for s'mores.

Activity:

Ask your students if they have noticed how the sun moves through the sky during the day. Tell them that the sun isn't actually moving; we are! Even though we can't feel it, the earth is constantly spinning in circles. Take a globe and a flashlight and have a student shine the flashlight in one place to represent the sun. Then take the globe and hold it in the beam of the flashlight and say that right now the part of the earth that is in the beam of light is in daylight while the side of the earth that is not in the beam of light is in nighttime. Then start slowly spinning the globe to show them how the sun shines on different parts of the earth as it spins. You could say something like "Now the sun is rising in the United States, as it is falling in…." Tell them that the earth turns completely around one time each day, so when they wake up in the morning, the earth has turned completely around one time since the previous morning. You can illustrate this with the flashlight and globe.

Activity:

Go outside and place a stick in the ground. Mark where the shadow of the stick falls with a rock. Every hour go outside and mark the new shadow with another rock. Tell your students that in the old days, people would use the sun to tell time this way and that a device like this is called a sun dial. Point out to them where the sun is and how it has moved across the sky (make sure that no one looks directly at the sun and tell them that they never should do this or they could burn their eyes).

Part 2: The Planets

Activity:

Tell your students that not only does the earth turn around once a day; it is moving in a big circle around the sun when it does this. Take a chair and tell your students that it represents the sun. Take the globe and walk with it once around the chair and say that every time the earth goes around the sun a year has gone by. Spin the globe on its axis as you do this to show how it spins as it goes around the sun. Tell them that the sun is a big ball of burning gas and the earth is a planet that circles it.

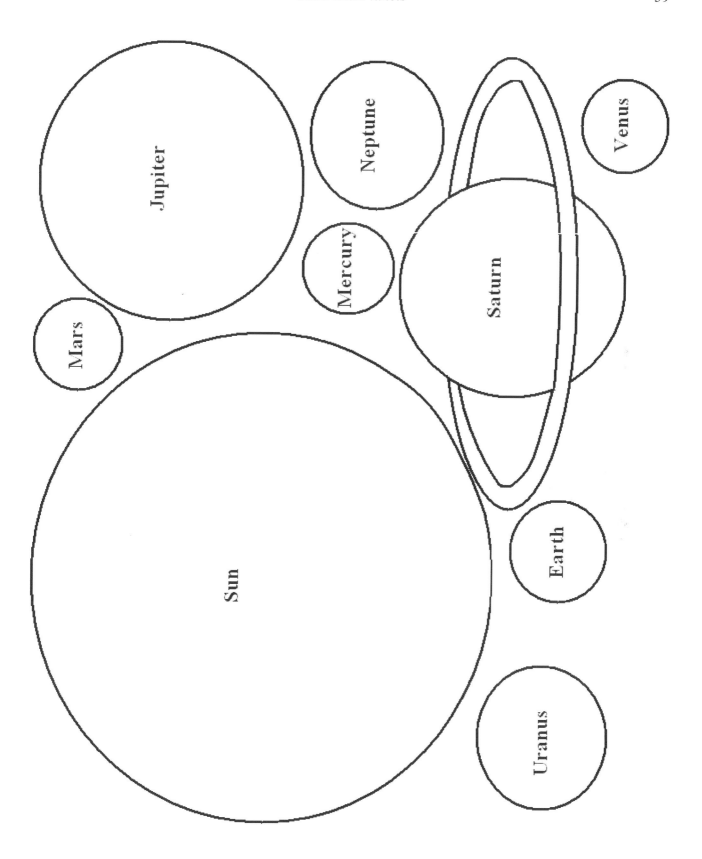

Activity:

Ask your students if they have heard of any other planets besides the earth that circle our sun. There are eight planets in our solar system; Mercury, Venus, Earth, Mars, Jupiter, and Neptune, and they all travel around the sun. We used to say that there was another planet named Pluto, but astronomers (make sure they know that an astronomer is someone who studies the sun, stars, and planets) have decided that Pluto is too small to be called a planet, so they now call Pluto a "Dwarf Planet." Teach your students the following pneumonic device to help them remember the order of the planets from the sun, with Mercury being the planet closest to the sun and Neptune being the planet farthest from the sun:

My	(Mercury)
Very	(Venus)
Excellent	(Earth)
Mother	(Mars)
Just	(Jupiter)
Sent	(Saturn)
Us	(Uranus)
Nickels	(Neptune)

Activity:

Make a solar system mobile using the template on the preceding page. Copy the template and cut out the sun and planets. Place them on a piece of white poster board and trace around them with a pencil; then cut them out of the poster board and label each planet. Using paint or crayons make them the following colors: Sun (Yellow), Mercury (Grey), Venus (Yellow), Earth (Blue and White), Mars (Red), Jupiter (Orange and White), Saturn (Yellow), Uranus (Light Blue), and Neptune (Blue). Show your students some books or internet photos of the planets to give them an idea of what the different planets look like. Sometimes the colors will vary depending on the filters used to take the photos.

Now you need to decide what you would like to hang your solar system from. One easy way is to hang it from a clothes hanger with the sun on one side and the planets in order going away from the sun. Another way is to cut a large circle from a piece of corrugated cardboard or foam board. The size of the circle will depend on how large you want your mobile to be, though the circle should be at least ten inches in diameter. Put a mark in the middle of the circle where the sun will hang from and draw eight circles outside of the sun so that it resembles a dart-board target. These circles represent the orbits of the planets around the sun. You can attach each planet anywhere on its respective orbit, with Mercury attaching to the circle closest to the sun, Neptune to the one farthest from the sun, and the others in their respective orders in between.

To attach a planet to its hanger, take a threaded needle and poke it through the top of the planet. Knot the end of the thread so that the planet will hang from it. If you used the cardboard circle hanger, thread the needle through the planet's orbit on the circle. If you used a clothes hanger, tie it off on its place on the hanger.

The clothes hanger mobile is now ready to hang. If you chose to make the cardboard circle mobile, you will need to string some thread through the cardboard circle to hang it. It will hang better if you hang it from four threads spaced evenly around the edges of the circle, instead of from just one thread in the middle.

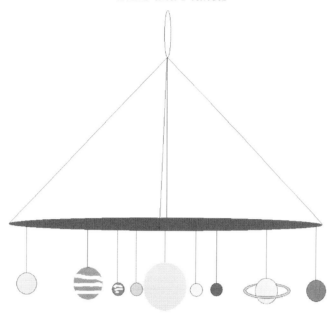

Part 3: The Moon

Tell your students that a ***solar system*** is the name astronomers give to all of the planets and other things that revolve around a star. The earth, along with the other planets in our solar system revolves around our local star, the sun. Ask your students what other large object can they see up in the sky besides the sun (the moon). Tell them that while the Earth is busy revolving around the sun, the moon is revolving around the Earth! Earth has only one moon, but some planets, like Jupiter, have lots of moons.

Activity:

*Take a pair of good-quality binoculars out one night and look at the moon through them. You should be able to see some craters if you look hard enough. Tell your students that the craters are made when objects such as **meteoroids** hit the surface of the moon. Meteoroids are solid objects moving through space that are in a certain size range. They can be as small as a speck of dust and as large as a house.*

Activity:

Take a shoebox and fill it about half-full with a mixture of flour and baking soda. Sprinkle cinnamon across the top. Have your students stand above the box and drop a marble in it to see the pattern of the crater formed. Try dropping it from different heights to see how the height affects the depth of the crater. Try dropping a small irregularly-shaped pebble in to see how a different shape might affect the crater's shape. Tell your students that this is similar to how the craters on the moon were formed.

Activity:

Tell your students that in 1969 astronauts Neil Armstrong and Edwin (Buzz) Aldrin were the first men to ever walk on the moon. Check out a movie from your local library about the Apollo 11 moon landing for your students to watch. You can also search for clips of the moon landing online.

Activity:

    Have your students take a pretend voyage to the moon. Before they do this, you will need to make some props first. Make a space ship out of either a large cardboard box, or a clean plastic garbage can. <u>If you use the garbage can, do not let your students go inside it when the lid is on</u>; wait until after you have cut a small window in it to prevent suffocation. Take a large piece of poster board and shape it like a cone to fit on top. If you really want to jazz it up, purchase some silver spray paint and paint it. Cut a hole to climb in and a window for your students to look out of.

    Make space helmets out of large paper grocery bags, by cutting out a "window" for their eyes. Again, you could spray-paint them silver. When you use the spray-paint, follow all of the directions and make sure you are in a well-ventilated room.

    Astronauts eat a lot of freeze-dried foods because they take up less space than regular food. They reconstitute much of their food with water. You can purchase freeze-dried food at a camping store for your young astronauts to try while they are on their pretend voyage, or you can purchase some dried soup or packaged macaroni and cheese from your local grocery store. Many of the drinks astronauts have are powdered ones that they add water to, so you could buy some powdered juice for them to drink.

    Once you have your props ready, have your students climb into their space ship and blast off for the moon. When they arrive at the moon, have them get out for a space walk. Tell them that gravity is a force that pulls us down toward the earth and keeps us from flying around the room. There is less gravity on the moon, so astronauts can jump higher there. Have them jump around and describe what they see. Then tell them it is lunch time and give them the "astronaut food." Use your imaginations to continue the game.

Activity:

    Have your students make a mini rocket ship that can be flown by blowing into a drinking straw. Take a piece of paper and cut it in half as shown below:

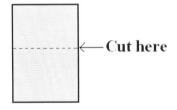

Cut here

    Now take one of the halves of paper, start in one corner, and roll it onto a pencil so that it forms a tube. Make sure that the pencil you use is fatter than the straw you will be using to shoot the rocket. Tape the tube with clear tape so that it keeps its shape. Remove the pencil and fold one end of the tube over about ½ inch and tape it down. Cut two triangles from the remaining half of the paper that you have left and tape them to the open end of the paper tube so that they form "fins." Slip the rocket over a drinking straw and blow. The rocket should shoot through the air. Make sure that you remind your students not to shoot them at other people!

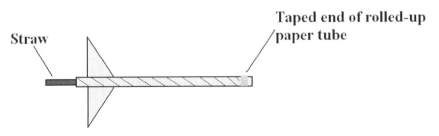

Straw

Taped end of rolled-up paper tube

Part 4: The Stars

Remind your students that the sun is our closest star. Tell them that one way that people find particular stars is by looking for patterns in the sky to help them remember where a star is. These patterns are called **constellations** and one of the most famous constellations is called "***The Big Dipper***." It is called the Big Dipper because it is shaped like a ladle that you would use to dip water or soup with. If you own a ladle, show your students what it looks like.

Activity:

Take a toilet paper tube and tape a piece of black construction paper over one end so that no light can get through. Now take a pin and poke holes in the construction paper to make the Big Dipper and North Star pattern below:

Next, go into a dark room and shine a bright flashlight that has only one bulb in it through the inside of the toilet paper tube and onto the wall. If the flashlight end is larger than the tube, you can wrap some cloth (a dark shirt works well) around the junction where the flashlight meets the tube to keep the light from escaping. You should be able to see the pattern of the Big Dipper on the wall. You may need to move the flashlight around a bit to make it so that the "stars" show up on the wall well. Sometimes it helps to point the light toward one side of the tube or the other, instead of straight down the middle. Point out to your students the outline of the dipper:

*Next, tell them that the Big Dipper is a special constellation because it points to a famous star called the **North Star** (also called the **Pole Star**). They can find the North Star by mentally continuing the line made by the two pointer stars in the Big Dipper. The first bright star that they see along this line is the North Star. If they can find the North Star in the sky, they will always know which way is north. Be sure and show them the North Star on the constellation you made with the toilet paper tube. You can continue this activity if you like by looking up other constellations and making more "tube planetariums." Then take your students outside at night to find the real constellations!*

Chapter 8: Health
Ages 4-7

Materials Needed for this Unit

White vinegar
A hard boiled egg
Two jars with lids
Baking soda
Salt
White and pink play dough or clay
Blender
One quart whole milk
Lemon juice
Crackers or toast
Fruit, including a citrus fruit
Yogurt
An orange
Whole cloves
Ribbon
8 ounces of cream cheese
2 cups cheddar cheese
1 cup of grated carrot
Raisins
Peanuts or other nuts
Sunflower seeds
Shredded coconut
Dried fruit
Access to the internet (for one activity only)
Rice
One package baking yeast
Flour
Sugar
Shortening
Eggs
Stopwatch or clock that measures seconds
Cardstock
Jump rope
Glitter
Hand lotion
Poster paper
Peppermint, strawberry or some other type of flavoring
Chicken bone (a drumstick bone works well)
Breakfast cereal such as Total® with 100% of the RDA value for iron in it

Crayons or markers
Spray bottle
Large piece of paper
Strainer
Non-metallic bowl
Magnet
White paper towel or cloth
Tape
Salt
Towel
Soap

Part 1: Introduction

This chapter contains a number of food activities. Be sure to check with your students to make sure that none of them have any food allergies before giving them any food, especially peanuts or other nuts.

Tell your students that most people want to live a long and happy life and one thing they do to help that happen is to take good care of their bodies. In this unit we're going to talk about different things they can do to keep their bodies healthy and strong.

Activity:

Ask your students to keep track during the next week of everything that they do to take care of their bodies.

Part 2: Teeth

Tell your students that most foods that we eat have some type of sugar in them and that there are germs called bacteria in our mouths that stick to our teeth and eat the sugar that we leave on them. As the bacteria eat the sugar, they make something called an acid that eats away at our teeth. That is why dentists clean off all of the bacteria and plaque from our teeth. Plaque is a mixture of bacteria and other substances.

Activity:

Tell your students that our teeth are a very important part of our digestive systems. Without teeth, it would be very hard to chew up our food so that we could swallow it. That is why it is so important to take good care of our teeth by brushing them regularly and not eating too many sweets.

Take a hard boiled egg and place it in a jar. Next, fill the jar with white vinegar and close the lid. Tell your students that an eggshell is made of materials that are very similar to their teeth. After a few days (up to seven, but often much faster; sometimes even overnight), the shell of the egg in the vinegar will dissolve away. This is because the acid in the vinegar dissolved the eggshell, just like the acid that bacteria makes dissolves teeth. Point out again to your students that brushing their teeth will get the sugar off of them that the bacteria like to eat.

Activity:

Try making some old-fashioned homemade toothpowder. Take 4 teaspoons baking soda,* ½ teaspoon salt, and 2 teaspoon of flavoring, such as strawberry or peppermint and mix them all together. Tell your students to dampen their toothbrushes and dip it in the powder to brush their teeth. Remind your students that they should brush their teeth at least twice a day. After tasting this toothpowder, they will probably really appreciate their kids-flavored toothpaste more!

Don't use this toothpowder more than once or twice, it is too abrasive to use regularly. Modern toothpastes are better for your teeth. Also, your students should not use this if they have any orthodontic work in their mouths.

---

* Make sure you use baking soda and not baking powder, some baking powder has alum in it, which you don't want your students eating.

Ask your students if they know what kinds of foods are bad for their teeth (sugary, sticky foods). Have them make a list of foods that are bad for their teeth and tell them that they should try not to eat too many of these types of foods. However if they do eat them, they should be sure to brush their teeth afterwards.

Activity:

Have your students make a model of their jaw using play dough. Tell them that children have twenty "baby" teeth that will eventually fall out to make room for the thirty-two permanent teeth that they will have when they are adults. It is especially important to take care of their permanent teeth, because they will not be getting any new teeth after that! Show them the picture below to help them make the model of their jaw--they can also look at someone else's teeth to help them with this project.

Schedule of Approximate Years for Loss of Baby Teeth

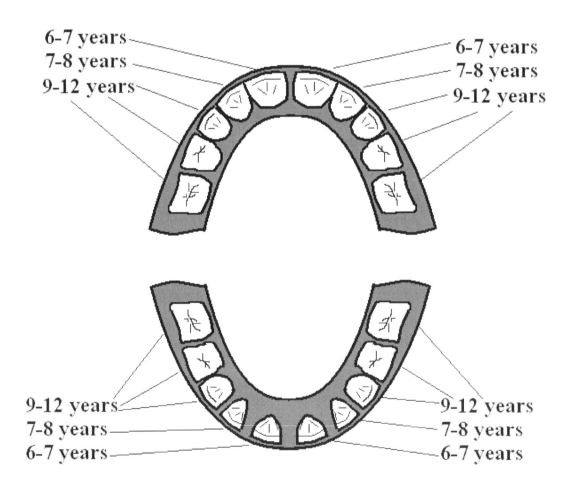

Part 3: Healthy Eating

Tell your students that teeth aren't the only parts of their body that need taking care of. While avoiding eating sugary food is one good step toward being healthy, there are foods that they <u>can</u> eat that will help keep their teeth and the rest of their bodies strong.

Activity:

Take a clean chicken bone (a drumstick works well for this) and place it in a covered jar of white vinegar. Before you put it in the jar, gently try to bend it to show your students how strong it is. Be sure that anyone who touches it washes their hands well afterwards. Wait seven days and take the bone out of the jar. Rinse it and try to bend it again; it should bend easily. This is because the vinegar dissolved the calcium in the bone and calcium is what gives bones their strength. If we did not have calcium in our bones, they would be "bendy" like the bone in the vinegar.

Tell your students that one of the main sources for calcium is dairy products such as milk, cheese, and yogurt. Soybeans and almonds are also good sources of calcium, plus some breads and cereals have calcium added to them because it is so important to our health.

Activity:

Make a calcium-rich snack and teach your students how cheese is made at the same time! Take one quart of whole milk (do not use ultra pasteurized milk, but plain pasteurized milk works just fine) and boil it, stirring occasionally. Add 2 ½ tablespoons lemon juice and stir for about one minute. The curds (the solid part) will separate from the whey (the liquid part). Pour the mixture through a strainer. The resulting cheese curds will resemble cottage or ricotta cheese. Spread them on crackers or toast for a healthy snack!

Tell your students that our bones need a special vitamin to help them absorb or take in calcium. This vitamin is called vitamin D. Vitamins are substances found in the food we eat that our bodies need to stay strong and healthy. People who don't get enough vitamin D can't absorb the calcium that they eat and they can get a disease called rickets. Their bones become soft and funny-shaped, sort of like the chicken bone that you put in the vinegar.

Vitamin D is very interesting because while we can get vitamin D from the food we eat, we mostly get it from being out in the sun! Our skin makes it when it is exposed to the sun, so it is good for our bodies to spend time outside. However, we also need to be careful that we don't get too much sun on our skin, or we get sunburn.

Activity:

Go outside and play in the sun! You can play a version of tag called "shadow tag" where instead of tagging a person; you have to tag their shadow. You may need someone to referee and make sure that the shadows were actually tagged.

Ask your students if they have heard of any other vitamins besides vitamin D. There are at least twelve other vitamins that our bodies need. One well-known one is Vitamin C. Vitamin C is important for our bones and skin; it helps heal wounds, and people who don't eat enough Vitamin C can catch a disease called scurvy. In the old days, before people knew what caused scurvy, many sailors would die from it because they weren't getting enough Vitamin C in their diet on long voyages. Do your students know what types of foods we get Vitamin C from? One of the best places to get Vitamin C is from citrus fruits (make sure your students know what citrus fruits are). You can also get it from tomatoes, broccoli, spinach, and red berries.

Activity:

Make a fruit salad by chopping up some fruit and mixing it with a bit of yogurt. Be sure to put in some citrus for the Vitamin C!

Activity:

Take an orange and completely cover it with whole cloves by poking them into the skin of the orange. Tie a ribbon around it like a package and hang it in a closet to make it smell like citrus and cloves. Tell your students it is to remind them how important it is to eat foods with Vitamin C.

Tell your students that another important vitamin is Vitamin A. Among other things, Vitamin A is good for our eyes and skin. We get Vitamin A from carrots, sweet potatoes, pumpkins, mangos, papaya, apricots, and cantaloupe. Can your students think of anything that all of these food items have in common? (they are all orange).

Activity:

Make a carrot spread by mixing 8 oz of cream cheese, 2 cups of shredded cheddar cheese, and 1 cup of grated carrot together. You can spread it on crackers for a great Vitamin A snack!

Mention to your students that calcium, which they learned about earlier, is not a vitamin. It is called a mineral, and it is not the only mineral that our bodies need to stay healthy. Another mineral that we need is iron, the same iron that we talked about in the unit on magnets; a metal! Iron is especially important for our blood. People who do not get enough iron become tired and weak. Some of the main sources we get iron from are beef, pork, chicken, and fish, but we can also get iron from raisins, soy, and spinach (among other things).

Activity:

Take two cups of plain (without fruit or raisins, just flakes) breakfast cereal that has one hundred percent of the RDA value for iron in it (for example Total®) and put them in a blender. Add just enough water to cover the cereal and blend it all together. Pour the cereal mixture in a non-metallic bowl and stir it with a strong magnet. If you like, you can rubber-band the magnet to the end of a tongue depressor to make it easier to stir. After a few minutes, you should see some tiny pieces of iron stuck to the magnet. If they are hard to see, wipe the magnet on a piece of white paper towel or cloth, and you should see black specks or smears of iron. Tell your students that iron is so important for our bodies that some cereal companies have put iron in their cereal to help us get enough iron in our food.

Activity:

Make a healthy trail mix by mixing together raisins, peanuts or other nuts (make sure none of your students are allergic to nuts), shredded coconut, sunflower seeds, and other dried fruit. Remind your students that this snack is full of iron for their blood.

Activity:

Tell your students that scientists have divided the various types of food into groups to make it easier for people to keep track of what they eat. Some of these groups are: grains (which include everything made out of grains like breads and cereals), vegetables, fruits, dairy, and protein. Have your students go to the USDA website at: http://www.choosemyplate.gov/. There are lots of fun activities on this website to help teach them about the foods that they eat.

Activity:

Show your students how grains are made into flour by taking some rice and grinding it into rice flour in a blender. You could also have them grind it themselves between two stones. After you do this, use the following recipe to make some rolls to show them how flour is made into bread: Dissolve 1 package of yeast in ½ cup lukewarm water. Boil 4 cups of water and add 1 cup of shortening to it. Let the water cool until it is lukewarm and add 2 cups of sugar, the yeast mixture, 1 tablespoon salt, and 4 eggs. Now mix in 6 cups of flour and once that is mixed, add 9 more cups of flour. Kneed the dough and cover it with a towel until it has doubled in size (about 1 hour). Punch down the dough and shape it into balls that are about 1 ½ inches to 2 inches in diameter. Place the balls on a greased cookie sheet and cover them with a towel. Let them rise about one hour and then bake them at 350 degrees for about 10-15 minutes.

Part 4: Exercise

Ask your students if they can think of something else we need to do to keep our bodies healthy (exercise). Children and teenagers should exercise about sixty minutes most days of the week. Ask your students what kinds of things they like to do to get their daily exercise. Come up with a list of different ways they could get exercise each day. Exercising keeps our hearts, lungs and the rest of our bodies healthy and strong.

Activity:

Show your students how to take their pulse by placing the first two fingers of one hand gently on the wrist of the other. If you place the fingers about 1 ½ inches down from the wrist on the thumb side of the little bones that go down the center of your wrist, you should be able to feel a pulse. Tell your students that the pulse rate tells you how fast your heart is beating. When you exercise, your heart beats faster. Have your students count how many times their heart beats in 15 seconds. Do this three times to get an average count (find the average by adding the three numbers together and dividing the answer by three). Now, have your students do jumping jacks for one minute and take their pulse again. Was it faster than their average resting pulse rate?

Activity:

Take your students outside for the following activity. First, brainstorm with them about the different exercise they know, such as jumping jacks, sit-ups, push-ups, etc…. Write the different exercises that they know on some cardstock, and place them in different places outside to make various exercise stations. Give the students a starting point and have them run to the first exercise station. When they reach it, have them do the exercise for that station ten times (i.e. ten jumping jacks or ten sit-ups, etc...). When they finish the first station, have them run on to the next station and do the exercise for that one. Continue this until they have completed all of the stations.

Activity:

Get out a jump rope and play some jump rope games. The most basic game is to have two people swing the rope and the rest run into it and jump. You can also use a jump rope to play the limbo, where the kids try to go under the rope by leaning backwards without touching either the rope or the ground.

Part 5: Germs

Activity:

*Put a small amount of glitter on your hand and go and shake one of your student's hands. If you have more than one student, have that student shake another student's hand, and so on. The glitter should spread from student to student as they do this. Ask them if they can guess what the glitter is supposed to represent (germs). Tell your students that this is one way that germs are spread, by touching someone's hand or something else that has germs on it. Ask your students if they know what **germs** are (invisible creatures such as protozoa, bacteria, fungi, or viruses that can make you sick). Tell them that one of the best ways to keep from spreading germs and getting sick is to wash their hands. They should get into the habit of washing their hands every time they use the bathroom, before they eat, and after they play with their pets. This will greatly reduce the number of illnesses they get. Make sure that the children get all of the glitter off of their hands so that they don't get any in their eyes!*

Activity:

    Have the students put hand lotion on their hands and then dip them in some glitter. Tell them that the glitter represents germs that they have to wash off of their hands. Have them try to first just wipe the glitter off with a towel. That probably won't get all of the glitter off, so now show them how to wash their hands with soap and warm water, making sure that they wash both the tops and bottoms of their hands and dry them thoroughly. Tell them that as they wash their hands, they can sing a song like "Row, Row, Row Your Boat," and that they shouldn't stop washing until the song is over. This will help them make sure that they have washed their hands long enough. Point out to them that to get all of the germs off, they needed to use soap and warm water. Make sure that they dry their hands also; all of these steps in washing their hands are important.

Activity:

    Tell your students that there are other things we can do to help keep us and the people around us from getting sick. One of these things is to cover our mouths when we sneeze or cough. Tape a large piece of paper (or tape a few pieces of paper together) to the wall and spray some water at it with a spray bottle that is set to a misty setting. See how far back you can stand and still have the spray hit the paper. Tell your students that that is what happens when they sneeze or cough; their germs get sprayed around the room.

    In the past, we were all told to cover our mouths with our hands when we sneeze or cough; but what happens if we sneeze or cough into our hand, and then we go to shake someone else's hand, or touch something with our hand? We end up spreading the germs around anyhow! So now there is a new way to keep from spreading germs when we cough or sneeze. Instead of coughing or sneezing into your hand, you can cough or sneeze into the bend in your elbow (demonstrate this).

    Tell your students that something else they can do to keep from spreading germs and getting sick is to not share cups or drinking bottles with other people, or eat using someone else's utensils or from someone else's plate.

Part 6: Things to Avoid

    Remind your students that vitamins are substances in the foods we eat that our bodies need to survive. They are so important that many people worry that they don't get enough vitamins in their foods, so they take vitamin pills--maybe some of your students take them. Vitamins for kids usually taste pretty good, almost like candy. However, it is important not to take more than one children's vitamin a day because some vitamins can make you <u>really</u> sick if you take too many of them. Can your students think of anything else that might make them sick if they ate it? Remind them that they should never take any medicine unless their parents or doctor have told them to take it, because, taking the wrong medicine or even taking too much of the right one can make them sick, or even kill them. Another thing they should not do is eat any strange berries, mushrooms, or leaves that they find outside. Many plants can make them sick and often tasty-looking berries can be poisonous. Tell them to only eat things that they find outside when their parents tell them they are safe to eat.

Activity:

    Have your students make a poster warning about things that they should not eat.

Chapter 9: Beginning Plants
Ages 4-7

Materials Needed for this Unit

Clear plastic disposable cups
Potting Soil
Bean seeds
Potted plant
A vegetable platter
Broccoli
Tomato
Celery
Beans or peas
X-Acto® or other sharp knife
Carrot
Black construction paper
Ranch salad dressing
One sixteen ounce carton sour cream
One package dried onion soup mix
Trowel or small shovel
Contact paper
Styrofoam drinking cups
Cross-section of either a branch or trunk of a tree
Paper plate
Crayons
Blank address labels
Adult-sized shoebox with lid
Small plant pot
Cardboard
Packaged sugar cookie dough
Yellow food coloring
Shelled sunflower seeds
Picture of a sunflower with the seeds in it from the local library or internet
Two pieces of corrugated cardboard at least 8 ½ x 11 inches each
Small re-closable plastic sandwich bag, the kind where you don't use a zipper to zip it
Colored Construction paper
Colored tissue paper
Green pipe cleaners
One or two bags of dried Lima Beans (see activity under "Part 2: Seeds")
Green masking or floral tape
 "Seed" foods such as bread, nut butters, sunflower seeds, granola, soybeans
Seeds and materials to start a vegetable garden

Grass or chive seeds
Empty egg carton
"The Tiny Seed" by Eric Carl
Potato
Toothpicks
Wax paper
Drawing paper
Lettuce
Stapler
Newspaper
Non-toxic acrylic paints
Clay flower pot
Flower seeds
Blender
Soy beans in their pods
Varnish (optional)
Eyedropper or spray bottle
Flashlight
Markers
A variety of fruits and vegetables

Part 1: Introduction

Ask your students what their favorite plant is and why. Then ask "Has a plant done anything for you today?" Possible answers are: we eat plants for food, wood from trees is used to build houses, plants give off oxygen that we breath, some clothes are made from cotton or flax, and bees use nectar from flowers to make the honey that we eat. Now bring out a potted plant and ask if they can tell you the three main parts of a plant (roots, stem, and leaves). Ask them if they know what these three main parts do (the roots anchor the plant and take up water and nutrients from the ground, the stem holds the plant up and moves water and nutrients, the leaves take in the sunlight that the plant needs to grow, the flowers produce the seeds, and the seeds grow into new plants).

Activity:

Show your students various vegetables and fruits and ask them what part of the plant they are from. Some examples you could use are: celery for stems, broccoli for flowers, lettuce for leaves, carrots for roots, tomatoes for fruit, beans or peas out of the pod for seeds.

Activity:

Make a vegetable platter for your students to eat with one or more dips for them to try. You can use ranch salad dressing for one dip and mix a carton of sour cream with a package of dried onion soup mix for another (or make your own favorite dip). Tell your students that you have a snack for them, but that first they have to guess what vegetables are on the platter. Give them hints that include what part of the plant it is, what color, etc...

Part 2: Seeds

Activity:

Read the story "The Tiny Seed" by Eric Carl. Follow it up with the next activity.

Activity:

Tell your students that you want them to curl up on the floor and pretend that they are seeds in the ground. Tell them that you are going to cover them with dirt and pretend to throw dirt on them. Next shine a flashlight on them and say: "Now the sun is shining on the little seeds." Then take an eyedropper and drop a bit of water on their cheeks and say that it is raining on them (or you could give them a squirt with a spray bottle). Finally, tell them that it is time for them to start to grow and have them slowly unfold and stand up tall with their arms held up like leaves. Ask each student what kind of plant they are.

Activity:

Give each of your students an egg carton to collect seeds in. Now go outside and have your students go on a scavenger hunt for seeds. See how many different kinds they can find. Tell them that plants can't move very much so their seeds have to move for them, otherwise they would all grow too close together. Look at the various seeds you found and see if you can figure out what mechanism the seed has for dispersal. Tell them that seeds can be blown on the wind, float in the water, or stuck to animals. Some seeds are even transported in poop! An animal will eat the fruit and poop out the seeds far away from where the animal found the fruit. Sometimes squirrels will store acorns for the winter and forget where they hid them. The acorns then grow into oak trees.

Activity:

Tell you students that you want them to pretend they are seeds and act out what the seeds are doing as you tell them the following story:

I am a little seed and I'm curled up in a ball. Suddenly, a human comes along, accidentally kicks me and I roll away. Then a cat walks by and I get stuck to its foot. The cat carries me on its foot to the side of a river and I fall off into the water. I move with the water downstream and I get washed up into the sand. A bird sees me and picks me up and carries me far away to its nest. I fall out of the nest and land on the ground where a squirrel finds me and hides me in a hole in the ground for the winter. The squirrel forgets all about me, and I stay there until the spring; when I feel the warm sun and feel the nice water and start to grow. I grow and grow until I am a beautiful plant.

Activity:

Take a small re-closable sandwich bag (<u>not</u> the kind that uses an actual zipper to close it) and fill it with lima bean seeds. Add as much water as the bag can hold and seal it shut. Place the bag on a plate in the sun and wait a few hours. The seeds should swell up and burst out of the bag. Tell your students that before seeds can grow, they need to soak up lots of water. These seeds soaked up so much water that they burst the bag open! Use some of the seeds for the following activity.

Activity:

Take one of the seeds from the previous activity and using a sharp knife (like an X-Acto® knife), slice it open lengthwise. The thin layer on the outside of the seed is called the **seed coat**. The little plant on the inside is called the embryo (or you could just call it a baby plant). The bulk of the rest of the seed is used for food for the new plant as it starts to grow.

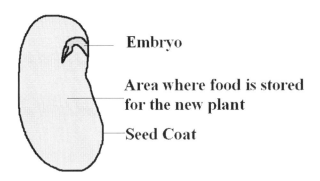

Activity:

Ask your students to try and think of as many seeds that people eat as possible. Then have a "seed snack," where you eat things made of seeds. Possibilities are sunflower seeds, bread (made from wheat) with various nut butters on it, soybeans, and granola. Show them how peanut butter is made by taking some shelled peanuts and grinding them up in a blender (you can add a tiny bit of water if needed). **Make sure that none of your students have any nut or other types of food allergies before doing this or any food activity.** One fun way to eat soybeans is to fry them in the pods with garlic salt. Let them cool and pop the seeds out to eat them.

Part 3: Roots

Remind your students that roots help keep the plant in place and take up water and nutrients from the soil that plants needs to grow.

Activity:

Take your students outside and pull up a weed by its roots so they can see what roots look like. You might need to bring a trowel to help you get the plant up! Try digging up more than one weed to compare their roots.

Activity:

Tell your students that you want them to draw a picture that shows the hidden parts of plants; the roots. They can just draw one plant, showing its roots, leaves, and stem, or they could draw a whole group of plants.

Activity:

Take a clear disposable plastic cup and fill it with potting soil. Next, plant a bean seed right next to the side of the cup so that as it grows, your students will be able to watch the roots of the plant and how they grow. Tape some black construction paper over the side of the cup that the roots will be growing on; this will protect the roots from too much light. Lift off the paper to look at the roots as they grow

Part 4: Stems

Remind your students that the stems of plants are used to support the plant and to move nutrients and water from the roots to the leaves.

Go outside and show your students a tree. Ask them to show you what part of the tree is the stem. Now show them a cross-section of either a branch or trunk. Point out where the bark, sapwood, heartwood and pith are. Tell them that the bark protects the tree from disease and insects. The sapwood is the part of the tree that carries the water and nutrients from the roots to the leaves. The heartwood and pith are old sapwood that no longer carries nutrients.

Tell your students that in places where there are definite seasons, you can tell how old a tree is by counting the rings. Each ring stands for a new year of growth.

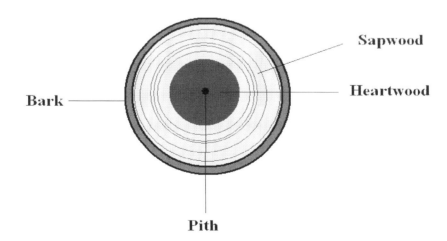

Activity:
  Give each of your students a paper plate and have them draw a picture of a cross section of a tree on it. If they can write, have them label the parts themselves, or you can label it for them. One way to do this is to take blank address labels and write "Bark, Sapwood, Heartwood, and Pith" on them to make little stickers to place on the appropriate parts of their plates.

Part 5: Leaves

  Tell your students that the leaves of the plant are where the plant takes in sunlight to help it grow.

Activity:
  Take your students on a leaf hunt. Before you do this activity, learn about any poisonous leaves in your area such as poison oak, ivy, or sumac so that you don't have any bad reactions to the leaves you might find. Go outside and have your students collect different types of leaves. Point out to them how different types of trees have different leaves; then make leaf rubbings of them by placing a piece of paper over the leaves and rubbing the paper with the <u>side</u> of a crayon.

Activity:
  Take an adult-sized shoe box and tape pieces of cardboard in it so it looks like the diagram below. Cut a hole about 1 ½ by 1 ½ inches wide in the middle of the top of the shoebox. Plant a bean seed in a small pot and place it in the bottom of the box. Put a small plate or jar lid under the pot so that water doesn't leak out when you water it. Put the lid back on the shoebox (while still keeping the whole thing upright) and place it in a sunny room. Only open the shoe box when the plant needs watering. Eventually the bean plant will grow toward the hole in the top of the box, weaving around the cardboard like a maze! Tell your students that this is because plants need sunlight to grow, so it is going through the maze you have made to get to the sunlight.

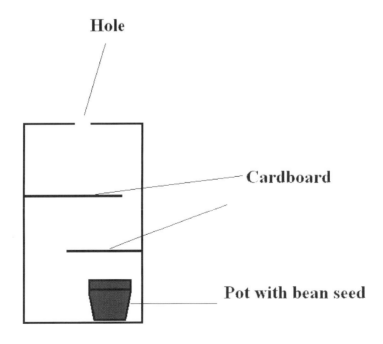

Part 6: Flowers

Remind your students that flowers are the parts of the plants where the seeds are made.

Activity:

Show your students a picture of a sunflower with the seeds in it (from your local library or the internet) and tell them that you are going to make sunflower cookies! As always, make sure that your students don't have any food allergies before doing any projects involving food. Take some pre-made sugar cookie dough and mix a bit of yellow food coloring into it. Give each of your students a piece of wax paper with a bit of dough on it. Have them form the dough into a flat circle. Next, have them draw another circle inside the cookie with a toothpick and press shelled sunflower seeds onto the inner circle. Then have them draw petals on the outer part of the circle with their toothpick. Put on a cookie tray and bake according to the packaged directions. ***Be sure to tell your students not to eat the raw cookie dough and to have them wash their hands before and after this project. People have gotten deathly ill from eating raw cookie dough!***

Activity:

Take your students outside and collect some flowers to press. Once you have them collected, put down a piece of corrugated cardboard and lay at least two sheets of newspaper on top of it. Spread out your flowers over the newspaper and lay two more sheets of newspaper on top of them. If you have more flowers you can keep layering them between the newspapers until you are done. Finish it off with another piece of cardboard on top. Pile some heavy books on top of the whole stack and let it sit for about two weeks in a cool, dry place. If some of your flowers are very thick, you can take a sharp knife and cut them in half to make them thinner.

When it is time to take them out, do it carefully, so that you do not damage the flowers. Give each child a piece of contact paper to arrange their flowers on. Carefully cover it with another piece of contact paper to make a flower placemat.

Activity:

Have your students make tissue paper flowers by taking a green pipe cleaner, folding it in half and twisting it to make a stem. Next, take a piece of colored tissue paper and cut it into a circle that is about four inches in diameter. Grab it in the center and twist it to make a flower shape. Now, take the pipe cleaner and twist the two free ends around the tissue paper flower. Cover the stem where the flower attaches with green masking or floral tape. Give your students lots of color choices and have them make a few flowers so they can design a bouquet. Take a piece of construction paper and staple it into a cone-shape that they can put their bouquet in.

Part 7: Growing Plants

Activity:

　　Remind your students what plants need to grow (water, sunlight, nutrients from the soil). Tell them that you are going to do an experiment to prove that plants need water to grow. Give them each two styrofoam drinking cups with potting soil in them. Plant a bean seed in each cup. Label one cup with the word "water," and the other cup with the words "no water." Over the next few days, regularly water the bean in the cup labeled "water." The best way to water the plant is let the dirt dry out between each watering so that the plant does not get over-watered. Do not water the bean in the other cup. Point out to your students that the bean in the cup with no water was not able to grow like the bean in the cup with water. This is because plants need water to grow and survive.

Activity:

　　Give each of your students a styrofoam drinking cup and have them use markers to draw faces on their cups. Fill the cups with dirt and plant lots of grass or chive seeds in them. Water them regularly and eventually the cups will grow "hair" that your students can cut with scissors!

Activity:

　　Start a vegetable garden. Be sure to include a variety of plants so that your students can see how the different vegetables grow.

Activity:

　　*Tell your students that sometimes you can grow whole new plants from things other than seeds. Show them a potato and tell them that because potatoes grow underground, many people think that they are roots, but they are wrong. Potatoes are actually a special type of stem called a **tuber**. Farmers use these tubers to grow more potatoes by cutting them into pieces and planting them. Give each of your students a piece of potato that is about 1 ½ inch by 1 ½ inch to plant, making sure that each piece still has its skin and has some eyes on it. Plant it the same way you planted the bean seed earlier, in a clear plastic disposable cup filled with dirt. Place the potato piece along the side of the cup so that you can see the roots grow. Cover the cup with dark construction paper that you can easily lift off to watch the roots grow. After you have had a chance to watch the plant grow, you might want to plant the potato outside so that eventually you can have potatoes for dinner!*

Activity:

　　Give each of your students a clay pot and have them decorate it with non-toxic acrylic paints. Fill it with dirt and give them a choice of flower seeds to plant in it. If you want, you can varnish the pots after they are done to make them shiny and more durable.

Part 8: Review

Activity:
   Tell your students the following riddles and see if they can guess the answers:

1) I start with the letter "W" and plants need me to grow (water).

2) I am tiny and start with the letter "S." I am a baby plant (seed).

3) I am big and tall and people use me to build houses (tree).

4) I protect trees from disease and start with the letter "B" (bark).

5) I am very warm and plants can't grow without me. I start with the letter "L" (light).

6) I am the part of the plant that carries water to the leaves (stem).

7) I am a flower that people like to eat. I start with a "B" (broccoli).

8) People put seeds in me to help them grow. I start with a "D" (dirt).

9) I am the part of the plant that gathers sunlight for the plant to grow. I start with an "L" (leaves).

10) I am a leaf that people like to eat. I start with the letter "L" (lettuce).

11) I am the part of the plant that makes the seeds. I start with the letter "F" (flower).

12) I am the part of the wood that moves water through a tree. I start with the letter "S." (sapwood).

13) I am a root that people like to eat. I start with the letter "C" (carrot).

14) Plants put this back into the air for people to breathe. I start with the letter "O" (oxygen).

15) I am the part of the wood that is dark and in the middle of the tree. I start with the letter "H" (heartwood).

Chapter 10: Animal Ecology
Ages 4-7

Materials Needed for this Unit

Non-Iodized salt

Brine Shrimp or Brine Shrimp eggs (can be purchased from a pet or aquarium store)

Algae disk (can be purchased from a pet or aquarium store)

An aquatic plant that lives in salt water (can be purchased from a pet or aquarium store)

A two liter see-through container

Library books on deserts, rainforests, coniferous forests, and prairies

Envelopes

Recommended movies, published by Scholastic: *Magic School Bus: Hops Home, Magic School Bus: Gets Eaten.*

Old magazines with lots of pictures of different kinds of animals that you won't mind cutting pictures from.

Large piece of drawing paper

Index cards

Safety pins

A rag doll or another doll that is about 1 foot long and not too heavy.

String or yarn

Scissors

White construction paper

Brown construction paper

Access to a color copy machine

Pictures from library books or the internet of a Toucan, Kangaroo Rat, American Bison, and American Beaver

Crayons or markers

Tracing paper

Part 1: Habitats and Biomes

Tell your students that the word ***habitat*** is a fancy way of saying where an animal lives. It is important that an animal's habitat contains everything that it needs to survive. Ask them to think about what they need in their own habitat to survive (food, shelter, water, clothing, oxygen). Now ask them what do they think a fish might need to survive, or a butterfly.

Next tell your students that an animal's habitat is located in a larger area called a ***biome.*** For example, a frog living in a pond in the woods has a pond for a habitat, but the pond is in a ***coniferous forest*** (pine-tree forest), so he is living in a coniferous forest biome. Tell your students that it is kind of like a person who is living in a house in a city, the house is the habitat, and the city is the biome.

Activity:

Have your students create their own Brine Shrimp habitat. Take a two-liter see-through container and fill it almost to the top with tap water. Let it sit out twenty-four hours with the top off to remove the chlorine. Using a funnel, add ½ C of non-iodized salt to the jar. Cover it and shake until the salt is dissolved. Place an aquatic plant in the container. Make sure that it is a hardy one that will survive in salt water. Next, add either a pinch of brine shrimp eggs or about 10 adult brine shrimp to the container (the eggs are more fun because you have the anticipation of waiting for them to hatch!). Finally, add a pinch of a crushed algae disk, which you can purchase at your local pet store. Leave the container uncovered and do not place it in direct sunlight. Keep your shrimp habitat at room temperature. If you used Brine Shrimp eggs, they should hatch in about 48 hours. As the shrimp eat the algae, the water will become clear. When that happens, add another pinch of the algae disk to feed them.

Ask your students what Brine Shrimp need in their habitat to survive (oxygen, places to hide, food, water).

Activity:

One night while your students are asleep, hide (or have their parents hide) one of their stuffed animals (make sure it's not one that they will be upset about leaving for awhile). In the morning, tell them that their stuffed animal has gone on a trip to visit various biomes around the world, and that they will be writing home about their travels. On the following two pages are four letters that you can print out and mail to your students every few days (you can either really mail them or just put them in your mailbox for your students to find). Be sure to sign them with the stuffed animal's name! You can also make up some of your own if you like. Show them the places mentioned in the letters on a map or globe. You could also check out some books from the library on deserts, rainforest, coniferous forests, and prairies to supplement the letters.

Activity:

Scholastic has a great kid's movie on habitats called "The Magic School Bus Hops Home." You can probably order it from your local library.

Hello From the Desert!

I've been visiting my friend the Kangaroo Rat who lives in a desert biome in North America. Do you know what a desert is? It is a place where it barely ever rains, so a Kangaroo Rat's habitat is very dry. Luckily, a Kangaroo Rat doesn't need very much water to live; in fact a Kangaroo Rat may live its whole life without drinking any water!

One thing that a Kangaroo Rat does need in its habitat is a place to hide during the day when the sun is out and the desert is hottest. While I was visiting my friend, we hid in his burrow all day and closed the entrance up tight. At night, once it had cooled off, we went outside to search for seeds to eat. We had to be very careful and watch out for all of the other animals who like to eat Kangaroo Rats, such as bobcats, snakes, and Kit foxes. At one point we saw a fox sneaking up on us and we ran and hid in the borrow! Don't worry though, we weren't hurt!

Love,

--Cut Here--

Hello from the Rainforest!

Today I am writing you from the rainforest in South America. I am visiting my friend the Toucan. I thought that since the last biome I visited was the desert, you might like to hear about one that is the opposite, one where it rains a lot! Isn't it lucky that I have friends in so many biomes? I'm not sure if you know what a Toucan looks like. It has a very large bill which it uses to eat fruit (that means it needs fruit in its habitat). Unlike the Kangaroo Rat, the Toucan eats during the day and sleeps at night, so I was able to go to bed at my usual time. We slept in a hole in a tree that a woodpecker had made. Toucans can't make their own holes, so they need a habitat that has lots of holes in the trees already for them to live in. The rainforest is just perfect for them because it has lots of different kinds of trees with holes in them for the Toucan to use.

Guess what I saw while I was out eating fruit? Monkeys! They were eating fruit in the tree next to us! My friend says they can be very silly, but they don't bother him much!

Love,

Hello from the Prairie!

 Today I am visiting my friend the American Bison in a prairie biome in South Dakota. Do you know what a prairie is? It is a huge area covered with grass and other low plants. There are very few trees here, just grass as far as I can see. When the wind blows, the grass moves like waves on an ocean. My friend the Bison says that many years ago about thirty to sixty million bison used to roam these prairies, but that now there are less than half a million. This is because they were hunted so much when settlers started moving to the prairie.

 A scary thing happened here yesterday, we almost got caught in a prairie fire! Luckily I was able to climb on my friend's back and he carried me away. Fire is an important part of the prairie biome. It does two very important jobs, clearing out the dead grasses, and burning down the trees. If too many trees grow in a prairie it wouldn't be a prairie anymore!

 I hope you don't miss me too much, I'll be home soon!
  Love,

---Cut Here--

Hello from the Coniferous forest!

 Now I am visiting my friend the American Beaver who lives in a coniferous forest biome. I think the coniferous forest is my favorite biome in the world! There are lots of beautiful trees here, which are important for a beaver's habitat. Beavers cut down trees with their teeth! I hope they have good dentists! They use the trees to build a dam across a small stream or river. The dam blocks the stream so that a pond forms behind it. After they have made their pond, the beavers build themselves a home out of sticks and trees. They have to dive underwater to get inside it, but the inside is cozy and dry. Coniferous forests are a great biome for beavers, not only because of the trees, but because there are lots of streams and rivers for them to build dams in.

 My friend the beaver introduced me to some of his neighbors in the coniferous forest. I met a toad, a white-tailed deer, a red squirrel, and a skunk, who sprays out a nasty perfume when danger approaches. This turned out to be helpful to us because a wolf came by while we were visiting her and she was able to drive it away.

 This is my last biome to visit; I'll be heading for home tomorrow.
  Love,

Part 2: Predators and Prey

Ask your students what they think lions eat (zebras, wildebeest, buffalo, warthogs, antelope). Tell them that animals that hunt and eat other animals are called ***predators*** and the animals that they eat are called ***prey.***

Activity:

Read the following story out loud to your students and discuss how predators help prey populations. Ask them if they think that wolves in real life know that they are helping prey populations by weeding out the weak and sick (no, the wolves are only trying to catch food to survive, it just happens that the weak and sick are easier to catch).

Tipuk and the Caribou Hunt

Tipuk the young wolf woke up with a howl as his older sister Koko pushed some snow on him. "Time to get up, you don't want to be late for your first hunt!" she said.

Tipuk jumped up in excitement, "where are we going?"

"Nigaq says that we are going to the big lake; the elders have caught the scent of caribou from that direction. Hurry, we don't want to be late!"

Tipuk and Koko crawled out of the den and ran over to where the rest of the pack was waiting. "Hello sleepy one," said Tipuk's mother, Sura, "Are you ready for your first hunt?" Tipuk danced around in excitement as the pack started off toward the lake. "Careful," Sura said, "You don't want to wear yourself out before the hunt even starts, and you certainly don't want to scare the caribou away before we get there. Follow along quietly behind me." Tipuk quickly slipped into place behind his mother and started running with the pack.

After awhile, Nigaq, who was leading the pack, froze in place, and the rest of the pack copied him. Ahead of them, on the edge of the big lake, were five caribou. Without a sound, the wolf pack split in two, with Nigaq, Sura, and Tipuk circling around to the left of the caribou, and the rest circling to the right. Suddenly, the wolves rushed forward, frightening the caribou toward the lake. The caribou were fast runners and easily out ran the wolves at first, but eventually Tipuk saw that one of them appeared to be slower than the others. Nigaq saw this also, and yelled out "Chase the one on the right," so the wolves started closing in on the slowest runner. Sura was soon able to grab its neck, and the chase was over.

Nigaq called Tipuk over to him. "Son, what did you notice about this hunt?" he asked.

"I noticed that if it wasn't for the slowest caribou, we might not have had dinner today!" Tipuk replied.

"Exactly!" Nigaq said. "Caribou are hard to catch, so we always try to find the slowest or weakest one in the herd. This gives us something to eat, and helps make the caribou herd stronger; so that the herd has less disease, and the strongest and smartest caribou are left to raise their young."

"Wow," said Tipuk, "so the caribou need us, just like we need them!"

"Exactly!" Nigaq said again, "and now it's time to eat."

And so they did.

Part 3: Food Chains and Food Webs

Tell your students that the wolves and caribou in the Tipuk story are part of what is called a *food chain*. A food chain is basically a list of what eats what. In the wolf/caribou food chain, the caribou eat grass (or other plants), and the wolves eat the caribou. In this food chain, the grass is called a *primary producer*, because the grass gets its energy from the sun instead of from eating something else. The caribou are called *herbivores*, because they eat plants, and the wolves are called *carnivores*, because they eat other animals.

Activity:

Ask your students if they can think of examples of other types of food chains and have them draw a picture of the animals in their food chain, connecting the animals with arrows.

An Ocean Food Chain

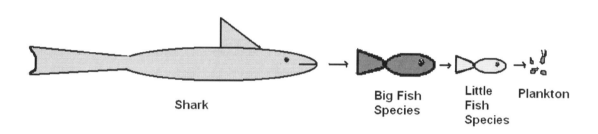

Shark   Big Fish   Little   Plankton
               Species   Fish
                                 Species

Now tell your students that different food chains connect with each other. For example, other creatures eat plankton besides fish, and other creatures eat fish besides other fish. Also, creatures like sharks eat more than one type of food. We call these combinations of food chains a *food web*, because if you draw a picture of all of the different connections, it looks like a web. On the following page is a picture of a simple ocean food web. Show it to your students and ask them when do they think a crab or plankton would eat an Orca (after it is dead). A food web is actually a map of how food energy moves around between animals. Notice how every creature is connected to every other creature by the food web. Every creature has its own important place in the web, and the web might be broken without it.

Activity:

Have your students take some old magazines and cut out pictures of various animals and plants from them. Have them glue the pictures onto a large piece of drawing paper and draw lines from each animal to its food until they have made a food web. They might have to draw in some of the items like plankton themselves.

An Ocean Food Web

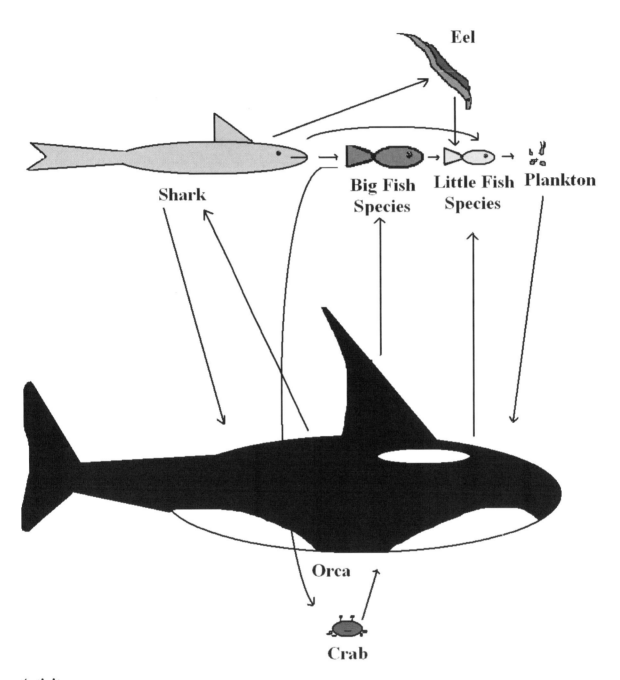

Activity:
   Scholastic has a good movie on food chains called "The Magic School Bus Gets Eaten" that you can try and find at your local library.

Activity:

If you have access to a group of kids, this is a fun activity to show how the different creatures are connected in a food web. Before you start, write up some index cards with the names of the various creatures that you want in your food web. You will need one for each child who is participating. Attach each card to a child's shirt with a safety pin (be careful not to prick anyone!). Now tell each child that their left arm is for what they can eat and their right arm is for what eats them. Have them join hands in a circle. Tie pieces of string between their arms, forming a web between them (if there is another parent available to help with this, it would go faster). For example, if you have a child that represents caribou, tie a piece of string from his/her left arm to the right arm of a child that represents grass. If you have more than one type of plant represented that the caribou can eat, you should tie another string from the caribou child's arm to the right arm of the child that represents the other type of plant. Keep doing this until you have tied as many strings as you and the children can think of. Now place a rag doll, or doll of similar size and weight (about one foot) in the middle of your web. Tell the children that the doll represents humans, who depend on the food webs of the world to survive. Ask them what would happen if some of the animals in the food chain disappeared? Choose an animal or plant to cut out of the food chain, and using scissors, cut the strings that tie that child to the web, and have that child step out of the circle. If any children have no strings on their left arms after this is done, they will have to leave the web also, because it means that they have died from lack of food. Eventually, the web will collapse, and the doll will fall. You can make this happen more quickly by choosing for your first animal one that has a lot of strings attached.

Part 4: Animal Defenses

Tell your students that even though a particular animal is an important part of a food chain, that doesn't mean that it <u>wants</u> to be eaten! Over time, prey animals have developed ways to help protect them from being eaten. Ask them if they can think of some of these animal defenses (stinging, ability to run fast, bad tasting, ability to fight back, being poisonous). One of the ways animals protect themselves is by **camouflage**, or blending in with their environment. The octopus camouflages itself by changing the color and texture of its skin to match its surrounding. Baby fawns have spots on their coats to blend in with woodland foliage. Camouflage can work both ways though; predators can use camouflage to help keep them hidden from their prey until they are ready to pounce.

Activity:

Before you do this activity, take some tracing paper and trace the outline of a bear that is on the following page. Next, cut it out, and trace it again on two sheets of construction paper, one white and one brown. Cut the white and brown bears out of the construction paper, making sure to <u>cut all of the lines around the bear off</u>. Now, glue the bears onto two white pieces of construction paper. It is important that the white bear be cut out of the same type of paper as it is glued onto. Make sure that your students do not see what you are doing!

Now, have your students sit indoors about twenty feet from where you are standing. Hold up the two papers with the bears on them and ask your students which one has the bear on it. When you do this, hold the white one against your body so that no light shines through the back of it (that might make the bear show up). If all goes well, they will only see the brown bear and then you can show them how the white bear was camouflaged, just like a polar bear would be in the winter snow.

Activity:
On the back cover of this book is a worksheet that has some camouflaged animals hidden on it. See if your students can find them! The answers to the worksheet are in the back of the book.

Chapter 11: Insects
Ages 8-13

<u>Materials Needed For This Unit</u>

A good-sized balloon that is not long and skinny

A four inch by eight inch paper bag

Paper towel

Plastic egg that opens

Drawing paper

Crickets (you can get them from a pet store)

Mealworms (you can get them from a pet store)

Some type of plastic container that is at least 4" high and has a lid

Carrot, apple, or grape

Paper towel

A plastic box with a lid about 18" x 14" and is about 8" high

Green and red toothpicks

Milk carton

A treat to be the "treasure" for a treasure hunt

Clothespin

Watermelon

Clean spray bottle

Dirt

Cotton

Crayons or markers

Duct tape

Magnifying glass

Oatmeal

Tape measure

Spray perfume

Flashlights

Petroleum jelly

Stiff plastic (like the type copy shops use for the covers of spiral-bound books)

Small glass jar with a lid

Either dry dog food or rolled oats, sugar, powdered skim milk, and waxed paper

Recommended Magic School Bus DVDs, published by Scholastic, are listed at the end of this unit in Part 7.

Ruler

Markers or crayons

Blindfold

Drinking glass

A jar lid

Part 1: Animal Classification

Activity:

Have your students list thirty different kinds of animals (have them include birds, insects, fish, etc...). Now tell them that they need to group the animals into five different groups. They can decide themselves what the criteria are for each group. For example, they could sort them into "Fish, Insects, Birds, Mammals, Reptiles," or they could sort them into "Green, Blue, Brown, Red, Black," or they could sort them into "Land, Sea, Lakes, Sky, and Underground." See what they come up with for their five groups. Now choose the group that has the most creatures in it and say that they have to sort those creatures into three smaller groups, again having them decide the criteria for belonging in a group.

Tell them that what they have done is similar to what scientists have done with all of the living creatures in the world. They have organized them into groups based on what is the same or different about each creature, and they have given every creature in the world a name in Latin. One reason scientists did this was to make it less confusing when they are talking about an animal. For example, if a scientist in the United States is talking about a Monarch Butterfly, a scientist in Germany who doesn't speak English may not know what a Monarch Butterfly is. That scientist will have a German name for it. But if Monarch Butterfly has a Latin name that all scientists use, then there is no confusion about what they are talking about. The Latin name for Monarch Butterfly is "Danaus plexippus."

Tell your students that the first group that scientists organized all of the living creatures into is called a "Kingdom." They may have heard of the "Plant Kingdom" or the "Animal Kingdom." Next scientists took everything in each Kingdom and organized them into groups called "Phyla" (singular phylum). Everything in a Phylum is grouped into "Classes," everything in a Class is grouped into "Orders," everything in an Order is grouped into "Families," everything in a Family is grouped into a Genus, everything in a Genus is grouped into a Species.

Activity:

Write down the scientist's groups in order like this:

Kingdom
Phylum
Class
Order
Family
Genus
Species

Now have your students invent a mnemonic device to help remember these groups in the correct order. For example they could say: King Peter Can Order Fuzzy Green Shoes.

Part 2: Definition of an Insect

Tell your students that insects are in the Kingdom Animalia, the Phylum Arthropoda, and the Class Insecta. They are in the Kingdom Animalia because they are animals, the Phylum Arthropoda because they have, among other things, an exoskeleton, and the Class Insecta because they (again among other things) have three pairs of legs. Thus, a simple way to define insects is an animal that has an exoskeleton and three pairs of legs. Insects don't have bones like we do. Instead, the hard outside of an insect's body supports and protects it. This hard outer layer is called an exoskeleton.

Activity:

Show your students a small paper bag, one that is about <u>4 inches by 8 inches</u>, and tell them that it represents the exoskeleton of an insect. Show them a balloon (one that is not long and skinny) and tell them that it represents the inner body of an insect. Place the balloon in the paper bag with the neck of the balloon sticking out a bit so that you can blow on the balloon while it is in the bag. Twist the lunch bag shut over the stem of the balloon, but not too tight, you will need to be able to get air into the balloon. Start blowing on the balloon while you hold the bag shut around it. Eventually the balloon will get too big for the bag and the bag will either rip or pop (it can sometimes be pretty loud, so be prepared). The same thing happens to an insect's exoskeleton. As the insect grows, it gets too large for its exoskeleton, causing it to split open so that the insect can crawl out of its old exoskeleton. This process of shedding an exoskeleton is called **molting**.

One note about the paper bag demonstration; if the bag is too large or too thick, the balloon either won't break it, or you will end up having to blow too hard to make the bag break. It is important to use a small-sized bag for this. It should not be difficult to break; if it is then stop immediately and get a smaller bag, do not try to force it to break.

Activity:

Tear off a section of paper towel, wad it up, and dampen it with water. Now, place it inside of a plastic egg. Take another section of paper towel, wad it up, and dampen it like the first one. Place this one on a plate, and make a note of the time. Every half-hour check to see how long it takes the paper towel on the plate to dry. Once the paper towel on the plate is dry, open the egg. The paper towel in the egg should still be damp. Tell the students that the egg represents an insect's exoskeleton and the towel its inner body. An insect's exoskeleton can protect it from drying out in hot weather, just like the egg protected the paper towel from drying out. The exoskeleton can also protect it from some predators, and is important in helping the insect move and keep its shape.

Activity:

Go on an insect hunt. See how many insects you can find in ten minutes. Make sure to count the legs to see that there are three pairs (six legs), or it's not an adult insect.

Part 3: Insect Life Cycles

Ask your students these questions: "When is a butterfly not a butterfly?" (when it is a caterpillar!). "Does a caterpillar have six legs?" (no). "Is it an insect?" (yes). "But I thought all insects had six legs, how come a caterpillar is an insect?" (because a caterpillar is a "baby" or immature butterfly, it doesn't have its legs yet). An insect has six legs as an adult, but not necessarily when it is young.

Activity:

*Ask your students to tell you the lifecycle of a butterfly (egg, caterpillar, chrysalis, butterfly). The chrysalis is also called a **pupa**. Give each student a piece of paper. Have them draw a picture with the different stages of a butterfly's life cycle.*

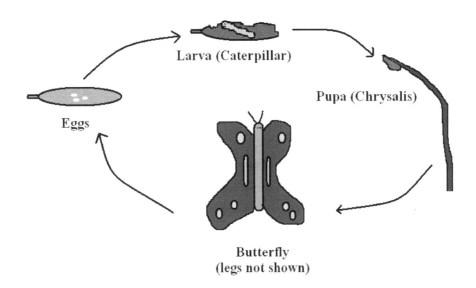

Complete Metamorphosis

Lifecycle of a Butterfly

Tell your students that a butterfly's lifecycle is an example of "Complete Metamorphosis." This means that it changes from a worm-like larva into something that looks completely different, a butterfly.

Activity:

Purchase about five mealworms from your local pet store. Prepare a home for them by taking a plastic container that is at least four inches tall (and has a lid) and filling it about 1 ½ inches deep with uncooked oatmeal. Place a <u>small</u> slice of carrot, apple or one half of a grape on top of the oatmeal and put your mealworms in the container. Put a piece of paper towel on top of the whole thing, mealworms and all. The towel is important because the mealworms will tend to stay near the surface more if the towel is there. Punch holes in the lid and close the container. **Do not add water**, mealworms get their water from the food they eat. They do better in warm places, so don't put them in cold areas.

Have your students open the box about once a week and measure the size of their five mealworms. Have them calculate the mealworm's average size each day you take measurements by adding the total of all five measurements and dividing the total by five (the number of mealworms you have). Replace the carrot, potato, or apple as needed. Draw pictures of what they look like. There should also be old shed exoskeletons in the container (as the mealworms grow, they will need to shed their old exoskeletons). Mealworms undergo Complete Metamorphosis, just like butterflies, only instead of turning into butterflies, they turn into beetles! Right before the pupa stage, they will crawl to the top of the oatmeal, curl into a "C" shape and stop moving. Don't worry; they're not dead, just getting ready to pupate. The pupas look like strange non-moving bugs, take them out and put them in another container with just a little uncooked oatmeal in it. Pupas don't eat, so you don't need to worry about feeding them. The pupas should change into adults in six to eighteen days.

Be patient, it could take a few months before your mealworms become pupas (though since you are buying them instead of growing them from eggs, it usually doesn't take that long). Be sure to have your students wash their hands after touching the mealworms.

Activity:

Purchase six crickets from a pet store. Take a plastic box with a lid that is about 18" x 14" and about 8" high, and punch lots of holes in the lid. To help prevent cricket escapes, spread a band of petroleum jelly about two inches wide around the inside of the top of the box. The petroleum band should be about one inch down from the top. Spread about two inches of dirt on the bottom of the container. Use a spray bottle to moisten it regularly. It should only be slightly damp, not soaking wet. Put items in the container to provide cover for the crickets such as rocks, crumpled paper towel, sticks, etc...

Place a bit of dry dog food in an old jar lid and put it in the box. If you prefer not to use dog food, you can mix together some rolled oats, sugar, powdered skim milk and water into a stiff paste, and spread them onto some waxed paper. Let it dry. Break it into pieces and place some of the pieces in the jar lid. You can store the rest in the refrigerator.

Unlike mealworms, your crickets will need a water container. One simple way is to take a jar lid, put cotton in it, and add water. The cotton prevents the crickets from drowning, but you may need to change the cotton once in awhile so that it doesn't get moldy.

Observe your crickets periodically. Crickets undergo "Incomplete Metamorphosis." This means that they do not have a larva stage like the butterfly does. Instead, they have a nymph stage that looks a lot like the adult, only is smaller, and the wings aren't developed. As they shed their exoskeletons, the nymphs gradually get larger and develop wings until finally they are adults. If all goes well, after a few weeks you will have tiny cricket nymphs.

Crickets make interesting pets. In China, starting sometime between 618 - 906 AD, people would often keep crickets as pets because they enjoyed the sounds they made. However, if you want to keep any of your crickets as pets, it is best if you only keep one of them, they reproduce very quickly! You can return any crickets you don't want to your pet store, but wait until you have finished Part Four of this unit, you will still need them.

Activity:

       Have your students draw a picture showing Incomplete Metamorphosis. Their picture should end up looking something like this:

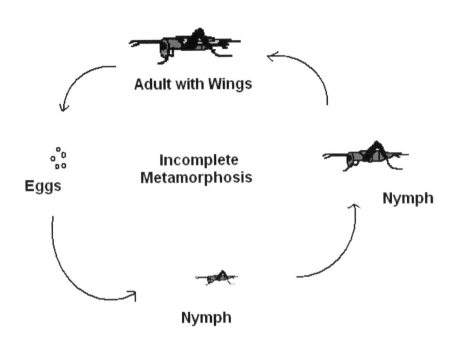

Part 4: Parts of an Insect

Activity:

       Take a <u>small</u> glass jar, punch holes in the lid, and place an adult (with wings) cricket inside and close the lid. Observe the cricket with a magnifying glass. Count the cricket's legs (there should be six). A cricket has three body parts, the head, thorax, and abdomen. The head is where the eyes are located, the thorax is directly behind the head, and the abdomen is its rear. See if you can identify all three parts. A cricket breathes through tiny holes in the sides of its abdomen called spiracles; see if you can locate them. The adult cricket should have two pairs of wings, the Fore Wings and the Hind Wings (the Fore Wings are the ones in front; the Hind Wings are behind them). Sticking out of the very back of the female cricket is a tube called the Ovipositor, which it uses to lay its eggs in the dirt. A male cricket won't have this tube. See if your students can tell if their cricket is a male or female. Both male and female crickets have two back appendages called Cercus, so the female will have a third appendage in the middle (the Ovipositor). Keep your cricket in its jar to do the next activity. Be sure to wash your hands after touching the crickets!

Activity:

       Have your students draw a picture of their cricket, labeling the body parts. It should end up looking something like the following picture.

Cricket Body Parts

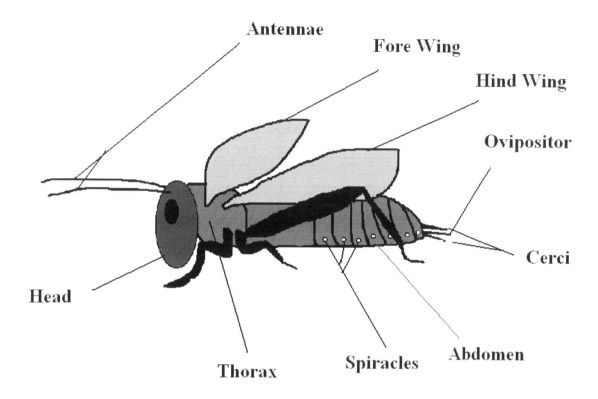

Antennae
Fore Wing
Hind Wing
Ovipositor
Cerci
Head
Thorax
Spiracles
Abdomen

Part 5: Insect Communication

Ask your students if they remember how scout ants and bees tell the rest of their hive mates where to find food (this was covered previously in the chapter "Insects and Their Kin"). Ants communicate by laying down a chemical trail for others to follow, and bees do a "dance" that communicates direction and distance. Tell your students that other insects use different methods to communicate with each other. For example the flashing lights of fireflies are actually male and female fireflies signaling to find a mate. One type of male firefly flies in a "J" shape through the air as he flashes. A female of the same species will recognize his signal and respond from the ground where she is sitting by sending her own flash. Another insect, the Water Strider communicates in a different way. Water Striders "skate" across the surface of ponds or lakes and cause ripples in the water. Some species use the patterns of these ripples to help find a mate or protect their territory. Female Lunar Moths attract mates by releasing chemicals called pheromones into the air that the male moths can detect miles away. The chirping song of the cricket that the Chinese prized so much is actually how the crickets attract mates and warn off rivals. As you can see, insects use a variety of methods to communicate with each other.

Activity:

 Tell your students that one thing we didn't mention in the chapter "Insects and Their Kin" is that when bees can't see the sun (such as when they are inside their hive) to point to a direction in the "bee dance," they dance on the combs in the hive. If they dance up, it means to go toward the sun. If they dance down, it means to go away from the sun. Any other angle from the sun is danced based on that up and down line.

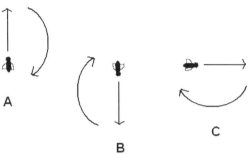

 In the diagrams above, "A" represents the scout bee dancing up the side of the hive, telling the other bees that the nectar source is in the direction of the sun. "B" represents the scout bee dancing down the side of the hive, telling the other bees the nectar is away from the sun, and "C" represents the scout bee dancing in a direction in an angle away from the line of the sun. Remember, the straight line part of the dance is the direction the nectar is in. The curved line is just the bee going back to the starting point to dance the straight line again.

 Set-up a treasure hunt using the sun for directions. You will have to set this up the day before, and you will need to do it at the exact same time of day, so that the sun is in the same place in the sky when you set it up and when the students go on the hunt. Have a starting point that is the "hive." Write out a set of directions from that starting point using the sun as a guide. For example say "Go ten feet toward the sun. Face the sun, hold your arms out straight from your sides and go twenty feet in the direction of your right arm," etc.... Give your students the directions and see if they can use them to find a treasure, which can be some kind of treat that you have hidden.

Activity:

 As we mentioned earlier, female Lunar Moths attract mates by sending out pheromones into the air that the males can follow back to the female. Go outside and blindfold one of your students. Now, move a short distance away, take a spray bottle of perfume, and spray some of it into the air. See if the student can find you using only his or her nose, similar to the way Lunar Moth males find females.

Activity:

 For this nighttime game, each person participating will need a flashlight. You will be sending signals to each other, just like the fireflies. The goal is to direct the other person (or persons) to a particular place using flashes of light. If you have enough people, you could split into two teams to see which team gets their participants to a designated spot first, or you could just play with two people and time yourselves to see how long it takes. Sit down before the game and come up with a set of directions. For example, one flash could mean "go right," two could mean "go left," etc.... Once you have your directions, go outside and have one person think of a place to direct their team member(s) to (without telling where it is!), and start flashing the light to show the other team member(s) where to go.

Part 6: Insect Defenses

Ask your students if they can think of things that insects do to keep from being eaten. Some sting or bite. Some are camouflaged to look like leaves, sticks, or other things. There is a caterpillar that looks like a snake, and another that looks like bird droppings! There are insects who are master escape artists, like the cockroach who has tiny hairs that can sense changes in air pressure when something is about to pounce, or the Tiger Moth who can sense a bat's ultrasound echolocation and escape when a bat flies near. Through the ages, insects have developed many ways to protect themselves.

Activity:

Take thirty green toothpicks and thirty red toothpicks and scatter them fairly evenly in a grassy area without letting your students watch. Brush the grass a little so that the toothpicks go down into the grass a bit. If you have more than one student, scatter thirty green and thirty red toothpicks per student. Give your students fifteen seconds to pick up as many toothpicks as they can find. Count how many of each color your students found. You can calculate the percentage of each color found by dividing the total number of each color found by thirty (or however many total toothpicks of that color you scattered) and multiplying the answer by one hundred. It is likely that your students will have found more of the red toothpicks than the green ones because the green ones were harder to find in the grass; they were camouflaged.

Activity:

Go outside and see if you can find any insects that are camouflaged to look like their surroundings.

*If you would like to collect some and observe them for a short time (be sure to return them to where you found them when you are through), you can make a temporary insect home from a milk carton by cutting windows in two opposite sides of the carton and taping a piece of stiff plastic (like the type copy shops use for the covers of spiral-bound books) over the windows. Punch some holes in the top for air (not too large, or the insects can get out, but make sure there are enough holes to let the air in). You can open the milk carton from the top, and after your insect is safe inside, keep it shut with a clothespin. Put in a piece of the item that your insect was on inside the carton to make it feel more at home. **Only collect insects that you know will not hurt you. If you have any doubts, do not collect it!** You can catch some insects by placing a drinking glass over the insect and then sliding a piece of paper between the glass and the ground. Carry it, glass and paper together, over to your carton and place the insect inside.*

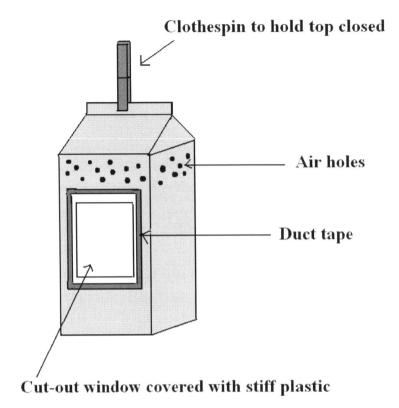

Clothespin to hold top closed

Air holes

Duct tape

Cut-out window covered with stiff plastic

Part 7: Recommended Movies

The "Magic School Bus" series has three excellent movies on insects. You can usually get them at your local or school library. They are listed below:

The Magic School Bus: Butterfly and the Bog Beast
The Magic School Bus Gets Ants in its Pants
The Magic School Bus In a Beehive
The Magic School Bus: Bugs, Bugs, Bugs contains all three of the above in one DVD.

Test for Insects

1) The groups that scientists use to classify living things are in this order:
    a. Species, Order, Class, Phylum, Genus, Kingdom, Family
    b. Kingdom, Class, Order, Family, Phylum, Genus, Species
    c. Kingdom, Phylum, Class, Order, Family, Genus, Species
    d. Kingdom, Family, Order, Class, Phylum, Genus, Species

2) Insects are in the:
    a. Kingdom Animalia, Phylum Insecta, Class Arthropoda
    b. Kingdom Animalia, Phylum Chordata, Class Insecta
    c. Kingdom Animalia, Phylum Protozoan, Class Insecta
    d. Kingdom Animalia, Phylum Arthropoda, Class Insecta

3) Insects have:
    a. Six legs
    b. Eight legs
    c. Four legs
    d. Ten legs

4) An Exoskeleton:
    a. Is the skeleton of an insect, just like ours
    b. Grows as an insect grows
    c. Is always covered in hairy spines
    d. Is the outer skeleton of an insect used for support

5) A mealworm has:
    a. No metamorphosis
    b. Complete Metamorphosis
    c. Incomplete Metamorphosis
    d. Substandard Metamorphosis

6) A cricket has:
    a. No metamorphosis
    b. Complete Metamorphosis
    c. Incomplete Metamorphosis
    d. Substandard Metamorphosis

7) One of the differences between complete and incomplete metamorphosis is:
    a. Incomplete Metamorphosis has a larva stage and Complete Metamorphosis doesn't
    b. Complete Metamorphosis has a nymph stage and Incomplete Metamorphosis doesn't
    c. Complete Metamorphosis has a larva stage and Incomplete Metamorphosis doesn't
    d. Incomplete Metamorphosis has a pupa stage and Complete Metamorphosis doesn't

8) The cricket's body is divided into three sections called:
    a. Head, Thorax, Abdomen
    b. Head, Leg Section, Abdomen
    c. Skull, Body, Feet
    d. Head, Thorax, Rear End

9) The cricket's spiracles are for:
    a. Seeing
    b. Smelling
    c. Breathing
    d. Tasting

10) The Viceroy Butterfly mimics the Monarch Butterfly because:
    a. The Monarch Butterfly is so beautiful
    b. The Monarch Butterfly is so bad-tasting
    c. The Monarch Butterfly is so scary
    d. The Monarch Butterfly is so numerous

Chapter 12: Microscopes and Invisible Creatures
Ages 8-13

Materials Needed for this Unit

Most of the materials needed for this unit are either common household items, or are easily obtained from grocery, hardware, drug, discount stores, and pet stores. However, this particular unit requires the use of a microscope, preferably one that magnifies at least 100 times. Much of this unit can be done without a microscope, but you will need one to do about one-third of it. For that one-third, you will also need a few microscope accessories which are listed in the unit, along with information on where to purchase them.

Sugar

Baby food jar with lid

Heavy-duty rubber band

Eyedropper

Piece of paper with printed words on it

A glass jar with smooth, clean sides

Two fairly good-quality magnifying glasses

The book "Horton Hears a Who" by Dr. Seuss

Library books that identify different protozoa

Copy paper and access to a copier

Electron microscope photos of dust mites (try online or in a library book)

Plastic wrap

Needle and thread

Two balloons

Funnel

Writing paper

Sterile cotton swabs

Fish net from a pet store

Nylon stocking, not too sheer

Two soda bottles (2-liters each)

Microscopes and microscope accessories can be purchased at:

Nasco

(800)558-9595

(920)563-2446

www.eNasco.com/science

901 Janesville Ave.

Fort Atkinson, WI 53538

A microscope that magnifies at least 100X

Well-slides or concave microscope slides for holding water

Flat microscope slides

Not essential to the unit, but fun to look at are Nasco's prepared slides of plant and animal parts, and their live cultures of protozoan.

Part 1: Convex Lenses

Ask your students if they know what the word ***magnify*** means (to make something small look larger). We use tools called lenses to make small things look larger.

Activity:

*Take a paper with printed writing on it and place a piece of plastic wrap over some of the words. Now take an eyedropper and squeeze one drop of water on top of the plastic wrap, so that the drop is covering a word. Have your students describe the shape of the water drop. Look through the drop at the word beneath it; it should appear magnified. The shape of the water drop is thicker in the middle than on the edges. This shape is called **convex**. The water drop has formed a single convex lens.*

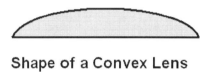

Shape of a Convex Lens

*Now have your students look at the printed writing with a magnifying glass. Make sure they notice the shape of the lens. Magnifying glasses are made from a **double convex lens.** A double convex lens is shaped like two single convex lenses put together:*

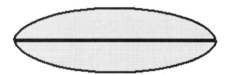

Activity:

Tell your students to take a glass jar with smooth, clean sides and fill it with water. Dry the sides and place it on a piece of paper with print on it. The print should appear magnified as you look at it through the jar. This means that the jar is acting like a double convex lens and is magnifying the object. Show your students the bottom of the jar and draw a line across the middle of it to show them how it makes a shape like a double-convex lens.

Bottom view of a jar with a line across the middle:

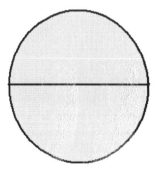

Part 2: Microscopes

Remind your students that we have seen how magnifying glasses make small things look larger. By using more than one lens, we can make small things look even larger than a single magnifying glass can. A compound microscope uses two lenses to magnify things.

Activity:

Tell your students to take a magnifying glass and look at a piece of paper with print on it. Now take a second magnifying glass and hold it under the first one. Move one of the magnifying glasses up and down until the print is in focus again. Notice the size of the print. Now remove the bottom magnifying glass. The print should look smaller when you are only looking through one glass. Compound microscopes use two or more lenses to magnify objects, so they appear even larger than when looking at them through just one lens.

Activity:

*Bring out a compound microscope and show it to your students. On the following page is a diagram of a microscope with the parts labeled. Point out that when you look through the microscope, you are looking through two lenses, just like when they looked through the two magnifying glasses together. The lens closest to their eye is called the **eyepiece**. The lens closest to the object they are viewing is called the **objective lens** ("objective" for "object"). Show them how the eyepiece and objective lenses have the powers written on them. If your eyepiece says 10x that means that if you looked through the eyepiece alone, it would make the object look ten times larger than its normal size. If your eyepiece is 10x and your objective lens is also 10x, your microscope will be magnifying the object you are looking at by 10 x 10 which equals 100x. If your eyepiece is 10x and your objective lens is 40x, your microscope will be magnifying the object you are looking at by 10 x 40 which equals 400x. Have your students tell you how much your microscope would be magnifying your object if the eyepiece is 10x and the objective lens is 20x (200x).*

*The microscope may also have two focusing knobs, one for broad focusing, called the **course adjustment** (it is usually the larger knob) and one for fine focusing called the **fine adjustment**. The flat area where you place microscope slides is called the **stage**. It should have some clips on it that help hold microscope slides in place called the **stage clips**.*

Show them how to properly carry a microscope by grasping the curved arm of the microscope with one hand and placing the other hand under the base of the microscope. Tell your students that all microscopes need a light source. Some will have a mirror at the bottom that you will need to shine a light into, adjusting the mirror so that the light bounces up toward the slide. Others will have a built in light that you will need to turn on.

Next, have your students go outside and find things that they would like to look at under a microscope. The items need to fit on a microscope slide. Feathers, leaves, sugar, hair, or very thin slices of celery are fun things to look at (you can always cut them to fit the slide). Have them place their item on a microscope slide and place the slide on the stage, holding it in place with the stage clips. Next, before looking through the eyepiece, use the coarse adjustment to move the objective lens as close-as-possible to the slide, then look through the eyepiece and, still using the coarse adjustment, <u>slowly</u> move the objective lens away from the slide until it comes into focus. You always focus by moving the lens away from the slide so that you don't accidentally run the lens into the slide while you are focusing. Once you have your item in focus with the coarse adjustment, you can fine tune it with the fine adjustment. Have your students practice focusing with the microscope.

Parts of a Microscope

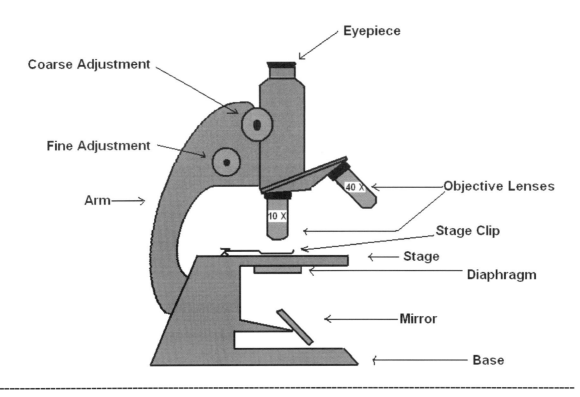

Eyepiece

Coarse Adjustment

Fine Adjustment

Arm

Objective Lenses

Stage Clip

Stage

Diaphragm

Mirror

Base

40 X

10 X

Parts of a Microscope

40 X

10 X

Activity:

    On the previous page are two diagrams of the parts of a microscope, one with the parts labeled and one without. One microscope part not mentioned earlier is the diaphragm, located under the stage. The diaphragm can be adjusted to let in different levels of light into your microscope. Once your students have learned the parts of a microscope, copy and cut out the unlabeled diagram and have them label the parts from memory.

Activity:

    If you don't mind spending some extra money, Nasco, the company mentioned in the materials list, has some great slide kits of prepared slides of various plant and animal parts. These are not essential to the unit, but are fun to look at!

Activity:

    Either read your students the story "Horton Hears a Who" or ask them if they remember it. Do they really think there are whole worlds on a speck of dust? Now show them some electron microscope photos of dust mites and tell them that there <u>are</u> whole worlds in a speck of dust, and scientists can see them using a special high-powered microscope called an **electron microscope.** *Dust mites can be found anywhere, but they especially love beds. A typical mattress can have anywhere from 10,000 to 10,000,000 dust mites inside! That is because dust mites love to eat the skin cells that we shed! Actually, dust mites perform an important function. Each person sheds approximately 1/5 of an ounce of skin cells each week. Think about what would happen if we didn't have dust mites cleaning up after us; our houses would be filled with old skin cells!*

Part 3: Protozoa

    Tell your students that dust mites aren't the only tiny creatures out there that we can't see; there are whole worlds of invisible creatures! One type of these creatures is the Protozoa, many of whom are so small that we can't see them living in our land, water, and air.

Activity:

    Take a fish-net from a pet store and cut the netting off of the wire rim. Next, take a pair of nylons (make sure they are not too sheer or they will be too fragile) and cut one leg off. Take the cut leg and cut off the foot so that you now have a column of nylon that is open at both ends. Take the wider end of the column, curl it over the wire rim, and sew it in place. Next, take the foot-end of the nylon column and pull it over the open end of a small jar (a baby-food jar works great for this because it is made of fairly thick glass). Secure it in place with a heavy-duty rubber band. Save the lid to the jar and bring it along with the net to the collection site.

    Take your new net to a local pond, the scummier the better, and drag it through the water close to the bottom or edge of the pond. If you do not have a pond near you, try a lake or stream. Take the net out of the water and remove the nylon from the jar. Use the jar lid to cap it closed and take it back to your microscope.

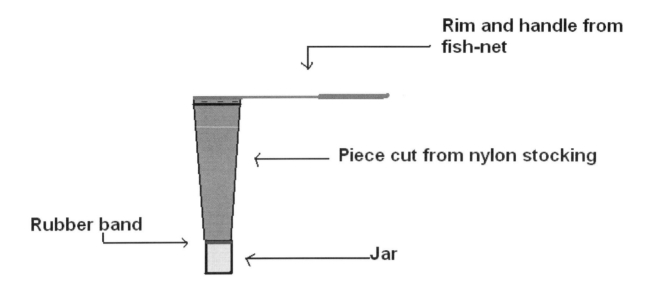

Using an eyedropper, take a drop of water out of the jar and place it in a well-slide or concave microscope slide. Look at it under the microscope at 100x and see if you can find any tiny moving creatures. Have your students draw pictures of the different creatures that they see. Check out some library books about protozoa and see if you can identify the creatures that you found.

Activity:

For an optional project, or if you have absolutely no access to water, Nasco, the company mentioned in the materials list, has some live protozoa cultures that you can purchase that are a lot of fun to look at. Be sure not to release any of the cultures into your local streams, lakes, or ponds.

Part 4: Writing a Protozoa Research Report

Tell your students that the text of a research report has three main parts, the ***introduction,*** the ***discussion,*** and the ***conclusion***. The introduction tells the reader what the report is going to be about. The discussion is where the bulk of the report is; it is the part of the report that gives the reader information about the subject. The conclusion sums up the whole report for the reader.

There are other parts to a research report besides the main text. For our purposes in this unit, we are just going to include a ***bibliography,*** which goes at the end of the report. A bibliography is a list of the sources where the student found the information used in the report. On the next page is a sample bibliography which shows how to write up a few different types of sources. The items that are underlined could also be put in italics or in quotation marks instead of underlining them.

Bibliography

(A book with one author)
Smith, Jane. Protozoan and Other Invisible Creatures in Water. New York: McCune Publishing, 1988.

(A book with two authors, notice that they are listed alphabetically)
Allen, Tom, and Jane Smith. Protozoan and Other Invisible Creatures in Water. New York: McCune Publishing, 1988.

(A book with three authors, notice that they are listed alphabetically)
Allen, Tom, Simon Cutter, and Jane Smith. Protozoan and Other Invisible Creatures in Water. New York: McCune Publishing, 1988.

(A book with more than three authors)
Smith, Jane, et al. Protozoan and Other Invisible Creatures in Water. New York: McCune Publishing, 1988.

(A magazine article)
Smith, Jane. "Life of an Amoeba." Children's Science Magazine, June 1890, pp. 3-5.

(An article from a website)
Life of an Amoeba. Amoeba World Website, 12 Mar. 2006. Retrieved January 3, 2009, from <http://www.amoebaworld.com>.

Activity:
Have your students choose a type of protozoa to research. They can look up information on the protozoan they've chosen in books or online and take notes on what they find. Tell them that when they write the report, they must use their own words and not copy them exactly from what someone else wrote. Once they have written their notes, show them how to make an outline of what is going to be in the report. It should look something like the one below. Have them use the outline to write their final report.

Sample Outline for a Research Report on Daphnia

I. Introduction
   A. Statement saying what this report is about.
   B. Definition of a Daphnia.

II. Text
   A. How long have Daphnia been in existence?
   B. Daphnia life
      1. Where do Daphnia live?
      2. What do Daphnia eat?
   C. How do Daphnia affect humans?

III. Conclusion

Part 5: Fun with Fungus

Ask your students if they know what a ***fungus*** is. A fungus is an organism that is neither plant nor animal (they have their own kingdom called the "Fungi"), does not contain chlorophyll like plants, and feeds on organic matter (things that were or are alive). Mushrooms and molds are a type of fungus, and so is yeast. Ask your students if they know of anything that we use yeast for (baking bread). That's right; the yeast that we use for baking is actually a living organism, a fungus!

Activity:

Mix 1 cup warm (not hot) water with 2 tablespoons sugar and add 2 ¼ teaspoons (about 1 package) yeast. If you can find "highly active," or "rapid rise" yeast, that is even better. Using a funnel, pour the mixture into a 2- liter soda bottle and attach a balloon over the opening of the bottle. Let it sit for about an hour. If all goes well, the balloon should start expanding fairly soon. This is because yeast, like humans, uses sugar for energy. As the yeast does this, it changes the sugar to alcohol and releases carbon dioxide gas. The release of this gas is what is causing the balloon to fill up and also is what causes bread to rise. The little holes in a loaf of baked bread are from the bubbles of carbon dioxide gas that the yeast produces.

Activity:

Test to see what happens if you do not add sugar to a mixture of yeast and water. Do the same experiment as the one above, but do not add the sugar to the yeast. The balloon should not expand, because the yeast does not have any sugar to consume.

Activity:

About forty-five minutes before this experiment, mix 1 cup warm (not hot) water with 2 tablespoons sugar and add 2¼ teaspoons (about 1 package) yeast. Let it sit at room temperature. After forty-five minutes, fill an eyedropper with the yeast mixture, place a drop of it on a well slide, and look at the yeast cells under the microscope.

Test for Microscopes and Invisible Creatures

1) Which of these is <u>not</u> a characteristic of a convex lens:
    a. Its shape is larger in the middle than the sides.
    b. Its shape is larger on the sides than the middle.
    c. It is used to magnify things.
    d. It is used in microscopes.

2) A compound microscope…….
    a. has more than one lens
    b. has only one lens
    c. uses electrons to magnify things
    d. is used to make things that are far away look closer

3) The objective lens…..
    a. is closest to the eye
    b. is located on the stage of the microscope
    c. is located on the base of the microscope
    d. is closest to what the observer is viewing

4) The parts of a research paper are in the following order:
    a. Bibliography, Introduction, Discussion, Conclusion
    b. Introduction, Bibliography, Discussion, Conclusion
    c. Introduction, Discussion, Conclusion, Bibliography
    d. Discussion, Introduction, Conclusion, Bibliography

5) Dust Mites are found…
    a. under water
    b. under ground
    c. in the refrigerator
    d. in your carpet

6) A fungus is…
    a. a type of plant
    b. a type of animal
    c. a type of protozoa
    d. none of the above

7) Yeast is…
   a. a plant
   b. an animal
   c. a fungus
   d. none of the above

8) Which of the following is <u>not</u> a part of a compound microscope:
   a. Set bolt
   b. Stage
   c. Objective lens
   d. Base

9) If a microscope has an objective lens that is 20x and an eyepiece that is 10x, what magnification does it have?
   a. 100x
   b. 200x
   c. 40x
   d 50x

10) Which of the following is a proper bibliography entry:
   a. <u>Protozoan and Other Invisible Creatures in Water</u>. Smith, Jane. New York: McCune Publishing, 1988.

   b. Smith, Jane. <u>Protozoan and Other Invisible Creatures in Water</u>. 1988. New York: McCune Publishing.

   c. Smith, Jane. <u>Protozoan and Other Invisible Creatures in Water</u>. New York: McCune Publishing, 1988.

   d. New York: McCune Publishing, 1988.Smith, Jane. <u>Protozoan and Other Invisible Creatures in Water</u>.

Chapter 13: Atoms and Molecules
Ages 8-13

Materials Needed For This Unit

Aluminum Foil

Pie pan

A glass soda bottle or something similar

*One or two packages of colored marshmallows

Hammer

A quarter

Dark construction paper

Cotton string

Food coloring

A glass jelly jar that holds more than two Cups

Sugar

Peppermint extract

Ice

Drawing paper

A glass jar that holds at least two cups of water

Saucepan

Toothpicks

Sugar

Magnifying glass

Epsom salts

Table salt

Drinking glass

Paperclip

Perfume in a spray bottle

Measuring cup

Balloon

Eyedropper

Pencils

Markers or crayons

*You can substitute colored balls of clay or gumdrops for the marshmallows.

Part 1: Definition of an Atom

Hold up a piece of aluminum foil and ask your students if they know what it is made of (aluminum). Give a piece to each of your students and have them rip the foil in half. Now tell them to rip the foil in half again and have them keep ripping it in half until it cannot be ripped any smaller. Have them imagine that they keep ripping it in half until they have ripped it into such a small piece that they have to look at it under a microscope to see it. Tell them that eventually they could rip it so small that it would be the smallest piece of aluminum in the world. At that point, if you ripped it again, it would no longer be aluminum. When they get to that smallest piece, it is called an *atom*. Atoms are so small that they can only be seen under a special microscope called an electron microscope. They are so small that millions of them could fit in the head of a pin.

Tell them that scientists have found all of the different kinds of atoms in the world, and that they have written them down in something called the *Periodic Table of the Elements*. **Elements** are the names for the different types of atoms.

Show them the Periodic Table on the following two pages and name some of the elements. Have them find aluminum on the table. See if there are any other elements that they recognize. Tell them that everything in the world is made of atoms, including themselves!

Periodic Table of the Elements

1 **H** Hydrogen 1.00794									
3 **Li** Lithium 6.941	4 **Be** Beryllium 9.012182								
11 **Na** Sodium 22.98977	12 **Mg** Magnesium 24.305								
19 **K** Potassium 39.0983	20 **Ca** Calcium 40.078	21 **Sc** Scandium 44.95591	22 **Ti** Titanium 47.867	23 **V** Vanadium 50.9415	24 **Cr** Chromium 51.9661	25 **Mn** Manganese 54.93805	26 **Fe** Iron 55.845	27 **Co** Cobalt 58.9332	
37 **Rb** Rubidium 85.4678	38 **Sr** Strontium 87.62	39 **Y** Yttrium 88.9059	40 **Zr** Zirconium 91.224	41 **Nb** Niobium 92.90638	42 **Mo** Molybdenum 95.94	43 **Tc** Technetium [98]	44 **Ru** Ruthenium 101.07	45 **Rh** Rhodium 102.9055	
55 **Cs** Cesium 132.90545	56 **Ba** Barium 137.3270	57-71 **La-Lu** Lanthanide Series	72 **Hf** Hafnium 178.49	73 **Ta** Tantalum 180.9479	74 **W** Tungsten 183.84	75 **Re** Rhenium 186.207	76 **Os** Osmium 190.23	77 **Ir** Iridium 192.22	
87 **Fr** Francium [223]	88 **Ra** Radium [226]	89-103 **Ac-Lr** Actinide Series	104 **Rf** Rutherfordium [261]	105 **Db** Dubnium [262]	106 **Sg** Seaborgium [266]	107 **Bh** Bohrium [264]	108 **Hs** Hassium [269]	109 **Mt** Meitnerium [268]	

57 **La** Lanthanum 138.9055	58 **Ce** Cerium 140.116	59 **Pr** Praseodymium 140.90765	60 **Nd** Neodymium 144.24	61 **Pm** Promethium [145]	62 **Sm** Samarium 150.36
89 **Ac** Actinium [227]	90 **Th** Thorium 232.0381	91 **Pa** Protactinium 231.0359	92 **U** Uranium 238.0289	93 **Np** Neptunium [237]	94 **Pu** Plutonium [244]

Z	Symbol	Name	Mass
28	Ni	Nickel	58.6934
29	Cu	Copper	63.546
30	Zn	Zinc	65.39
31	Ga	Gallium	69.72
32	Ge	Germanium	72.61
33	As	Arsenic	74.9216
34	Se	Selenium	78.96
35	Br	Bromine	79.904
36	Kr	Krypton	83.8
46	Pd	Palladium	106.42
47	Ag	Silver	107.8682
48	Cd	Cadmium	112.411
49	In	Indium	114.82
50	Sn	Tin	118.71
51	Sb	Antimony	121.76
52	Te	Tellurium	127.6
53	I	Iodine	126.905
54	Xe	Xenon	131.29
78	Pt	Platinum	195.08
79	Au	Gold	196.96659
80	Hg	Mercury	200.59
81	Tl	Thallium	204.383
82	Pb	Lead	207.2
83	Bi	Bismuth	208.98
84	Po	Polonium	[209]
85	At	Astatine	[210]
86	Rn	Radon	[222]
110	Ds	Darmstadtium	[281]
111	Rg	Roentgenium	[280]
112	Cn	Copernicium	[285]
113	Uut	Ununtrium	[284]
114	Uuq	Ununquadium	[289]
115	Uup	Ununpentium	[288]
116	Uuh	Ununhexium	[293]
117	Uus	Ununseptium	[294]
118	Uuo	Ununoctium	[294]
5	B	Boron	10.811
6	C	Carbon	12.011
7	N	Nitrogen	14.00674
8	O	Oxygen	15.9994
9	F	Fluorine	18.9984
10	Ne	Neon	20.1797
13	Al	Aluminum	26.982
14	Si	Silicon	28.0855
15	P	Phosphorus	30.974
16	S	Sulfur	32.065
17	Cl	Chlorine	35.453
18	Ar	Argon	39.948
2	He	Helium	4.0026
63	Eu	Eruopium	151.964
64	Gd	Gadolinium	157.25
65	Tb	Terbium	158.93
66	Dy	Dysprosium	162.5
67	Ho	Holmium	164.93
68	Er	Erbium	167.26
69	Tm	Thulium	168.93421
70	Yb	Ytterbium	173.04
71	Lu	Lutetium	174.968
95	Am	Americium	[243]
96	Cm	Curium	[247]
97	Bk	Berkelium	[247]
98	Cf	Californium	[251]
99	Es	Einsteinium	[252]
100	Fm	Fermium	[257]
101	Md	Mendelevium	[258]
102	No	Nobelium	[259]
103	Lr	Lawrencium	[262]

Part 2: Definition of a Molecule

Show your students the Periodic Table again. Ask them to find water on it. When they can't find it, ask them why they think water is not on there (because it's not an atom). Water, like everything in the world, is made of atoms, but it isn't made of all one type of atom. It is made of two different types of atoms: hydrogen and oxygen. Have them find (or show them) hydrogen and oxygen on the Periodic Table. Water is made of two hydrogen atoms and one oxygen atom. When you add two or more atoms together, it is called a ***molecule***. Two hydrogen atoms and one oxygen atom together make a water molecule. All molecules are made up of two or more atoms.

Activity:

Have them make models of molecules with toothpicks and colored marshmallows (you can substitute gumdrops or balls of clay for the marshmallows if you like). Start with a water molecule. Choose a color to be oxygen and a color to be hydrogen. Attach the two hydrogen marshmallows to the oxygen marshmallow with the toothpicks so it looks like this:

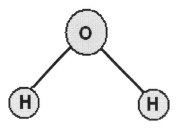

After they have finished making the water molecule, have them make these molecules:

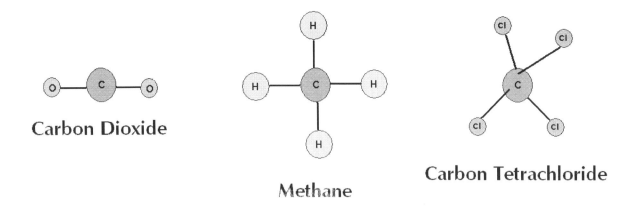

Carbon Dioxide

Methane

Carbon Tetrachloride

Point out to your students that "di" means two, so carbon di̲oxide means a carbon molecule with two oxygen molecules. "Tetra" means four, so carbon tetra̲chloride means a carbon molecule with four chlorine molecules.

Part 3: Crystals

Activity:

　　　　Make eight or more water molecules with marshmallows like you did in the previous activity; only this time push each molecule's hydrogen "atoms" up the toothpicks until they are touching the larger oxygen "atom." Next, take two of the water molecules and connect them to each other by pushing one molecule's oxygen atom onto one of the toothpicks sticking out of one of the other molecule's hydrogen "atoms." Continue adding the other water molecules in the same way until you have a three-dimensional structure. Each oxygen atom can have up to four hydrogen atoms connected to it.

　　　　Tell them that they have just made a model of ice crystals! Different molecules have different shapes. When molecules of the same substance attach to each other without any interference from outside forces, they will go together like puzzle pieces, depending on the shape of each individual molecule.

Activity:

　　　　Have your students draw (or draw for them) three-dimensional figures starting with different shapes. For example:

You can start with a cube, or a roof-shape, or any shape you please:

Then build on your original shape to create a larger structure:

　　　　Just like the cube and the roof-shape can be the building blocks of a larger shape, molecules are the building blocks of the shapes of crystals.

　　　　Now tell your students that it is time to see some real shapes that molecules make when they join together.

Activity:

　　　　Look at some salt under a magnifying glass and notice the shape of the crystals. Salt molecules join together to make cubes. Smash the salt with a hammer and look at the crystals again. Tell your students that in real life, outside forces such as erosion, pressure, and heat act on groups of molecules so that their shapes aren't what they would be if left alone. A salt molecule is made of one atom of sodium and one atom of chloride. When salt molecules are allowed to attach to each other freely, they make salt crystals.

Activity:

Grow some crystals to see how they form different shapes. To grow crystals, you need to make a **saturated solution**, which is basically a mixture that is as full of sugar, or whatever you put in it, as it can get. Sugar crystals are fun to grow because you can eat them! Take a rough string (not too slippery or the crystals won't be able to stick to it) and tie a paperclip to one end to weigh it down. Tie the other end to the middle of a pencil and hang the string into an open jelly jar with the paperclip on the bottom. Jelly jars can usually withstand having hot water poured into them, but be careful when pouring the mixture into the jar, just in case it breaks. Don't let the string touch the sides of the glass. Make a saturated solution of sugar by boiling one cup of water in a saucepan and gradually stirring in 3 cups of sugar, tablespoon by tablespoon. Pour the sugar mixture into the jar. You can add a few drops of food coloring if you would like your crystals to be colored. Let the jar sit for a few days. This recipe is designed to make lots of crystals quickly, so if you just want the crystals on the string, you can take them out early, or leave the string in and watch the crystals take over the jar! Table sugar molecules are made of 12 atoms of carbon, 22 atoms of hydrogen, and 11 molecules of oxygen.

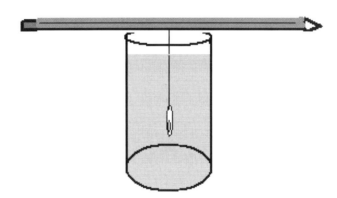

Epsom Salts make very pretty spiky-shaped crystals. To see them, cut a piece of dark colored construction paper to fit the bottom of a pie-pan. Thoroughly mix 1 Tablespoon Epsom salts with 3 Tablespoons of warm water in a glass. Pour the mixture onto the construction paper in the pie pan. Let it sit in a warm place until the water evaporates. Sometimes the crystals are even better on the bottom side of the paper, so check both sides. Epsom Salt molecules are made from one atom of magnesium, one atom of sulfur, and four atoms of oxygen. Even though they are called "salt," they are <u>not</u> edible, so make sure your students don't taste them!

When we "grow crystals," we are breaking the molecules apart from each other and allowing them to come back together in their natural pattern. Crystals are good examples of the different kinds of shapes molecules can make when they join together.

Part 4: Characteristics of Molecules

A. Molecules Move

Activity:

Place a glass of water on a table. Put a few drops of food coloring in it and watch what happens. The food coloring will eventually move throughout the glass.

Tell your students that even though molecules are so small that we can't see them, we can see groups of molecules. The food coloring is a group of molecules and we can watch it move through the water until the food coloring and the water are evenly mixed throughout the glass. This mixing due to molecular movement is called **diffusion**.

Activity:

Have your students stand about ten feet away from you. Take a perfume spray bottle and squirt one spray of perfume into the air. See how long it takes the smell to reach your students.
Point out to your students that molecules not only move (diffuse) through water, they can move through air also.

B. Molecules move faster or slower depending on temperature

Activity:

You will need to prepare the bowls of water for this activity ahead of time. Fill a bowl with cold water and put it in the freezer for about 20 minutes. While the water is cooling, boil some water and pour it into another bowl. Place both bowls next to each other on a table and drop the same number of drops of food coloring in each bowl. Observe how long it takes for the color to diffuse throughout each bowl (you can even time them with a clock or stopwatch). The food coloring in the cold water bowl should take longer to diffuse than the food coloring in the hot water bowl. That is because molecules move faster in hot water than in cold water.

A fun way to illustrate molecular motion for your students is to tell them that when molecules are cold they are sluggish and don't want to move much. You can pretend you are the slow, sluggish, cold molecule while you say this (and have them move along with you if they want to). Next tell them that hot molecules move around very quickly. As you say this, start speeding up your movements and speech. As molecules start moving around more quickly, they spread apart, and pretty soon they just shoot off into the air by themselves and become a gas.

Activity:

Have your students play a game where they pretend that they are atoms at different temperatures. You call out "hot", "cold," or "warm," and they need to move accordingly. If they are "hot," they should be moving faster and farther away from each other. If they are "cold," they should be moving slower and closer together. If they are "warm," they should be moving somewhere in between.

Activity:

     Boil a pot of water on the stove (a tea kettle is especially good for this). Have your students watch as the water starts turning into water vapor and "escapes" from the pot into the air.

Activity:

     Leave an empty glass soda bottle (or a similar-type bottle) in the freezer for about ten minutes. Take it out and spread a film of water over the top of the bottle opening with your finger. Immediately place a quarter over the bottle opening. After a few minutes, as the air inside the bottle starts warming up, the coin will start clicking up and down. This is because as molecules of air inside the bottle start warming up, they will start moving faster, and start moving farther apart or expanding. As they move farther apart, they will start pushing on the coin at the top of the bottle and force it upward.

C. Molecules have Space Between Them

Activity:

     Pour 1 cup of water in a glass jar and mark with a marker or piece of tape where the water line is. Add another cup of water to the jar and mark where the water line is with 2 cups of water in it. Now pour out all of the water. Measure 1 cup of hot tap water and pour it into the jar.

     Ask your students what they think will happen if you add 1 cup of sugar to the cup of water in the jar. Do they think it will move the level of the water up to the 2 cup mark? Add 1 cup of sugar to the water and stir it with a spoon until it dissolves in the water. The level of the sugar and water will be less than the 2 cup mark. This is one case where 1 + 1 does not equal 2! One of the reasons for this is that even though molecules are so small that we can't see them, they still have spaces between them. When the sugar dissolved in the water, the sugar molecules fit into the empty spaces between the water molecules, so they don't take up as much room in the water as they did in air.

D. Molecules are Small

Activity:

     Fill up an eyedropper with peppermint extract. Squeeze the extract into an unfilled balloon, making sure not to let any drip onto the outside of the balloon. Blow up the balloon and tie it shut. Wait a few minutes and smell the outside of the balloon. It should smell like peppermint.

     You can smell the peppermint on the outside of the balloon because the peppermint molecules were so small that they could move through the balloon to reach the outside air.

Part 5: Parts of an Atom

     Remind your students that molecules are made of atoms and that atoms are the smallest possible pieces of elements. For example, if you broke an atom of iron in half, it would not be iron any more. But what are atoms themselves made of? An atom has three main parts, **protons**, **neutrons**, and **electrons**. The protons and neutrons are in the center of the atom and together they are called the nucleus. The electrons move around the outside of the nucleus.

Activity:

   Have your student draw a picture of an atom. It should turn out something like this:

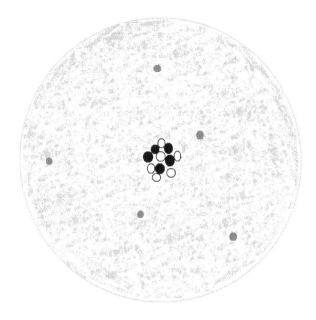

   The protons and neutrons are the black and white circles in the center of the atom, forming the nucleus. The electrons are the gray circles outside of the nucleus. Normally there is the same number of electrons as protons, so in the drawing above, the protons are the black circles, the neutrons are the white circles, and the electrons are the gray circles. The cloudy area shows the space that the electrons are moving in.

Activity:

   Pretend you are the nucleus and your students are the electrons moving around you. Using the Periodic Table, figure out what type of atom you are by the number of electrons you have.

Activity:

   Draw some specific atoms using the following information:

   1) A hydrogen atoms has one proton, one electron, and no neutrons
   2) A carbon atom has 6 protons, 6 electrons, and 6 neutrons
   3) An iron atom has 26 protons, 26 electrons, and 30 neutrons
   4) A nitrogen atom has 7 protons, 7 electrons, and 7 neutrons

Test for Atoms and Molecules

1) What is diffusion?
   a. Another word for "different"
   b. A type of molecule
   c. The mixing of molecules due to molecular movement.
   d. The movement of electrons in an atom.

2) What is an atom?
   a. The smallest piece of an element that can still be called that element
   b. A bomb
   c. Something that contains tritons and neutrons
   d. Something made of molecules

3) What is a molecule?
   a. A part of an atom
   b. A combination of two or more atoms
   c. A mole's cuticle
   d. Part of an electron

4) What is a proton?
   a. The part of the atom that spins around outside the nucleus
   b. A part of an electron
   c. A light ray that comes off of electrons
   d. A particle in an atom that is part of the nucleus

5) What is an electron?
   a. The part of the atom that spins around outside the nucleus
   b. It is what crystals are made of
   c. A particle in an atom that is part of the nucleus
   d. The part of the atom that rests

6) What is a neutron?
   a. The part of the atom that spins around outside the nucleus
   b. A part of an electron
   c. A particle in an atom that is part of the nucleus
   d. A neutral molecule

7) What makes up the nucleus of an atom?
     a. Electrons and protons
     b. Protons and neutrons
     c. Electrons and neutrons
     d. Electrons, protons, and neutrons

8) Name three characteristics of molecules.
     a. They are motionless, they have space between them, they are small.
     b. They are solid objects, they are motionless, they are small.
     c. They have space between them, they move more quickly in cold temperatures than warm temperatures, they are small.
     d. They move, they have space between them, they are small.

9) What is the name of the table that scientists have listed all of the different types of atoms in?
     a. The Table of Molecules
     b. The Periodic Table of the Elements
     c. The Table of the Chemicals
     d. The Periodic Table of Molecules

10) Molecules mover faster or slower depending on what?
     a. Whether it is dark or light
     b. Whether it is sour or sweet
     c. Whether it is hot or cold
     d. Whether it is wet or dry

Chapter 14: Matter
Ages 8-13

Materials Needed For This Unit

Vacuum cleaner with attachments
Sand
Square cake pan
Marbles of two different colors or types
Fruit juice
Ice-cube tray
Toothpicks or popsicle sticks
Red or purple cabbage
Lemon juice
Baking soda
White Vinegar
Balloon
Two liter soda bottle
A tall thin clear glass jar that fits inside either a larger clear glass jar or drinking glass
Steel wool
Crushed ice
Celsius thermometer that goes from at least 0 to 100
A watch or clock with a second hand, or a stopwatch
Salt
Sugar
Four clear glass jars that can hold about three cups of liquid
Three clear glass jars that can hold about one cup of liquid
Plastic drinking water bottle (not one made out of hard plastic)

Duct tape
Masking tape
Marker
Cornstarch
Drinking glass
Saucepan
Paper towel
Bowls

Part 1: Definition of Matter

Tell your students that you are going to be studying matter. Let them know that the word matter is a scientific word for "stuff." **Matter** is anything that takes up space and has mass (which is basically saying that it can be weighed). Have them list things that are matter and see if they think of things like air and water. If they don't, ask them if they think air and water are matter (they are). Tell them that matter is all around us. Air is matter, water is matter; we are matter. Atoms and molecules are matter.

Say that the only place where there isn't matter is in something called a "vacuum" (you might want to mention that you don't mean inside a vacuum cleaner!) A vacuum is a space that has absolutely nothing in it. No air, no molecules, no atoms. There is an old saying "Nature abhors a vacuum." Ask them what they think this means (nature hates a vacuum). How might nature show that it doesn't like a vacuum? (by filling it).

Activity:

   Empty a plastic drinking water bottle (use a bottle made of soft plastic that you can crush easily with your hand, not one made of hard plastic) and let it dry. Take a vacuum cleaner and use the attachments that come with it to fasten the plastic bottle on the end of the vacuum cleaner hose with duct tape (the flimsier the bottle and the more powerful the vacuum cleaner, the better). It is very important that the duct tape seals the joint between the bottle and the vacuum so that no air can escape. Once you've attached the bottle, turn on the vacuum. The bottle should collapse (as-soon-as the bottle collapses, turn off the vacuum cleaner, you don't want to damage it). This is because "nature abhors a vacuum." The vacuum cleaner sucked all of the air out of the bottle, creating a vacuum. Something had to fill that empty space, so the bottle collapsed.

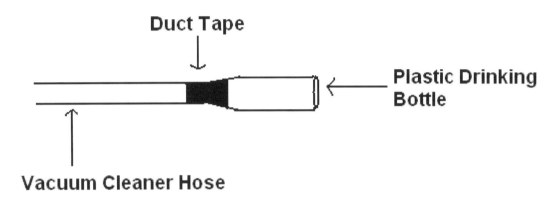

Part 2: States of Matter

   Tell your students that matter can be found in different forms or "states." We are going to talk about three of them here: **solid, liquid**, and **gas**. Have them think of water and describe the solid, liquid, and gas forms of water (ice, water that you drink, water vapor or steam). Remember how atoms and molecules move faster and farther apart when they are heated? The molecules and atoms of matter in a gaseous state move farther apart and faster than those of matter in a liquid state. The molecules and atoms of matter in a liquid state move farther apart and faster than those of matter in a solid state. In the picture below, each "o" represents a water molecule:

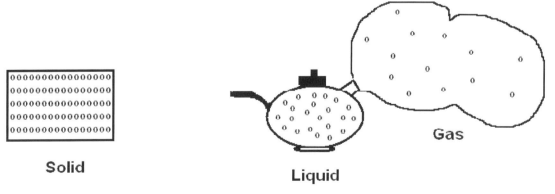

Activity:

If it has been awhile since you did the "Atoms and Molecules" chapter in this book, now would be a good time to repeat any of the activities in Part 4 that you think your students might need a review of.

Activity:

Take a square or rectangular cake pan and place some marbles in it close together in rows covering about ¼ of the pan. Tell your students that these marbles represent molecules in a solid state. Now start slightly vibrating the cake pan and, when the marbles have moved apart some, say that this represents molecules in a liquid state (the marbles need to be vibrating enough to move apart). Next, vibrate the cake pan even more, so that the marbles have spread across the whole pan. This represents molecules in a gaseous state.

Now, take some marbles that are all one color and place them in rows on one side of the pan. Then take some marbles that are all a different color and place them in rows on the other side of the pan. Start vibrating the pan and observe the motion of the marbles. They will slowly start mixing together. Ask your students if they remember what this might represent (diffusion, the mixing of molecules due to molecular movement).

Activity:

Have fun turning a liquid to a solid by making your own popsicles! Pour some fruit juice into an ice-cube tray, put it in the freezer and let it set for awhile. Before it is completely frozen, put toothpicks or popsicle sticks in each cube and return to the freezer until the ice cubes have frozen solid.

Part 3: Physical Properties of Matter

Tell your students that all matter has characteristics that make it different from other types of matter, just like they have characteristics that make them different from other people. Have them describe some characteristics that make them different from their brother or sister, or a friend. We call these characteristics of matter "properties." There are two types of properties of matter; physical and chemical. *Physical properties* are those that can be seen without actually changing the molecules of the substance we are looking at. For example, we can see what color it is, how it smells, or how heavy it is. Have them list out other physical properties they can think of (for example, taste, texture or shape). The state of matter is also a physical property. This is because even though changing from one state to another changes the appearance of something (for example ice to water), it does not change its molecules. *Chemical Properties* of matter are those that actually change the chemical make-up of the matter. This means that it changes the molecules of the matter itself. We will talk more about chemical properties of matter in later sections.

Activity:

Take out some items from your kitchen such as sugar, milk, vinegar, or whatever you choose, and put each item in a bowl. Have your students list as many physical properties of each item that they can. Don't forget to have them list the state of matter each item is in.

Part 4: Melting Point and Freezing Point

Tell your students that the temperature at which a substance changes from a solid state to a liquid state is called its melting point. Ask them if they think melting point is a chemical or physical property (it's a physical property because even though it is changing its state of matter, going from solid to liquid, it is not changing its molecular structure). Once the melting point is reached, the substance will stay at that temperature until all of it has turned into a liquid.

Ask your students what they think the freezing point is (the temperature at which a substance changes from a liquid state to a solid state). Freezing point and melting point are usually the same temperature. Freezing point is also a physical property.

Activity:

Fill a glass half full of water. Add enough crushed ice to fill the glass about 1½ inches from the top. Place a Celsius thermometer in the glass. Immediately record the temperature. Continue recording the temperature every minute for 12 minutes. Stir the ice and water during this whole process. Record your results on the graph below.

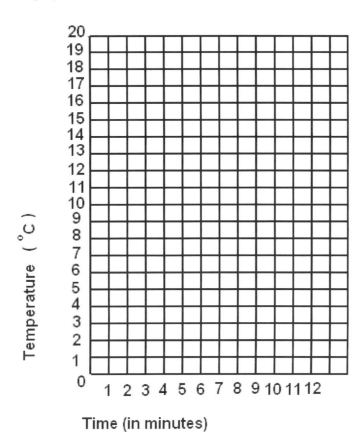

Remember that the melting point is the point where the temperature stays the same until all of the ice has melted. What melting point did you find? Providing your thermometer was accurate (sometimes they are not!), it should have been 0°C

Part 5: Boiling Point

Tell your students that another physical property of matter is boiling point. This is the temperature at which a liquid turns into a gas. Once the boiling point of a substance is reached, it will stay at that temperature (providing you keep applying heat) until all of it has turned into a gas.

Activity:

  Put a pot of warm water on the stove with a Celsius thermometer in it that can go up to 100 °C. Make sure that it is a thermometer that won't break under high temperatures. Immediately record the temperature. Continue recording the temperature every minute for 12 minutes. Stir the water in the pot during this whole process. Record your results on the graph below.

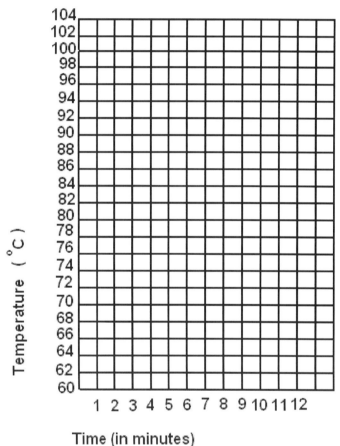

  Remember that the boiling point is the point where the temperature stays the same until all of the water has turned to a gas. What boiling point did you find? Providing your thermometer was accurate (sometimes they are not!), it should have been 100 °C.

Part 6: Solubility

Another physical property you can tell your students about is solubility. Take a glass of water and stir a tablespoon of salt into it. The salt seems to disappear. Ask your students if they know what happened to it. Do they think the salt is still in the water? Tell them that the salt has dissolved into the water. It is still there, but being in the water breaks it apart into separate molecules. The separate salt molecules are so small that you can't see them, and it seems like the salt has disappeared. Since the salt molecules are still there, and they haven't changed into another type of molecule, this is a physical property of salt. We say that salt is ***soluble*** in water. If something does not dissolve in a liquid, we say that it is ***insoluble*** in that liquid. A substance that dissolves in a liquid is called the ***solute*** and the liquid it dissolves in is called the ***solvent***. Ask your students which is the solute and which is the solvent when you dissolve salt in water (the salt was the solute and the water was the solvent).

Now take your glass of salt water and keep pouring (and stirring) salt into it. At some point the water will not be able to dissolve all of the salt you have poured into it. In this case, salt is still soluble in water, you have just poured in more than the water can dissolve.

Activity:

*Take three glass jars and label them using masking tape and a marker as "sugar," "cornstarch," and "sand." Pour ½ C of water in each jar. Take one tablespoon of sugar and stir it into the sugar jar. Take one tablespoon of cornstarch and stir it into the cornstarch jar. Finally, take one tablespoons of sand and stir it into the sand jar. Which of the three is soluble in water? Only one of them is; sugar. The sand is insoluble and the cornstarch forms something called a **suspension**. You can tell it is a suspension because the mixture is cloudy; the cornstarch did not disappear into the water. The cornstarch did not break down into individual molecules. It did break down into smaller particles, but it did not break down completely which is why you can still see it as a cloudy mass.*

Part 7: Chemical Properties of Matter

Tell your students that a chemical property is one in which the actual molecules of a type of matter is changed. These types of changes happen when one substance reacts or combines with another and a new substance or substances are formed.

Activity:

*Chop up some red or purple cabbage and boil it in water. The water should change to a purple-color. Take the purple cabbage water and pour some in each of two soup bowls. Add lemon juice to one bowl and baking soda to another. The cabbage water will change colors! Tell the students that this is due to a chemical reaction occurring between the cabbage water and the lemon juice and baking soda. A **chemical reaction** is what happens when a type of matter changes into something else at a molecular level. Liquid water changing into ice is not a chemical reaction because the water molecules never change, they just get closer together.*

Activity:

      Take a two-liter soda bottle and pour one inch of vinegar into it. Put a few teaspoons of baking soda onto a small piece of paper towel or tissue and twist it into a parcel small enough to drop into the bottle. Drop the baking soda parcel into the bottle and quickly stretch a balloon over the bottle opening. The balloon should slowly fill up. Mixing baking soda and vinegar together creates a chemical reaction that produces carbon dioxide gas. One of the chemical properties of baking soda is that it mixes with vinegar to produce carbon dioxide. It's probably not a good idea to breath a lot of carbon dioxide, so don't put your nose too close to it!

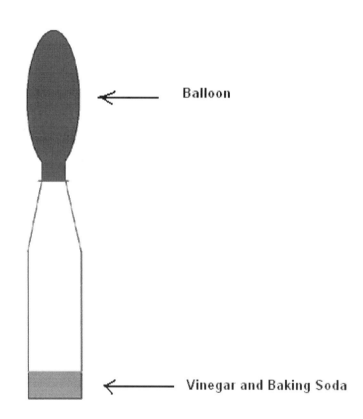

Balloon

Vinegar and Baking Soda

Activity:

     For this activity, you will need two clear glass jars or glasses. One needs to be tall and thin and able to fit easily inside the other with a slight tilt so that it doesn't rest firmly on the bottom. Dampen some steel wool and pack it tightly into the bottom of the tall thin glass jar. Pour about 1 ½ inches of water into the bottom of the wide glass jar. Turn the jar with the steel wool upside down and place it into the jar with the water. Tip the jar with the steel wool a little so that the bottom of the jar does not rest firmly on the bottom of the wide jar, but so that all of the opening is under water. Mark a line on the outside of the steel wool jar where the water stops inside it. After a few days you will notice that the water inside the steel wool jar has gone up (be patient, you are waiting for the steel wool to start rusting). This is because the iron in the steel wool is combining with the oxygen that was in the thin jar to form rust. As the oxygen combines with the iron, the air is depleted in the jar, and more water is sucked into the jar to take the place of the used oxygen. One of the chemical properties of iron is that it combines with oxygen to form rust.

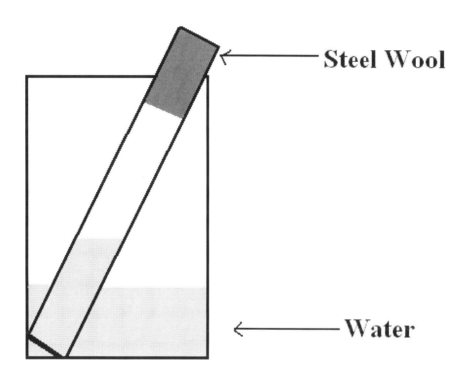

Part 8: Using Properties of Matter to Identify Substances:

     Tell your students that scientists can use the various physical and chemical properties of matter to help them determine what a substance is. In the activity on the following page, your students are going to use what they have learned in this unit to determine what is in four different jars of liquids. The set-up for this activity needs to be done when your students are not looking!

Activity:

  Before you start this activity (preferably right before you do the activity so that the mixtures are still fresh and the salt doesn't start coming out of the water), prepare four glass jars as follows. Using masking tape and a marker, label one jar as "A," one as "B," one as "C," and one as "D." Pour 2 C of warm water into each jar. In the jar labeled "A," stir in ⅛ C cornstarch. In the jar labeled "B," stir in ⅛ C salt. In the jar labeled "D," stir in ⅛ C baking soda. Do not stir anything in the jar labeled "C." Make sure that no residue of the solids is sticking to the sides of any of the jars.

  Give the four jars to your students and tell them that their job as scientists is to figure out what is in each jar using what they have learned about the physical and chemical properties of the various substances. Let them know that one jar has baking soda and water, one has salt and water, one has cornstarch and water, and one has nothing mixed in. The only test they <u>cannot</u> use is taste! Ask them why a real scientist would not taste an unknown substance (because it might be poisonous).

  Have the students brainstorm about how they can figure out what is in the four jars. They should be able to identify the cornstarch jar immediately by the cloudy appearance (remember that cornstarch is not soluble in water). See what ways they can think of to identify the other three jars.

  Here is one way to solve the problem. Take a bowl and pour 1 tablespoon of liquid into it from jar B. Add one tablespoon of vinegar. Take a clean bowl and do the same with jar C. Finally with another clean bowl, test jar D. Jar D should have a chemical reaction with the vinegar, thus it is the baking soda solution.

  Now you still have to separate out the plain water from the salt water. One way to do this is to take a few tablespoons from one of the remaining jars and boil the water off in a saucepan. If you do this, watch it constantly and be ready to take the pan off the stove quickly before the water is completely boiled away (you don't want to start a fire or burn your pan). Make sure your students don't get too close to the burner. Do this with both of the remaining liquids. Jar B will leave much more of a residue than jar C, due to the salt that is in the water in jar B. Remind your students that the salt is still in the water when it dissolves, it is just in such a small form that you can't see it. The plain water may leave a bit of a residue also, due to minerals in the water, but the salt will leave significantly more and will be very obvious.

Test for Matter

1) What is matter?
   a. A mat of molecules
   b. The space between molecules
   c. Anything that takes up space and has mass
   d. A special term for molecules that form a mat-like pattern

2) What is a vacuum?
   a. A scientific cleaning tool
   b. A space that doesn't have any matter in it
   c. A space that does have matter in it
   d. A space where molecules move slowly

3) What does nature abhor?
   a. Death
   b. Decay
   c. Atoms that don't act properly
   d. A vacuum

4) What are the three states of matter?
   a. Gas, solid, liquid
   b. Atoms, molecules, ions
   c. Birth, life, death
   d. Chemical, physical, mental

5) What is diffusion?
   a. Another word for "different"
   b. A type of molecule
   c. The mixing of molecules due to molecular movement.
   d. The movement of electrons in an atom.

6) Molecules in a gas move_____than molecules in a liquid.
   a. slower and closer together
   b. faster and farther apart
   c. faster and closer together
   d. slower and farther apart

7) Which of the following does <u>not</u> represent a physical property of matter?
    a. The mixing of vinegar and baking soda
    b. Water turning into ice
    c. The smell of vinegar
    d. The melting point of water

8) The melting point of a substance is the temperature it
    a. changes from a gas to a liquid
    b. changes from a solid to a liquid
    c. changes from a liquid to a gas
    d. changes from a solid to a gas

9) The boiling point of a substance is the temperature it
    a. changes from a solid to a liquid
    b. changes from a solid to a gas
    c. changes from a liquid to a solid
    d. changes from a liquid to a gas

10) When salt is dissolved in water, the resulting mixture is called a
    a. Solute
    b. Solvent
    c. Solution
    d. Soluble

Chapter 15: Chemistry Fun!
Ages 8-13

Materials Needed for this Unit

Small metal paperclip	One egg	Vanilla	Access to an oven
Dish soap	White glue	Strainer	Cookie sheet
Eyedropper	White sugar	Shortening	Paper coffee filter
Kitchen scale	Salt	Mixing bowl	Red or purple cabbage
Cooking oil	Soda Crackers	Brown sugar	Chocolate chips
Measuring cup	Paperclips	Butter	Baking soda
Molasses	Flour	Blender	Clear drinking glass

Iodine (can be purchased at a pharmacy)   A one-cup measuring cup
Borax powder (from a grocery store)   Clear plastic drinking cups

Part 1: Density

Ask your students if they remember the definition of matter from the previous chapter. Tell your students that the term ***mass*** is the measurement of the amount of matter in an object. The mass of an object never changes. The term ***weight*** is the measurement of the force of gravity (how hard it is pulling down) on a given mass. On earth, mass and weight are essentially the same. However, if you went to the moon, your mass would stay the same (because the amount of matter inside your body hasn't changed), but your weight would be less because there is less gravity pulling down on your body on the moon than there is on earth.

Activity:
Take exactly one cup of water and weigh it. Now take exactly one cup of cooking oil and weigh that (make sure you weigh at least 1 cup of each, if you weigh less than a cup, the difference won't show). Which weighs more? The water should weigh more, because water is denser than the cooking oil.
Density *is the term for the mass of a substance in a specific volume. In this case, the volume is one cup and the weight of the water in one cup is greater than the weight of the cooking oil in one cup, so it is denser. A simplified way to think of density is to think of how much "stuff" is packed into an area. For example, if you have two suitcases exactly the same size, but you pack twice as many clothes into one of them, the suitcase with more clothes is denser.*

Activity:
Take ¼ cup of oil and pour it into a clear glass. Next take ¼ cup of water and slowly pour it into the same glass by pouring it so that the water is going down the side of the glass. Finally, take ¼ cup of molasses and pour it into the glass the same way you poured the water. Let the liquids settle out and observe how they settle. Which of the three is the densest? (the molasses, it should be on the bottom of the glass) Which is the least dense? (the oil, it should be on the top of the glass.) The molasses is the most dense because it weighs the most per unit volume.

Part 2: Surface Tension

Tell your students that the molecules of a liquid are attracted to each other, much like the opposite ends of a magnet are attracted to each other. This attraction between similar molecules is called **cohesion**. The molecules <u>under</u> the surface of a liquid have similar molecules all around them, while the molecules <u>at</u> the surface of a liquid only have similar molecules on three sides of them. Because they don't have molecules pulling them upward, the molecules at the surface are able to bind together even more tightly to each other. This creates an effect called ***surface tension***. Because of surface tension, the very top layer of molecules are closer together than the molecules underneath them, forming an elastic-like sheet over the surface that holds in the liquid below. This elastic-like sheet is how insects like Water Striders are able to "skate" on the water.

Activity:
Fill a bowl with tap water. Take a small metal paperclip and bend one side of it straight up. Drop it into the bowl of water. It will sink to the bottom because the paperclip is denser than water. Wait for the water to stop moving, hold the same paperclip on the side that you bent up, and gently place it on the surface of the water so that it floats. It can float there, even though it is denser than water, because of surface tension. Now take a drop of dish soap and drop it into the water, preferably off to the side of the bowl. The paperclip should sink to the bottom. Dish soap is a chemical that lessens the effect of the water's surface tension by breaking up the bonds between the water molecules.

Part 3: The Difference between a Mixture and a Solution

Activity:
*Mix 1 3/4 C flour with 1/2 C white sugar in a mixing bowl. You have just made a **mixture**! A mixture is when two or more substances are combined and each of the substances has not been changed chemically (their molecules have not changed). The flour is still flour and the sugar is still sugar; they have not been changed chemically into something else. Now add 1/2 C brown sugar and 1/2 t baking soda to your mixture. Set your mixture aside.*

*Next measure out ⅛ C water in a measuring cup and stir in ¼ t salt. You have now made a **solution**. A solution is a kind of mixture that is homogeneous. **Homogeneous** means that is the same throughout. If you take out one teaspoon of your water/salt solution it will have the same amount of water and salt in it as the next teaspoon you take out. In a homogeneous mixture, you cannot easily see what the separate components of the mixture are. Add the water/salt solution to your flour/sugar mixture.*

*Next add ⅓ C shortening, ⅓ C butter, 1 Tablespoon vanilla, and 1 egg to the flour/salt mixture and stir everything together. Finally add 1 package of chocolate chips and mix. You have now made a **heterogeneous** mixture of batter and chocolate chips. A heterogeneous mixture is <u>not</u> the same throughout. The chocolate chips are not spread evenly throughout the batter. In a heterogeneous mixture, you can usually easily see what the separate components of the mixture are.*

Finally, drop the dough by rounded teaspoonfuls 2 inches apart on an ungreased cookie sheet. Bake 8 to 10 minutes at 375 degrees. Enjoy!

Part 4: The Conservation of Mass

Activity:

Normally measurements of mass would be made in kilograms, using a balance. However, not everyone has a balance at home, so we will use a kitchen scale for this activity. If you do have a balance, it would be better to use that. Your measurements have to be very accurate. Be sure that your scale is calibrated correctly each time before your students start measuring, and tell them to be careful not to spill or lose any of the items that they are measuring.

Using a kitchen scale, have your students weigh an empty one-cup measuring cup. Tell them to record their measurement in the worksheet on the following page on lines 2, 5, and 9. Next, they should fill the measuring cup with ¼ C salt, weigh it, and record this answer on line 1 of the worksheet. Set the salt aside in a bowl, being careful not to spill any. Now, using the worksheet, have them subtract the weight of the empty measuring cup from the weight of the measuring cup with the salt in it to find the weight of just the salt. The answer should go on lines 3 and 7 of the worksheet.

Now tell them to add ¾ C water to the measuring cup and weigh it. Do not dump the water out of the cup! They should record the answer on line 4 of the worksheet and do the subtracting on line 6 of the worksheet to find the weight of just the water. They should also record this answer on line 8 of the worksheet.

Next, tell your students to add the weight of the salt, the weight of the empty cup, and the weight of the water together on line 10 of the worksheet.

Finally, they should pour the salt that they set aside into the ¾ cup of water that is in the measuring cup and stir, being careful not to spill any salt or water. Ask your students how they think the weight of the dissolved salt in water will compare to the weight of the cup plus the salt plus the water.

Now have your students weigh the cup with the salt solution that they just made. This weight should be the same as the weight of the cup, plus the salt, plus the water. This is because even though the salt was dissolved into the water, it is still there, you just can't see it. This illustrates a chemical principal called the **"Conservation of Mass,"** that basically states that the mass of the substances that you combine in a physical or chemical reaction will be the same as the mass of the substance that you end up with. More simply, this means that the mass of what goes in equals the mass of what comes out.

Conservation of Mass Worksheet

1) Weight of the measuring cup with ¼ C salt   _____

2) Minus the weight of the empty measuring cup   - _____

3) Equals the weight of ¼ C salt   = _____

4) Weight of the measuring cup with ¾ C water   _____

5) Minus the weight of the empty measuring cup   - _____

6) Equals the weight of ¾ C water   = _____

7) Weight of the ¼ C salt   _____

8) Plus the weight of the ¾ C water   + _____

9) Plus the weight of the empty measuring cup   + _____

10) Equals the weight of the cup, salt, and water   = _____ *

*This answer should equal your final measurement in the experiment, the weight of the cup holding the salt <u>dissolved</u> in the water.

Part 5: Polymers

Activity:

  Give your students about ten paperclips each and have them make a paperclip chain from them (you can have them make a paperclip necklace if you would like to use more). Tell them that each paperclip represents a glucose molecule (glucose is a type of sugar), and that the whole paperclip chain represents a starch. Plants hook lots of glucose molecules together to form starches. Starch is a type of **Polymer,** *a long chain or ring of smaller molecules hooked together. The smaller molecules that make up a polymer are called* **monomers***. Glucose molecules are the monomers that make up the polymer starch.*

Activity:

  Take two clear plastic cups and label one "A" and one "B." Now take about a quarter of a piece of soda cracker and smash it up in the cup labeled A. Add a tablespoon of water to the cracker and stir. Next, take another quarter piece of soda cracker and chew it up <u>very</u> well (if you don't chew it up well enough, the experiment won't work), without swallowing it. Spit it into the cup labeled B, add a tablespoon of water to it, and stir. Now take an eyedropper of iodine and drop two drops into each cup. Do you see a difference? Iodine is a starch indicator; it will turn blue in the presence of starch.

  One of the things that saliva does is to break up starch polymers into their individual sugar molecules (the monomers). Your saliva in cup B broke up the starch molecules in the cracker that you chewed into its individual glucose molecules, so the mixture in cup B should be less blue than the mixture in cup A. The mixture in cup B might still have a bit of a purplish-blue color because all of the starch hasn't yet been broken up into its individual sugar molecules, but if you let it sit awhile longer, the saliva in the cup will keep working and the color will change.

Activity:

  Pour about 3 oz of white glue in a clear plastic drinking cup (do not use a foam cup). Take another clear plastic drinking cup and mix ½ oz of borax in 2 oz of water. Make sure that it is completely dissolved. Now pour the borax and water into the cup with the white glue and stir. You have just made a chemical reaction that created a rubber-like polymer!

Part 6: Electron Shells

Review with your students the parts of an atom that they learned in the chapter titled "Atoms and Molecules." You might want to go over Part 5 of that chapter again if you feel that they need more review.

Tell your students that electrons don't just randomly move around the nucleus of an atom, there is a pattern to their movement. Some electrons are found closer to the nucleus than others. Scientists have found that these differences in distance from the nucleus can be organized into what they call *electron shells*. There are a total of seven electron shells that an atom can have. The first shell, called the "K" shell, can hold up to two electrons in it, and the second, called the "L" shell, can hold up to eight electrons.

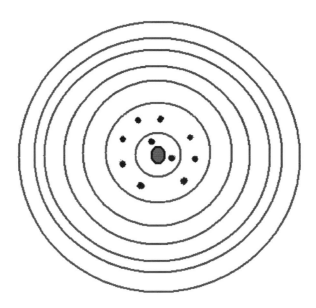

Model of an Atom With Its First Two Electron Shells Filled

In the diagram above, the nucleus of the atom is the circle in the center. The first circle around the nucleus is the first electron shell, with two electrons in it. The second circle around the nucleus is the second electron shell, with eight electrons in it. The remaining five electron shells are empty; there are no electrons orbiting in the other positions. This atom has a total of ten electrons. If you look at the Periodic Table included in the chapter titled "Atoms and Molecules," you will see that the element "Neon" has a ten in the box in the upper left-hand corner. The number ten is called the *Atomic Number,* which is the number of protons in an element. Remember that the number of protons normally equals the number of electrons, so if neon has ten protons, it will also have ten electrons. The diagram above is a model of a neon atom, because it has ten electrons.

Look at the Periodic Table again. Notice that hydrogen has only one electron. On the next page is a model of a hydrogen atom.

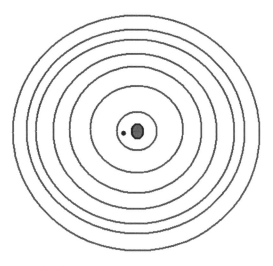

Model of a Hydrogen Atom

The third electron shell is called the "M" shell and it can hold eighteen electrons. The fourth shell is the "N" shell and it can hold up to thirty-two electrons. Argon has eighteen electrons. Below is the diagram of an Argon atom showing its electron shells.

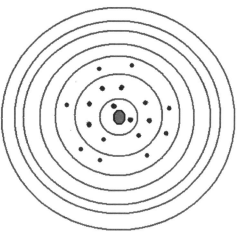

Model of an Argon Atom

Activity:

On the following page is a worksheet that your students can use to make their own models of the electron shells of atoms. Use the Periodic Table from your "Atoms and Molecules" chapter to find the Atomic Number of the atoms. Have your students draw in the electrons in each shell, making sure to start with the first innermost shell, filling it up, moving to the second shell, filling it up, etc.... They should not add electrons to a new shell until the previous shell is full. There is an answer sheet for this worksheet in the back of the book. Notice that there are no elements that have more than eighteen electrons on the worksheet. This is because the rules for filling the shells get more complicated after eighteen electrons. Be sure to mention this to your students.

Electron Shell Worksheet

Draw in the electrons for the following atoms. Start with the shell closest to the nucleus. Fill up each shell completely before moving on to the next.

Shell one is called K and has no more than 2 electrons
Shell two is called L and has no more than 8 electrons
Shell three is called M and has no more than 18 electrons
Shell four is called N and has no more than 32 electrons

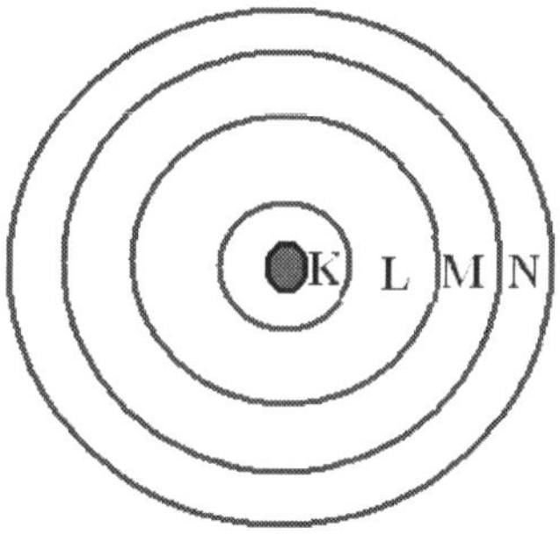

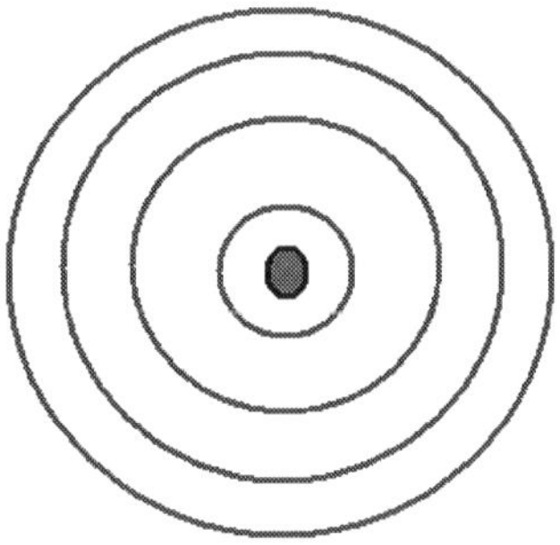

Helium

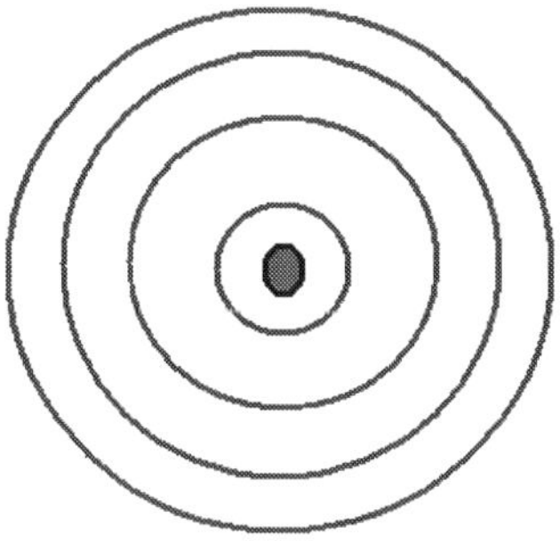

Nitrogen

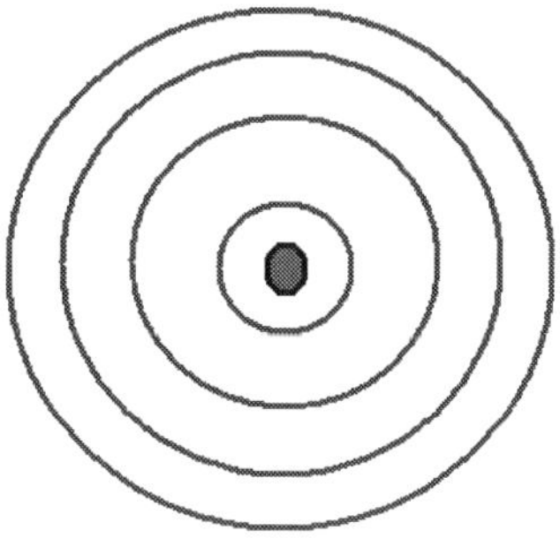

Sodium

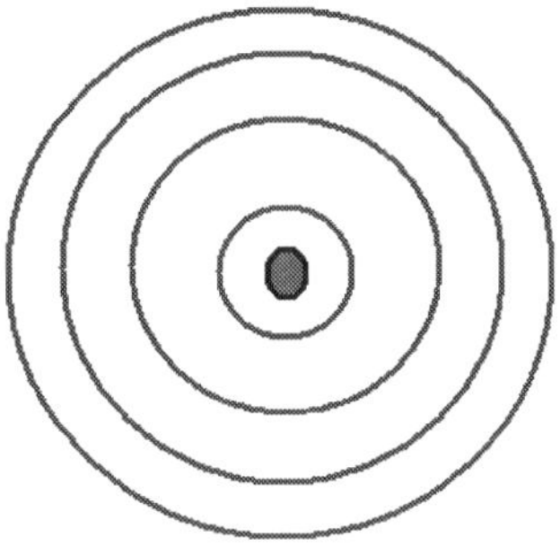

Chlorine

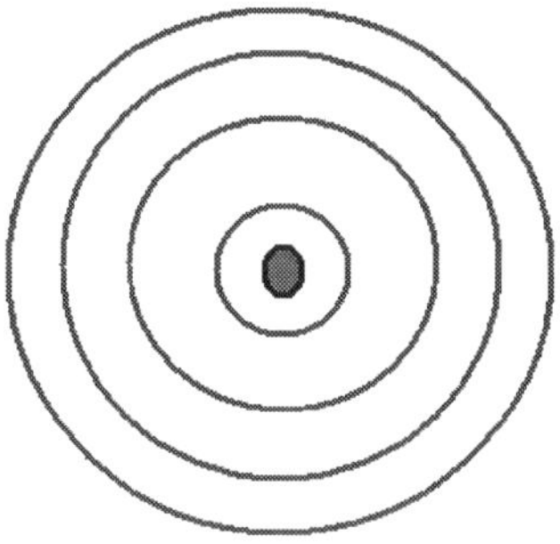

Phosphorus

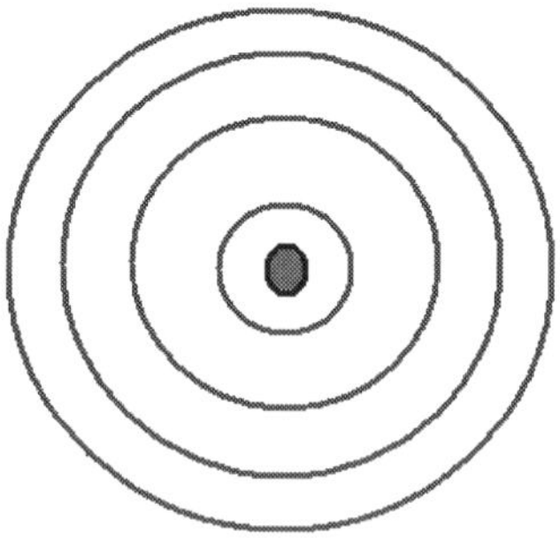

Carbon

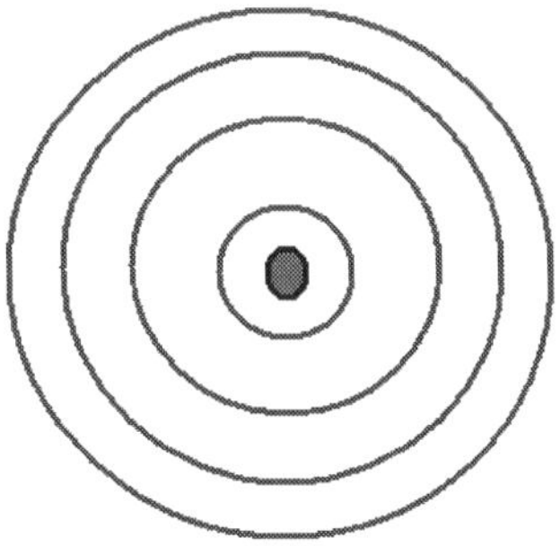

Magnesium

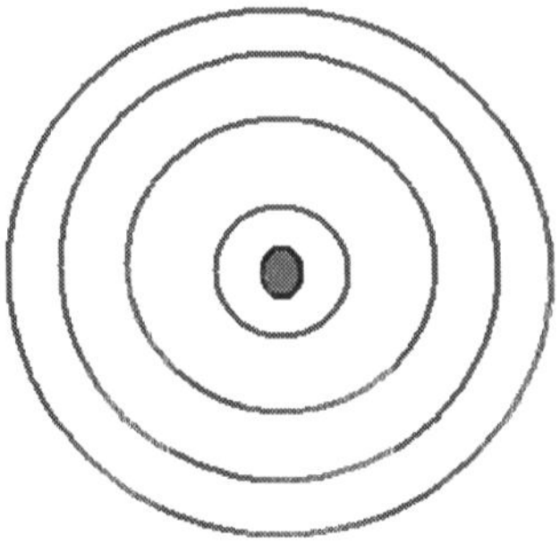

Oxygen

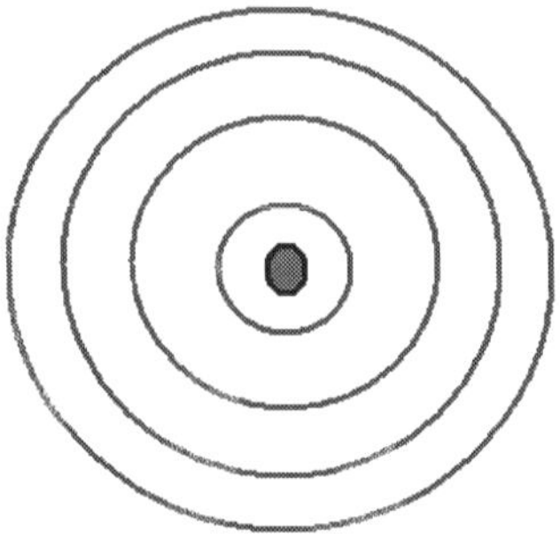

Sulfur

Part 7: Ions

Tell your students that electrons have what we call a negative charge and that we give the negative charge of each electron a value of -1. Protons have what we call a positive charge and we give each proton a value of +1. Positive and negative charges cancel each other out; so if we have one proton with a charge of +1 and one electron with a charge of -1 in an atom, they cancel each other out to give the atom a neutral charge (neither positive nor negative). If we have two protons and two electrons, the two protons cancel out the two electrons, and that atom has a neutral charge also.

Remember that the Atomic Number is the number of protons in an atom, and that number normally equals the number of electrons in an atom. That means that the charge of all of the protons cancels out the charge of all of the electrons and gives the atom a neutral charge. Of course, in nature, things aren't always so simple! Often an atom will lose or gain an electron, which changes the charge of the atom. An atom that is not neutral and has a charge is called an ***ion.*** If it has more electrons than protons, it is a negative ion, and if it has more protons than electrons, it is a positive ion. Molecules that have positive or negative charges are also called ions.

Activity:

Give your students some electron and proton problems to solve. For example, ask them if an atom has two electrons and one proton, does it have a positive or negative charge? (negative). Depending on their math skills level, you can ask them what the charge is (-1).

Part 8: Acids and Bases

Tell your students that different types of ions in a liquid can make it either an ***acid*** or a ***base***. We measure if something is an acid or base using something called a **pH scale.** The scale reads from 0 to 14. Acids have a reading from 0 to 7 and bases read from 7 to 14. If something is not an acid or base, its reading will be 7. You can purchase special pH paper that you dip into a liquid and it will change color depending on what level of acid or base the liquid is. The following activity shows you how to make your own pH papers. They won't be as accurate as the papers you purchase, but they can tell if you something is an acid or base.

Activity:

Take a red or purple cabbage, chop it up and mix it in a blender with a small amount of water (just enough to make it blend). Put the cabbage and water in a pan and heat on a stove until it boils, stirring occasionally. You may add a bit more water if you need to, but the more water you add, the less concentrated your mixture will be, so don't add too much! Wait until the cabbage cools and pour it through a strainer, saving the water. Next, soak a paper coffee filter in the cabbage water until it is deeply colored. Set the coffee filter aside to dry. Once it has dried, cut it into strips about ¼ inches wide and 2 inches long. Try dipping one end of a strip into some vinegar; it should turn a pinkish color, indicating an acid. Next mix a tablespoon of baking soda in some water and try dipping a new strip into that; it should turn green or blue, indicating a base. You can test other items you find also.

Test for Chemistry Fun!

1) Mass is:
   - a. A measurement of the density of an object in a specific volume
   - b. A measurement of the amount of matter in an object
   - c. A measurement of the pull of gravity on an object
   - d. A measurement of distance

2) Weight is:
   - a. A measurement of the mass of an object in a specific volume
   - b. A measurement of the amount of matter in an object
   - c. A measurement of the pull of gravity on an object
   - d. A measurement of distance

3) Density is:
   - a. A measurement of the mass of an object in a specific volume
   - b. A measurement of the amount of matter in an object
   - c. A measurement of the pull of gravity on an object
   - d. A measurement of distance

4) Cohesion is:
   - a. A chemical term for gravity
   - b. A measurement of force
   - c. An attraction between similar molecules
   - d. A force used to mix things

5) Surface Tension is caused by:
   - a. The mixing of molecules in a liquid
   - b. Gravity pulling down on a liquid
   - c. A weaker cohesion of molecules at the surface of a liquid
   - d. A stronger cohesion of molecules at the surface of a liquid

6) A Mixture is when:
   - a. Two or more substances are combined, but are not changed chemically.
   - b. Two or more substances are combined, but are changed chemically.
   - c. Gravity is used to mix something
   - d. Heat is used to mix something.

7) The difference between a homogeneous and heterogeneous mixture is:
   a. In a homogeneous mixture, everything is not mixed evenly throughout, and it is mixed evenly throughout in a heterogeneous mixture
   b. In a homogeneous mixture, everything is mixed evenly throughout and it is not mixed evenly throughout in a heterogeneous mixture.
   c. In a homogeneous mixture a chemical reaction takes place and it doesn't in a heterogeneous mixture.
   d. The items in a homogeneous mixture are mixed together using heat and they aren't in a heterogeneous mixture.

8) The following statement is the definition for what?

   The mass of the substances that you combine in a physical or chemical reaction will be the same as the mass of the substance that you end up with.

   a. Density Theory
   b. Theory of Solutions
   c. Principal of Ionic Mixtures
   d. Conservation of Mass

9) The first electron shell never has more than _____ electrons in it.
   a. Eight
   b. Six
   c. Two
   d. One

10) An ion is:
   a. An atom or molecule that has a positive or negative charge
   b. An atom or molecule that has no charge
   c. the same as density
   d. a piece of an electron

Chapter 16: Weather
Ages 8-13

Materials Needed For This Unit

Two identical outdoor thermometers
Rubber bands
Washable marker
Directional compass
Index card
Notebook
Graph paper
Glass jar (any size)
Ice
Drawing paper
Crayons or markers
Two saucepans
Two balloons of the same type and size
Large glass jar with a wide mouth
Non-flexible drinking straws
Mitten-style hot pad
Two pieces of cardboard about 8 ½ x 11 inches
Cotton shoelace
Plastic ruler
A twelve inch balloon
Straight drinking straws
Globe that spins
Thumb tack with a long point (the ones with the taller heads tend to have longer points
Jar with a flat bottom and straight sides

A half-gallon milk carton
Glue
Fan
Pencil with an eraser on top
Pin
Tape
String
Binoculars
Modeling clay
Balloon

Part 1: Introduction

Ask your students "What is weather?" (rain, sleet, hot or cold, snow, wind, mist, fog, etc...). Tell your students that weather is what the conditions outside are; if it is hot or cold, rainy or sunny, foggy or windy. These conditions affect us in many ways. Ask your students if they can think of some ways that weather might affect them. Point out to them that what might be bad weather for one person could be good weather for someone else (for example, a picnic might be ruined by rain that a farmer needs for his/her crops).

Part 2: Temperature

Tell your students that one of the most basic outdoor conditions we can measure is temperature. Ask if they know what we measure temperature with (a thermometer). Thermometers can measure temperature because most liquids expand (grow larger) when heated and contract (get smaller) when cooled. The first thermometers were made with water, but that didn't work very well because the water froze when it got too cold outside. These days we use other liquids in our thermometers such as mercury or alcohol.

Activity:

Take two outdoor thermometers and place one in the shade and one in the sun. Wait about ten minutes and compare the results. The daily temperatures that meteorologists publish are taken in the shade. Ask your students if they can figure out why that might be. One reason is that clouds can cross the sun, making it difficult to get an accurate reading. A shade reading won't have as many variables that could change it.

Activity:

Have your students start a weather journal. Have them take the temperature at a certain time every day. Remember to make sure the thermometer is in the shade and not the sun when they take the readings! Also, make sure they do not put their thermometer on the ground when they take the temperature readings; heat from the earth can affect the reading. Have them record the daily temperature in their weather journals. As you continue with this chapter, your students will be making some weather instruments that can be used to take other weather readings for their weather journals.

Activity:

Have your students make a graph of the temperature changes where they live as they record them. Take a piece of graph paper and have the horizontal axis be the dates and the vertical axis be the temperatures they have recorded.

Part 3: Clouds and Rain

Ask your students if they know what evaporation is. It is what happens when liquid water becomes water vapor (a gas). This occurs when water is heated.

Activity:

Boil a pot of water on the stove and show your students the steam coming off of it. Technically, what they are seeing isn't water vapor--water vapor is so small that you can't see it-- but they are seeing water particles going up into the air.

Activity:

Fill a jar about one quarter full of water. Mark the water level. Place it in a sunny spot and mark the water level each day until it's gone. Tell the students that the water evaporated into the air. The water particles are so small when they evaporate and become a gas that you can't see them.

Ask your students what they think happens to the water once it evaporates into the air (it rises up and eventually forms clouds). The higher up in the sky you go, the cooler the air gets. Warm air can hold more water vapor than cold air. As the warm air full of water vapor goes up, it starts getting colder. The colder air can't hold as much water vapor, so it starts to form tiny water droplets that come together as clouds. The water drops will stay in the air as clouds as long as the air within the cloud is warmer than the outside air. When the balance between the amount of water in the clouds and the air temperature around them changes, the water will fall to the ground as rain.

Activity:

Put some ice in one saucepan. Pour some water into another saucepan and bring it to a boil on the stove. Using a mitten-style hot pad, hold the saucepan with ice in it about one foot over the steam as it comes off the boiling water. Be very careful that you don't burn yourself, steam hurts! "Raindrops" should form on the bottom of the pan with ice in it and drop back into the boiling water. Tell your students that this is a mini water cycle; the hot water vapor from the boiling water rose into the air where it became cooler (in this case from the pan of ice). The cooler air could not hold as much water vapor, so it condensed out of the air and formed "rain." **Condensation** *is what happens when a gas (in this case water vapor) turns into a liquid (in this case water).*

Activity:

Have your students make a Water Cycle diagram showing water evaporating from the earth, going up into the sky, forming clouds, and falling back down again as precipitation. **Precipitation** *is the term for water that falls down from the sky. It can be in either a solid or liquid state such as rain, snow, sleet, or hail.*

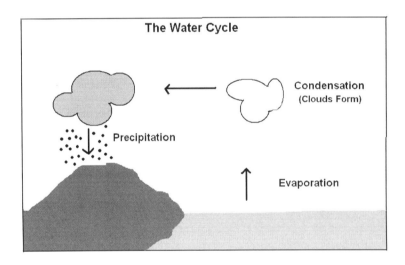

Activity:

Tell your students to go outside and choose a cloud that is not close to the sun (you don't want them to damage their eyes by looking at the sun). Have them look closely at its edges with a pair of binoculars. They should see that the edges of the cloud are changing, sometimes getting larger, sometimes getting smaller. When water droplets are condensing out of the air, the cloud's edges will grow. When water droplets are evaporating into the air, the cloud's edges will shrink.

Activity:

Take a glass jar with a flat bottom and <u>straight</u> sides and put it outside in an open area. On top of a fence post would be perfect, but on the ground is o.k. After it rains, have your students take a plastic ruler and measure how much rain is in the jar. Make sure that they record their measurements in their weather journals!

Part 4: Humidity

Tell your students that humidity is the measure of water vapor in the air. Remind them that warm air holds more water than cold air, so the way weather forecasters measure humidity is by comparing the amount of water vapor in the air to the amount of water vapor that air can hold at that temperature. This measurement is called *relative humidity.* When there is a lot of water vapor in the air, we say that it is **humid** outside. Humidity is measured with a hygrometer. In the following activity you will learn how to make a specific type of hygrometer called a *psychrometer*.

Activity:

Take two thermometers and make sure that they have the same accuracy; i.e. that they read the same. Using rubber bands, fasten them side by side on a half-gallon milk carton so that they are at least 2 ½ inches from the bottom of the carton. If they are too wide to fit side by side, you can put them each on their own side so that they share a common corner. Next, cut a slot or hole in the milk carton about one inch below one of the thermometers. Now take a piece of cotton shoelace and tie one end of it over the bulb of the thermometer that is above the slot. How you do this will depend on the type of thermometer you have. What is important is that the bulb is covered with the shoelace. Cut the other end so that it is just long enough to push through the slot in the milk carton and hang down to the bottom inside. Next pour about one inch of room temperature water in the bottom of the milk carton so that the shoelace inside is in the water. Get the part of the shoelace that is touching the bulb wet, and set the milk carton in a place where you can blow a fan on it. If you had to place the thermometers on separate sides of the milk carton, face the carton so that the fan can reach both of them, with the corner between them facing the fan.

After the fan has blown on the thermometers for one minute, make a note of the temperature reading from each of the thermometers. The thermometer with the shoelace on it, called the **wet-bulb thermometer**, should read cooler than the thermometer without the shoelace, called the **dry-bulb thermometer**. This is because as the water in the shoelace evaporates, it uses up heat and cools the air around it.

The dryer the air, the more water vapor it can hold, and the cooler the wet-bulb temperature reading will be. If the air is already holding all of the water it can, it is said to have 100 percent humidity. If your air is at 100 percent humidity, both thermometers will read the same temperature.

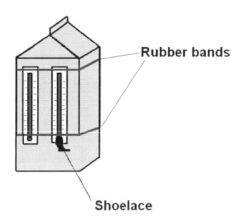

To calculate your humidity reading, subtract the wet-bulb temperature reading from the dry-bulb temperature reading. On the following page is a Relative Humidity Table. Find the dry-bulb temperature closest to yours on the vertical axis and the difference between the dry and wet bulb temperatures on the top horizontal axis. Where these two columns meet is your relative humidity. For example, if your dry-bulb temperature was 65 and the difference between your wet and dry-bulb temperatures was 3, your relative humidity would be 85 percent. Have your students calculate the relative humidity every day for their weather journals.

Part 5: Barometric Pressure

Ask your students how they know air exists, even though they can't see it (they can feel it, and if they hold their breath, they certainly know when it's not there!). Even though we can't feel air, we know it is there. It is all around us, everywhere we go. Tell your students that right now there is air pushing on them from all sides, they just can't feel it because their bodies are so accustomed to it. Have them think about being underwater and how they can feel water pushing on them from all sides. Air is doing the same thing; it's just lighter, so they can't feel it. Air is lighter than water, but it still has weight. The average weight of all of the air pushing on the earth (and us!) is 14.7 pounds per square inch at sea level. Have each student picture a column of air going up into the sky that is resting on his/her head. We are carrying about 14.7 pounds per square inch of air on our heads, all of the time! The weight of this air pushing down is called air pressure.

Activity:

Take a ruler and tie a string exactly in the middle of it. Find a place to tie the string so that the ruler will hang freely without touching a wall. Blow up two balloons so that they are exactly the same size. After you have blown them up, ask your students what is giving the balloons their shape (the air inside the balloon is pushing the sides of the balloon out). Tape one balloon one inch from one end of the ruler and the other balloon one inch from the other end of the ruler. Make sure that the ruler is now hanging perfectly perpendicular to the ground. If it is not, adjust the middle string so that the balloons are perfectly balanced. Point out to your students that at this point the balloons weigh the same on each side. Now take out a pin and pop one of the balloons. The ruler should now be hanging at an angle with the side with the full balloon hanging down. This is because you released the air out of the popped balloon and the full balloon still has the weight of the air in it, so it is heavier than the empty balloon. Remind your students that air has weight that is always pushing on them.

Relative Humidity Percentages

Dry Bulb Temps	Difference Between Dry and Wet Bulb Temperatures in Degrees Fahrenheit																													
	1	2	3	4	5	6	7	8	9	10	11	12	13	14	15	16	17	18	19	20	21	22	23	24	25	26	27	28	29	30
40	92	83	75	68	60	52	45	37	29	22	15	7	0																	
41	92	84	76	69	61	54	46	39	31	24	17	10	3																	
42	92	85	77	69	62	55	47	40	33	26	19	12	5																	
43	92	85	77	70	63	55	48	42	35	28	21	14	8																	
44	93	85	78	71	63	56	49	43	36	30	23	16	10	4																
45	93	86	78	71	64	57	51	44	38	31	25	18	12	6																
46	93	86	79	72	65	58	52	45	39	32	26	20	14	8	2															
47	93	86	79	72	66	59	53	46	40	34	28	22	16	10	5															
48	93	86	79	73	66	60	54	47	41	35	29	23	18	12	7	1														
49	93	86	80	73	67	61	54	48	42	36	31	25	19	14	9	3														
50	93	87	80	74	67	61	55	49	43	38	32	27	21	16	10	5	0													
51	94	87	81	75	68	62	56	50	45	39	34	28	23	17	12	7	2													
52	94	87	81	75	69	63	57	51	46	40	35	29	24	19	14	9	4													
53	94	87	81	75	69	63	58	52	47	41	36	31	26	20	16	10	6	1												
54	94	88	82	76	70	64	59	53	48	42	37	32	27	22	17	12	8	3												
55	94	88	82	76	70	65	59	54	49	43	38	33	28	23	19	14	9	5	0											
56	94	88	82	76	71	65	60	55	50	44	39	34	30	25	20	16	11	7	2											
57	94	88	82	77	71	66	61	55	50	45	40	35	31	26	22	17	13	8	4	0										
58	94	88	83	77	72	66	61	56	51	46	41	37	32	27	23	18	14	10	6	1										
59	94	89	83	78	72	67	62	57	52	47	42	38	33	29	24	20	16	11	7	3										
60	94	89	83	78	73	68	63	58	53	48	43	39	34	30	26	21	17	13	9	5	1									
61	94	89	84	78	73	68	63	58	54	49	44	40	35	31	27	22	18	14	10	7	3									
62	94	89	84	79	74	69	64	59	54	50	45	41	36	32	28	24	20	16	12	8	4	1								
63	95	89	84	79	74	69	64	60	55	50	46	42	37	33	29	25	21	17	13	10	6	2								
64	95	90	84	79	74	70	65	60	56	51	47	43	38	34	30	26	22	18	15	11	7	4	0							
65	95	90	85	80	75	70	66	61	56	52	48	44	39	35	31	27	24	20	16	12	9	5	2							
66	95	90	85	80	75	71	66	61	57	53	48	44	40	36	32	29	25	21	17	14	10	7	3	0						
67	95	90	85	80	75	71	66	62	58	53	49	45	41	37	33	30	26	22	19	15	12	8	5	2						
68	95	90	85	80	76	71	67	62	58	54	50	46	42	38	34	31	27	23	20	16	13	10	6	3						
69	95	90	85	81	76	72	67	63	59	55	51	47	43	39	35	32	28	24	21	18	14	11	8	5	1					
70	95	90	86	81	77	72	68	64	59	55	51	48	44	40	36	33	29	25	22	19	15	12	9	6	3					
71	95	90	86	81	77	72	68	64	60	56	52	48	45	41	37	33	30	27	23	20	17	13	10	7	4	1				
72	95	91	86	82	77	73	69	65	61	57	53	49	45	42	38	34	31	28	24	21	18	15	12	9	6	3				
73	95	91	86	82	78	73	69	65	61	57	53	50	46	42	39	35	32	29	25	22	19	16	13	10	7	4	1			
74	95	91	86	82	78	74	69	65	61	58	54	50	47	43	39	36	33	29	26	23	20	17	14	11	8	5	3			
75	96	91	86	82	78	74	70	66	62	58	54	51	47	44	40	37	34	30	27	24	21	18	15	12	9	7	4	1		
76	96	91	87	82	78	74	70	66	62	59	55	51	48	44	41	38	34	31	28	25	22	19	16	13	11	8	5	3		
77	96	91	87	83	79	74	71	67	63	59	56	52	48	45	42	39	35	32	29	26	23	20	17	14	12	9	6	4		
78	96	91	87	83	79	75	71	67	63	60	56	53	49	46	43	39	36	33	30	27	24	21	18	16	13	10	8	5		
79	96	91	87	83	79	75	71	68	64	60	57	53	50	46	43	40	37	34	31	28	25	22	19	17	14	11	9	6		
80	96	91	87	83	79	75	72	68	64	61	57	54	50	47	44	41	38	35	32	29	26	23	20	18	15	12	10	7	5	3
81	96	92	88	84	80	76	72	69	65	61	58	55	51	48	45	41	39	36	33	30	27	24	21	19	16	13	11	9	6	4
82	96	92	88	84	80	76	72	69	65	61	58	55	51	48	45	42	39	36	33	30	28	25	22	20	17	14	12	10	7	5
83	96	92	88	84	80	76	73	69	66	62	59	56	52	49	46	42	40	37	35	31	29	26	23	21	18	15	13	11	8	6
84	96	92	88	84	80	76	73	69	66	62	59	56	52	49	46	43	40	37	35	32	29	26	24	21	19	16	14	12	9	7
85	96	92	88	84	81	77	73	70	66	63	60	57	53	50	47	43	42	38	36	33	30	27	25	22	20	17	15	13	10	8
86	96	92	88	84	81	77	73	70	66	63	60	57	53	50	47	44	42	39	36	33	31	28	26	23	21	18	16	14	11	9
87	96	92	88	85	81	77	74	70	67	64	61	57	54	51	48	45	43	40	37	34	32	29	27	24	22	19	17	15	12	10
88	96	92	88	85	81	77	74	70	67	64	61	57	54	51	48	46	43	40	38	35	32	30	27	25	22	20	18	15	13	11
89	96	92	89	85	81	78	74	71	68	65	61	58	55	52	49	46	44	41	39	36	33	31	28	26	23	21	19	16	14	12
90	96	92	89	85	81	78	74	71	68	65	61	58	55	52	49	47	44	41	39	36	34	31	29	26	24	22	19	17	15	13
91	96	92	89	85	82	78	75	72	68	65	62	59	56	53	50	47	45	42	40	37	35	32	30	27	25	23	20	18	16	14
92	96	92	89	85	82	78	75	72	68	65	62	59	56	53	50	48	45	42	40	37	35	32	30	28	25	23	21	19	17	15
93	96	93	89	85	82	79	75	72	69	66	63	60	57	54	51	48	46	43	41	38	36	33	31	29	26	24	22	20	18	16
94	96	93	89	85	82	79	75	72	69	66	63	60	57	54	51	49	46	43	41	38	36	33	31	29	27	24	22	20	18	16
95	96	93	89	86	82	79	76	73	69	66	63	61	58	55	52	49	47	44	42	39	37	34	32	30	28	25	23	21	19	17
96	96	93	89	86	82	79	76	73	69	66	63	61	58	55	52	50	47	44	42	39	37	35	32	30	28	26	24	22	20	18
97	96	93	89	86	83	79	76	73	70	67	64	61	58	56	53	50	48	45	43	40	38	36	33	31	29	27	25	23	21	19
98	96	93	89	86	83	80	76	73	70	67	64	61	58	56	53	50	48	45	43	40	38	36	34	32	29	27	25	23	21	19
99	96	93	89	86	83	80	77	73	70	68	65	62	59	56	54	51	49	46	44	41	39	37	35	33	30	28	26	24	22	20
100	96	93	89	86	83	80	77	73	70	68	65	62	59	54	51	49	46	44	41	39	37	35	33	30	28	26	24	22	20	21
101	96	93	90	86	83	80	77	74	71	68	65	62	60	57	55	52	49	47	45	42	40	38	36	34	31	29	27	25	23	22
102	96	93	90	86	83	80	77	74	71	68	65	62	60	57	55	52	49	47	45	42	40	38	36	34	32	30	28	26	24	22
103	97	93	90	87	83	80	77	74	71	69	66	63	60	58	55	53	50	48	46	43	41	39	37	35	33	31	29	27	25	23
104	97	93	90	87	83	80	77	74	71	69	66	63	60	58	55	53	50	48	46	43	41	39	37	35	33	31	29	27	25	23
105	97	93	90	87	84	81	78	75	72	69	66	64	61	58	56	53	51	49	46	44	42	40	38	36	34	32	30	28	26	24
106	97	93	90	87	84	81	78	75	72	69	66	64	61	58	56	53	51	49	46	44	42	40	38	36	34	32	30	28	26	24
107	97	93	90	87	84	81	78	75	72	70	67	64	62	59	57	54	52	49	47	45	43	41	39	37	35	33	31	29	27	25
108	97	93	90	87	84	81	78	75	72	70	67	64	62	59	57	54	52	49	47	45	43	41	39	37	35	33	31	29	27	25
109	97	93	90	87	84	81	78	75	73	70	67	65	62	60	57	55	52	50	48	46	44	42	40	38	36	34	32	30	28	26
110	97	93	90	87	84	81	78	75	73	70	67	65	62	60	57	55	52	50	48	46	44	42	40	38	36	34	32	30	28	26
111	97	94	90	87	84	81	79	76	73	70	68	65	63	60	58	55	53	51	49	47	44	42	40	38	36	35	33	31	29	27
112	97	94	90	87	84	81	79	76	73	70	68	65	63	60	58	55	53	51	49	47	44	42	40	38	36	35	33	31	29	27
113	97	94	91	88	85	82	79	76	74	71	68	66	63	61	58	56	54	52	49	47	45	43	41	39	37	35	34	32	30	28

Activity:

*Tell your students that weather forecasters use a **barometer** to measure air pressure. To make your own barometer, take a 12" balloon, blow it up, let the air out, and cut off the neck. Blowing it up first is important because it stretches out the rubber. Stretch the cut balloon over the top of a large glass jar so that it is flat over the top. Secure it with a rubber band. Cut the end of a non-flexible drinking straw at an angle and glue or tape the other end to the middle of the rubber covering the jar. Now take two pieces of cardboard and place the jar on top of one of them so that the cardboard sticks out past the straw. Take the other piece of cardboard and place it against the jar and perpendicular to the bottom piece. Hold it in place with modeling clay.*

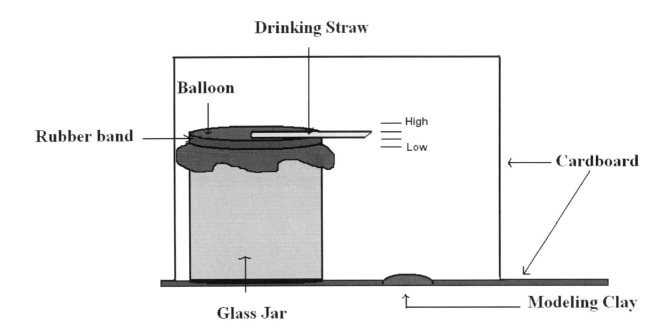

Keep your barometer inside away from moisture and windows in a place where the temperature will remain fairly steady. Check your barometer regularly and mark lines on the cardboard for the various positions you find the straw in. After awhile, mark your highest position as "High," and your lowest position as "Low." When you check your barometer, always look at it straight on, so that your eyes are on the same level as the straw. This will help keep your readings more accurate.

Low air pressures happen when warm air rises (pushing up, hence less pressure pushing down on the earth). As we learned earlier, warm air will cool as it rises and the water vapor in the warm air will condense as it cools to form clouds. That is why low air pressure is associated with cloudy skies and wet weather. Your barometer will read a low air pressure when the air pushing down on your jar is less than the air pushing up from the inside of the jar. Your barometer will read a high pressure when the air pushing down on your jar is higher than the air pushing up from the inside of the jar. Be sure to have your students write in their weather journals if the barometric pressure is "high" or "low."

Part 6: Wind

Tell your students that the movement of air as it rises causes air to move in other ways also. When warm air rises and forms a low pressure area, air from higher pressure areas starts to move toward it. Can your students guess what this movement of air from high pressure areas to low pressure areas is called? (wind).

Activity:

Blow up a balloon, but don't tie it off, hold it shut with your hands. Ask your students if the air pressure is higher inside the balloon or outside of the balloon (inside). Since high pressure air moves toward low pressure air, what do your students think will happen to the air in the balloon when you open it (it will flow out of the balloon to where the air pressure is lower). Hold the balloon above your one of your student's arms as you let the air out so that he or she can feel the "wind" generated as the air moves from high to low pressure.

Show your students a globe. Have them find the equator. Tell them that near the equator the land is usually pretty warm, so there is lots of warm air rising there, causing a low pressure area. As this happens, air from the higher pressure areas to the north and south of the equator moves toward the low pressure areas near the equator. Because the air near the equator is nearly always warm and moving up, there are always pretty consistent winds moving from the north and south of the earth toward the equator. These winds are called "Trade Winds."

Activity:

Take a globe and spin it in a counter-clockwise direction (if you don't have a globe, use a ball). <u>While the globe is spinning</u>, take a washable marker and quickly draw a straight line from somewhere near the top of the globe to about half-way down it. Before you do this, you might want to test the marker on a small piece of the globe to make sure that it will wash off! The line you drew will end up being a curved line, even though you drew it straight down. The line curved due to the "Coriolis Effect" (CORE-ee-oh-lis), caused by the spinning of the globe. The Coriolis Effect does the same thing to the trade winds, causing them to veer to the west on their way toward the equator.

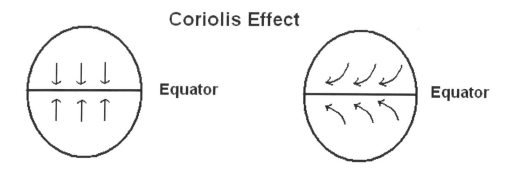

Coriolis Effect

As the high pressure wind from the north and south moves straight toward the Equator, the Coriolis Effect changes the wind's direction, so that it is also moving to the west.

Activity:

Take an index card and cut two shapes out of it like the ones below. The largest piece should be about 2 ½ inches long:

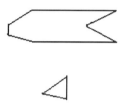

Now take a drinking straw and cut a slot in both ends. Slide the two pieces that you cut into the slots and glue or tape them in place. Next, take a thumb tack with a long point (the taller thumb tacks tend to have longer points; it needs to be longer than the width of the straw), and push it through the middle of the straw. Pull the tack out and enlarge the hole a bit with a small nail or the end of a paperclip so that the straw can spin freely around the tack. Now push the tack back through the hole and into the eraser end of a pencil. Make sure that the straw can spin freely around the thumb tack. The final result should look like this:

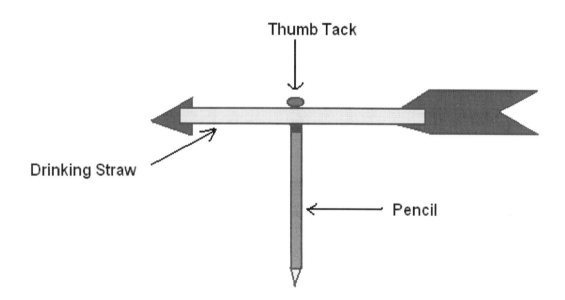

Take your wind vane outside with a directional compass and hold it up in the air. The arrow of the wind vane should point in the direction that the wind is blowing from. You can use a compass to tell exactly what that direction is. If for some reason your weather vane doesn't point in the right direction, try making the tail fin a bit larger. Be sure to have your students record the wind direction in their weather journals!

Test for Weather

1) Outdoor temperature readings should be taken:
    a. in the shade
    b. under something
    c. in the sun
    d. only at twelve noon

2) When water evaporates, it becomes
    a. hydrogen
    b. a liquid
    c. a gas
    d. oxygen

3) Warm air holds more water than
    a. hot air
    b. cold air
    c. the ocean
    d. ice

4) Warm air
    a. moves down
    b. moves to the East
    c. moves to the West
    d. moves up

5) Condensation happens when:
    a. Water changes from a liquid to a gas.
    b. Water changes from water to water vapor.
    c. Water changes from a gas to a liquid.
    d. Water changes from ice to a liquid.

6) The water cycle is:
    a. A special bicycle that runs on water.
    b. The way water moves between the earth and atmosphere.
    c. The direction rivers run on the earth.
    d. The pull of gravity on water

7) Air pressure is caused by:
    a. The weight of air pushing on things.
    b. Dust in the air
    c. People pushing things.
    d. Special scientific instruments

8) Air moves from areas of:
    a. low pressure to high pressure
    b. high pressure to high pressure
    c. high pressure to low pressure
    d. low pressure to low pressure

9) The Trade Winds happen when:
    a. Low pressure air from the north and south of the Equator moves toward the Equator.
    b. High pressure air from the north and south of the Equator moves toward the Equator.
    c. Cooler air at the Equator moves upward.
    d. The Coriolis Effect happens backward.

10) The Coriolis Effect makes it so that the Trade Winds move:
    a. toward the East
    b. toward the North
    c. toward the South
    d. toward the West

Chapter 17: Force and Motion
Ages 8-13

Materials Needed for this Unit

The materials needed for this unit are mostly either common household items, or are easily obtained from grocery, hardware, drug stores, or your local library. There is one exception to this, an experiment that uses iron filings. This experiment is not essential to understanding the unit, so it can be skipped if you do not want to go to the expense of purchasing the iron filings.

Food coloring	Wet Cloth	Ruler	Large washer
An eye drops bottle	Golf ball	Thick rubber-band	Scotch tape
Modeling clay	Tape measure	Two feet of string	Ping-pong ball
Nails	Two balloons	Contact paper	Directional compass
Hammer	Yardstick	Copy paper	Large bowl of water
Measuring cup	Pin	Duct tape	Marble
Masking tape	Rag		

A Sharpie® or other type of permanent marker
Small plastic container or lid
A half-gallon milk carton
Small toy car with wheels
Net bag that closes with a drawstring
A board about three ft. long and at least 6 in. wide
Two chairs that are exactly the same height
A piece of 1 x 10 inch wood, that is thirty-three inches long
A bar magnet with the two poles marked
Two pieces of one inch molding that are thirty-three inches long
Library books on Galileo, Aristotle, and Isaac Newton
An Optional movie titled "A Tale of Two Isaacs" (about Isaac Newton)
An Optional movie titled "On the Shoulders of Giants" (about Galileo)
A toy pick-up or dump truck with wheels that work well
Spools with the thread taken off of them
A clear or semi-transparent plastic container with a flat bottom
Clear, round plastic container that is about ten inches across
Two sticks that are 1/8"- 3/16" in diameter and about one foot long
Stop watch or clock with a second hand

Iron filings. You can purchase iron filings at:
    Nasco
    (800)558-9595
    (920)563-2446
    www.eNasco.com/science
    901 Janesville Ave.
    Fort Atkinson, WI 53538

Part 1: Force and Friction

Ask your students if they have ever heard of a person named *Aristotle*. Aristotle was a Greek philosopher who lived in the fourth century B.C. He was one of the first people to study motion. Some of his conclusions seem very obvious, but they are the basis for the study of motion. For example, he said that an object will not move unless something is pulling or pushing it. Ask your students to think about this, can they ever think of a time when they have seen an object move without something first pulling or pushing it? (if they mention something falling or rolling down an incline, tell them that the force pulling it down is gravity, which we will discuss later). The push or pull that causes an object to move, speed up, slow down, or change direction is called a *force.*

Now ask your students if things always move when they push on them? At this point, push on an object in the room, but do not push it hard enough to move it. Ask your students why they think the object didn't move. Aristotle figured out why. He said that when you push something it takes a certain amount of force to overcome another force called friction. *Friction* is a force that acts upon two objects that rub against each other. It causes objects to resist motion, or slow down. In the past, scientists thought that friction was caused only by the roughness of a surface, but now they realize that it is more complicated than that. As two surfaces slide against each other, there is an attraction between the molecules that causes the surface to "stick." This stickiness is one of the main causes of friction.

Activity:

For this activity, you will need a smooth-surfaced floor, such as a linoleum or smooth wood floor. Take a board that is about three feet long and at least six inches wide and lean it on a pile of books that is about eight inches high on your smooth-surfaced floor. Place a small toy car at the top of the board and let it roll down the board onto the floor. Measure how far it went. Do this ten times and calculate the average of the ten measurements (you find the average by adding all ten numbers together and dividing the total by ten). Now take a long piece of contact paper and remove the backing. Place it sticky-side up at the bottom of the board so that the car will roll onto it and repeat the experiment. The average distance the car traveled should be farther on the smooth surface than when compared to the sticky surface. This is because the smooth surface has less friction between the wheels of the car and the surface of the floor.

Part 2: Gravity

Remind your students that Aristotle said that objects move when a force pushes on them. However, Aristotle did not have an explanation for why objects keep moving after a force has stopped pushing or pulling them. Take a small model car and give it a push so that it keeps moving across a smooth surface. Point out to your students that the car still moves, even after you have stopped pushing it. Aristotle did not have a theory for why this happens, other than that it naturally happens that way. Aristotle's theories needed some adjusting, and the man who did this was named *Galileo Galilei* (1564-1642), an Italian scientist who is often called the "Father of Modern Science" because of the way he used experiments to prove his theories. Galileo agreed with Aristotle that an object that is not moving needs a force to push or pull it to get it started moving. However, Galileo believed that once an object starts moving, it will keep moving forever unless another force stops it. Ask your students what force eventually stopped the car you pushed from moving (friction). Galileo thought about how when someone throws a ball, it eventually falls back to earth. He decided that the earth itself is what is pulling the ball down. We call the force of the earth's pull *gravity.* Ask your students what would happen if you threw a ball in outer space where there is no friction and no gravity (it would keep going in the direction you threw it forever, or until a force was exerted upon it).

Activity:

Take a two-foot piece of string and tie a washer tightly to one end of it. Using a Sharpie® (or some other type of permanent marker), draw an arrow on the washer that points straight away from the knot on the string. Tie the other end of the string to the middle of a yardstick (or any other stick you can find that is about that long). Now take two chairs of the same size and place them back to back with some space between them. Balance the yardstick on the tops of the chairs. Tell your students to observe how the arrow on the washer is pointing straight down. Now take one end of the yardstick and lift it up a few inches off the side of the chair. The arrow should be still pointing straight down, even though the yardstick is now at an angle. You can increase the angle as much as you want and the arrow will still be pointing straight down. This is because gravity will always pull toward the center of the earth, so the arrow on the washer will always point toward the center of the earth, as-long-as you let it hang freely.

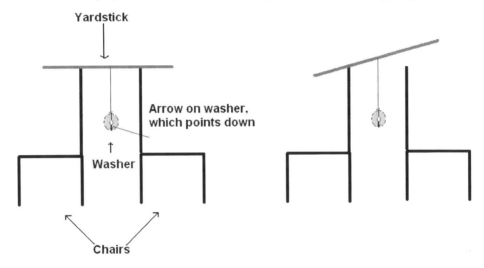

Activity:

One of the other things that Galileo discovered about gravity was that it causes both heavy and light objects to fall at the same speed. There is a story that he climbed up on the Leaning Tower of Pisa and dropped a heavy cannonball and a light cannonball at exactly the same time. They fell at the same rate and landed at the same time. It turns out that he probably never actually did this, but he did talk about what would happen in this type of experiment. Have your students try a similar experiment with a ping-pong ball and a golf ball. Have them hold one in each hand and drop them at exactly the same time. It is best to do this indoors, because outdoors other factors may affect the outcome, such as wind, or the unevenness of the ground. Since golf balls are heavy, make sure to protect your floor before you drop the ball on it! The two balls should land at about the same time (because they are traveling through air, the ping pong ball will have a harder time counteracting the air resistance than the golf ball, but the difference is usually not noticeable). You could even try it from a greater height by having someone stand on a ladder or chair (making sure that they don't fall!) as they drop the balls. Ask your students what they think would happen if they used a feather and a golf ball for this experiment. In theory, they should land at the same time, but the feather is slowed down by air pushing up on it, so it will take longer to fall. However, if you drop the feather and ball in a place where there is no air, they will land at the same time. Astronauts proved this by dropping a hammer and feather in space. Go online and do a search with the words "hammer," "feather," "astronaut," and "space," and you should be able to find a clip of the demonstration.

Part 3: Newton's First Law of Motion

Tell your students that **Isaac Newton** (1643-1727) was an English scientist and mathematician who, among other things, wrote the first three "laws" of motion. His first law was based on what Aristotle and Galileo had already discovered, and it says that: **An object at rest remains at rest and an object in motion will remain in motion with the same speed and in the same direction unless acted on by an unbalanced force.**

Ask your students if they can explain what this means (an object that is not moving will stay not moving unless a force acts upon it and an object that is moving will keep moving unless a force acts upon it). This **First Law of Motion** is sometimes called the principal of inertia. **Inertia** is the tendency of objects to resist <u>changes</u> in motion. Tell your students that they can think of inertia from a human point of view. A tired person sitting on a couch has a tendency to not want to get up and move and a person running very fast who tries to stop quickly can't stop immediately. Both of these are inertia, a resistance to change in motion.

Newton is famous for saying: *"If I have seen a little further it is by standing on the shoulders of giants."* Ask your students what they think this means. Point out to them how Newton's first law uses the concepts that Aristotle and Galileo had already worked on.

Activity:

Get some books from the library on Newton, Galileo, and Aristotle for your students to read. Have them chose one of these men to write a research paper about.

Activity:

There are two excellent movies you can have your students watch, one on Isaac Newton titled "A Tale of Two Isaacs," and one on Galileo titled "On the Shoulders of Giants." Both are produced by David Devine and Richard Mozer and may be available at your local library.

Part 4: Newton's Second Law of Motion

Ask your students if they know what the word **acceleration** means (the speeding up of an object). In physics, it actually means a <u>change</u> in speed over time, so that also includes the slowing down of an object and the change in direction of an object. However in common speech it means the speeding up of an object. When you are driving a car, and put your foot on the gas to make the car go faster, you are accelerating. Galileo found that one of the things that acceleration depends on is amount of force used to push or pull the object.

Activity:

You should set this experiment up ahead of time and do a test run before showing it to your students. Start by taking a thirty-three inch long piece of 1x10 board, lay it flat, and nail a strip of 1 inch molding down each side of it. Take three sheets of copy paper and trim about ½ inch off their width so that they will fit on the board. Tape the three pieces of paper together so that they make a sheet as-long-as the board. Be sure to put the tape only on one side of the paper, so that one side has no tape. Make at least three of these paper strips. You may want to make extras for possible glitches or if you want to repeat the experiment.

Now take an eye drops bottle and cut the bottom off of it. Turn it so that the cut end is facing up and fill it with water to see how quickly water drips out of it. You can test it with a stop watch or clock to make sure the drips are coming out at the correct rate. You want it to drip about three to four drops a second, so if it seems too slow, you can enlarge the hole a bit with a pin. Be careful not to enlarge it too much! If the hole is too large, use some modeling clay to plug it up a little. Pour the water out, and using a rubber band or duct tape, attach the eye drops bottle to the back of a plastic toy pick-up or dump truck, one with wheels that move well.

Now, take one of the strips of paper and tape it to the board, tape side down. Fill a measuring cup with about ½ C of water and add twenty drops of food coloring to it. Take everything outside to a flat surface, along with enough books to raise one end of the board about three inches, and a rag to wipe the board dry. Lay the board down, paper side up, and raise one end with the books. Test the height of the books by seeing if the truck will roll down the board without having to be pushed to get it started. If it won't roll by itself, add some more books to raise the height. Do not make the angle too steep, it should be at the <u>lowest</u> height where the truck will roll by itself.

Now, cover the hole in the eye drops bottle with your finger and fill it about half-full with the colored water. Place the truck at the top of the board, remove your finger from the hole, and let the truck roll down the board, stopping it just before it falls off the end of the board. The truck should have left a trail of drips going down the paper. Carefully remove the paper and set it aside. Notice the pattern of the drips. When the drips are farther apart, it means that the truck was moving faster. This is similar to how a person's footprints are farther apart when they run than when they walk. Mark this sheet as "Run 1."

Next dry the board and tape another sheet of paper to it. Be sure not to change the height of the books. Repeat the experiment, only this time give the truck a good push to start it down the slope. Mark this sheet as "Run 2." Compare the drips on the two sheets of paper. Remember that acceleration is not the final speed that the object obtains, but the rate at which the object takes to get to its final speed. The pattern of drops for the truck you pushed should show the drops farther apart at the beginning of the run when compared to the pattern of drops for the truck that you didn't push. This illustrates Galileo's observation that the greater the force, the greater the acceleration (your push was the extra force in the second run of the truck).

Measuring Acceleration

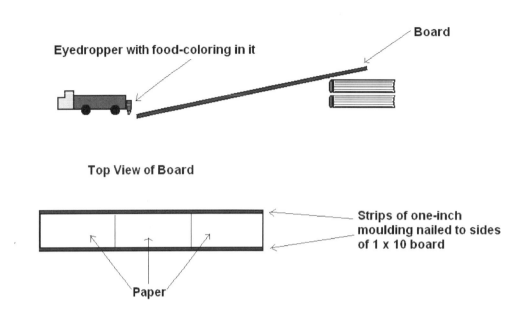

Eyedropper with food-coloring in it

Board

Top View of Board

Strips of one-inch
moulding nailed to sides
of 1 x 10 board

Paper

Newton wrote a **Second Law of Motion,** to explain this property of acceleration. The Second Law of Motion says that **the change in acceleration with which an object moves is directly proportional to the amount of the force applied to the object and inversely proportional to the mass of the object.** Basically the first part of this just says that if you apply twice as much force to an object, it will accelerate twice as fast. If you apply three times as much force to an object, it will accelerate three times as fast. The second part of it means that if you have two objects, and one is heavier than the other, the heavy object will accelerate slower than the lighter object. For example, ask your students to imagine two vehicles at the starting line to a race. One of the vehicles is a semi-truck and the other is a small race car. Which vehicle do they think will take longer to accelerate up to speed? Hopefully they said the semi-truck, because it weighs more and has more mass. Newton's Second Law of Motion is actually just common sense. Applying more force to an object makes it speed up faster, and heavy objects take longer to speed up.

Part 5: Newton's Third Law of Motion

Take a balloon, blow it up, and let it go to fly around the room. Ask your students why they think the balloon is pushed forward when the air rushes out of it. The balloon is an example of *Newton's Third Law of Motion,* which says that **every action has an equal and opposite reaction.** When the air inside the balloon rushes out of the balloon, it pushes on the air outside of the balloon (the "action"). According to Newton, this means that the air outside of the balloon will push back (the "reaction"). It is the force of the outside air pushing back that propels the balloon forward. Notice that the "reaction" is moving the balloon in the opposite direction of the "action."

Newton's Third Law of Motion is happening all of the time. When you stand on the ground, your weight is pushing down on the ground, but according to Newton's law, the ground is also pushing up against you. If it didn't, you would fall right through the earth!

Activity:

You can use *Newton's Third Law of Motion to make a car that is propelled by a balloon. Take a half-gallon milk carton and cut the top off. Next, cut out one complete side, so that you have a bottom and two sides that look like this:*

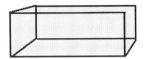

Now cut two of the sides so that it looks like this:

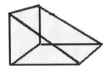

Next, cut a hole in the middle of the upright side that is about ½-inch across:

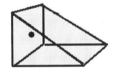

Now punch holes in both sides of the car for two sticks to go through. The sticks should be 1/8-3/16 inches in diameter and about 1 foot long:

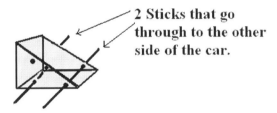

2 Sticks that go through to the other side of the car.

Put empty thread spools on the ends of the sticks; they should spin freely on the sticks with no sticking as they turn. Now wrap some masking tape on the very ends of the sticks to keep the spools from falling off. Wrap another bit of masking tape around the sticks in the area between each spool and the car, to keep the spools from sliding around too much on the stick. Now take a balloon and pull the neck of it through the hole in the back of the car so that the hole in the balloon faces out and the full end of the balloon sits inside the car. Blow up the balloon as large as you can, put the car on the ground and watch it go! The size of the hole may need to be adjusted, if it is too small, there won't be enough force to push the car, and if it is too large, the car won't go very far. Remind your students that Newton's Third Law says that for every action there is an equal and opposite reaction. It is the reaction of the outside air pushing back at the air escaping from the balloon that is pushing the car forward.

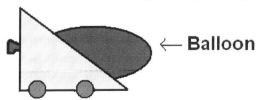

← Balloon

Part 6: Centripetal Force

Activity:

Take a marble and place it inside an upside-down round clear plastic container that is about ten inches across. Start moving the container around in small circles to get the marble to start spinning along the inside wall of the container. Tell your students that **centripetal force** is what is keeping the marble spinning along the wall. Centripetal force happens when an object that "wants" to go in one direction due to inertia also has a force acting on it that is pushing or pulling it inward. In this case, the outside container is pushing inward on the marble and the combination of the marble's inertia and the inward push of the container causes the marble to spin in a circle. Centripetal force can be described as an inward force that keeps an object moving in a circle.

Now have your students stand back and get the marble spinning again. Slow it down so that it is still spinning, but not at too high a speed. Tip the container a bit and let the marble escape. The marble will keep going in a straight line away from the container. Because of inertia, the marble will want to resist a change in direction and will go in a straight line. With the outside container no longer causing a centripetal force, inertia will force the marble to travel in a straight line. In the diagram below, line A shows the path the marble wants to take because of inertia and line B shows the direction of the inward force that is pushing on the marble. The dotted line shows the path the marble takes due to centripetal force.

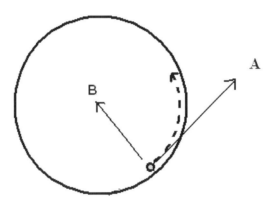

Tell your students that the planets spin around the sun because of centripetal force. The gravity of the sun is what is pulling them inward.

Activity:

Take a net bag that closes with a drawstring and put a wet piece of cloth in it. Have a student hold the bag by its drawstring and start to spin in a circle. The water will start flying out of the cloth as he or she spins. Ask them if they can feel the pull of the bag as they spin it. They are the source of the inward force keeping the bag spinning. If they let go of the bag it will fly off in one direction due to inertia (they can try it if they want, just make sure they won't hit anyone). The water in the cloth does not have anything pulling it inward, so it can fly off of the cloth. After they have spun the bag around for awhile, have him or her stop and feel the cloth. It should be drier than it was before it was spun. This is how the spin cycle in a washer works. The drum of the washer has holes in it and when it spins, the water flies out through the holes because it does not have any centripetal force pulling it inward.

Part 7: Magnetic Force

Tell your students that another common force is magnetic force. All magnets have invisible lines of magnetic force around them. We know they are there because we can see the results of their force, for example when you put a magnet close to a paperclip, magnet force will pull the paperclip toward the magnet.

Activity:

Have your students take a large see-through plastic container with a flat bottom and rest it on top of a bar magnet so that the open end of the container faces up, and the magnet is <u>underneath</u> the container. A Tupperware® type container will work for this. Now sprinkle iron filings evenly inside the bottom of the container. They should fall in a pattern that shows the lines of magnetic force around the magnet. Make sure that anyone who touches the filings doesn't touch their eyes or mouth until they wash their hands. Do not throw the filings down your sink.

Tell your students that compass needles always point north because the earth itself acts like a huge magnet, and it has lines of force around it just like any other magnet. These lines of force go around the earth something like this, as if the earth had a bar magnet in its center:

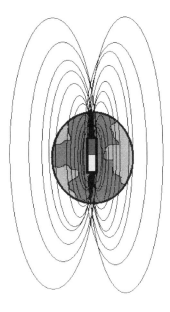

Activity:

Tell your students that they can use a bar magnet as a compass. Have them take a bar magnet and place it inside a <u>small</u> plastic container, or place it on a small plastic lid. Now place the container inside a large bowl of water. Once it stops moving, the dish should be lined up so that one end of your magnet points in the same direction as your compass (make sure that there isn't anything metal nearby). Compare it with a compass to see if this is correct. Show them how when you turn the dish with the magnet in it in a different direction, it will spin back so that it is lined up on the north/south line.

Test for Force and Motion

1) The push or pull that causes an object to move, speed up, slow down, or change direction is called….
    a. Motion
    b. Friction
    c. Energy
    d. Force

2) Aristotle was a….
    a. Greek philosopher who studied motion.
    b. Roman philosopher who studied motion.
    c. Egyptian philosopher who studied motion.
    d. English scientist who studied motion.

3) Friction….
    a. causes a sliding object to slide faster
    b. causes a sliding object to slow down
    c. causes a sliding object to go sideways
    d. causes a sliding object to jump in the air

4) The force of the Earth's pull on objects is called….
    a. Friction
    b. Centripetal force
    c. Gravity
    d. Newton's Second Law of Motion

5) A balloon flying around the room because air is rushing out of it is an example of….
    a. Friction
    b. Newton's law that says an object with more mass will accelerate more slowly than an object with less mass.
    c. Newton's law that says that for every action there is an equal and opposite reaction.
    d. Centripetal Force

6) If you see a toy car and push it forward, this is an example of….
    a. Newton's law that says that an object won't move unless a force acts upon it
    b. Newton's law that says an object with more mass will accelerate more slowly than an object with less mass.
    c. Gravity
    d. Centripetal force

7) The spin cycle of a washing machine is an example of …
    a. Gravity
    b. Friction
    c. Newton's Third Law of Motion
    d. Centripetal Force

8) A large truck takes longer to speed up than a small car. This is an example of…
    a. Newton's law of motion that says that for every action there is an equal and opposite reaction.
    b. Newton's law that says an object with more mass will accelerate more slowly than an object with less mass.
    c. Newton's law that says that an object won't move unless a force acts upon it
    d. Centripetal Force

9) Newton was….
    a. Greek philosopher who studied motion.
    b. Roman philosopher who studied motion.
    c. Egyptian philosopher who studied motion.
    d. English scientist who studied motion.

10) Which of these is not a force:
    a. Magnetism
    b. Electron
    c. Centripetal
    d. Gravity

Chapter 18: Simple Machines
Ages 8-13

Materials Needed for this Unit

An eleven or twelve ounce coffee can full of coffee
A thirty-three ounce coffee can full of coffee
A rubber band that is about five cm in diameter when shaped into a circle
A rubber band that has about four cm diameter when shaped into a circle
Ruler
A board that is about two feet long and at least eight inches wide
String
Books
Two wedge-shaped door stops
A pair of scissors
A screw
Paper
Pencil
Tape
A stick
A pulley that is about 1 ½ inches in diameter with the cord to go with it.
A beach bucket with a strong handle
Sand or gravel
Two one quart milk cartons
A washer
A twelve inch dowel that is about ¼ inch thick
Foam board
Sewing pins
Glue
Drawing compass
One or two small pulleys and cord or rope to go with them. The size of the pulleys will depend on what you choose to use them for (Part 6 of this unit).
A thick rubber band
Markers
Paper and pencil
A butter knife that is not too flexible
A toy car

Part 1: Work

Ask your students if they can guess what the definition of a ***machine*** is. The simplest definition is: *A machine is a device that makes work easier.* But, what is ***work*** defined as? A simple definition of work is: *Using a force to cause a change in motion.*

Activity:

Take a rubber band that has about a 5 cm diameter when it is shaped into a circle and slip it around an 11 or 12 oz coffee can full of coffee. Now take a rubber band that has about a 4 cm diameter when it is shaped into a circle and tie it to the first rubber band by slipping it under the first rubber band so that half of it is above the first rubber band and half below. Now take the bottom loop of the second rubber band and pull it through the top loop of the same rubber band.

Now, pull the coffee can ten centimeters in one direction by pulling on the rubber bands. As you do this, place a ruler gently against the coffee can and measure how far the rubber bands are being pulled out from the can. Write your measurement down.

Now, take the rubber bands off of the 11 or 12 oz coffee can, keeping them attached to each other, and slip them over a 33 oz coffee can full of coffee. Using the ruler, measure how far the rubber bands have to be pulled out from this coffee can to get it to move 10 centimeters. Compare this measurement to your previous measurement. It should be about double the previous measurement. <u>The amount the rubber band stretches shows how much force it takes to move the two coffee cans</u>. It takes about twice as much force to move the larger can as it does the smaller can. This also means that it takes more work to move the larger can compared with the smaller can.

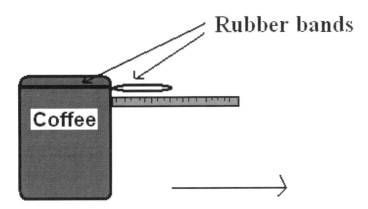

Part 2: Simple Machine #1; The Inclined Plane

Tell your students that scientists have described the most basic machines and called them the ***simple machines***. There are six kinds of simple machines, the ***inclined plane***, the ***lever***, the ***screw***, the **wedge**, the **pulley** and the ***wheel and axle***.   All other machines are made up of various simple machines and are called ***complex machines.***

Activity:

Stack a pile of books about 8 inches tall and place a board on it so that one end sits on the books and one end sits on the floor or table. Tell your students that you have just made a simple machine; an inclined plane. Ask them why they think this is a machine (because it makes work easier). See if they can think of some ways that an inclined plane can be used to do work.

Take a heavy book and tie two strings tightly around it so that they form a cross in the middle of the book. Now take a thick rubber band and tie it to the middle of the cross made by the string. Lift the book up by pulling on the rubber band until the book is the same height as the top of your inclined plane (you can lift it right next to the top of the inclined plane to show this). Using a ruler, measure how much the rubber band stretched to get the book to this height. Now untie the rubber band and tie it to one of the strings on the edge of the book. Place the book at the bottom of your inclined plane and slowly pull it up to the top. Measure how far your rubber band had to stretch to do this. The rubber band should have to stretch less to move the book up the plane than it did to move it straight up in the air. This means it took less force to move the book up the inclined plane than it did to pull it straight up. There are some diagrams on the following page illustrating this experiment.

Tell your students that scientists have come up with an equation that helps them measure work: W= F x D (Work equals Force times Distance). This means that how much work a job takes depends on how much force is used to move an object and how far the object is moved. Here is how this equation works in the experiment you just did:

Work:

In this case, the work is the job that you want to get done, which is to raise the book to a height of about 8 inches. In both cases (moving the book straight up or sliding it up the inclined plane), the work remained the same; the book was brought up to an 8 inch height.

Force:

The force was less when the book went up the inclined plane, which was why the rubber band stretched less when you pulled it up the plane. It took less force to pull it.

Distance:

The distance the book moved was longer when it went up the inclined plane. You can demonstrate this by standing the board upright next to the 8 inch pile of books.

In the W = F x D equation, the force and the distance are like opposites. When you increase the distance (like when you pulled the book up the longer distance of the inclined plane), you decrease the force needed to do the work. When you increase the force, you decrease the distance. To put it simply, more distance equals less force and more force equals less distance.

This means if we want to <u>decrease</u> the amount of force it takes to do something, we need to <u>increase</u> the distance it takes to do it.

Part 1: Pulling the book straight up in the air.

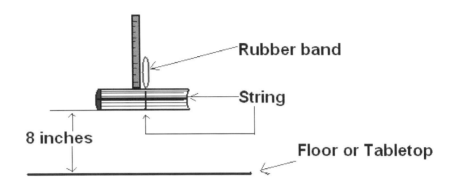

Part 2: Pulling the book up an inclined plane.

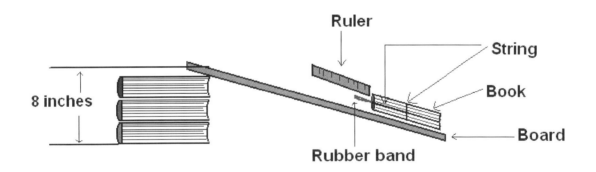

Part 3: Simple Machine #2; The Screw

Hold up a screw and tell your students that believe it or not, some scientists say that a screw is an inclined plane, then do the following activity.

Activity:

Take a piece of paper and cut it so that it is the same height as a pencil. Next, cut the paper diagonally:

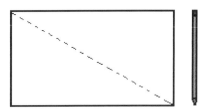

Now, take one of the diagonal pieces and point out to your students that it is an inclined plane. Draw a colored line down both sides of the diagonal edge of the piece of paper (front and back). Now tape the short straight edge to the pencil and roll it around the pencil like this:

Draw a colored line on this edge

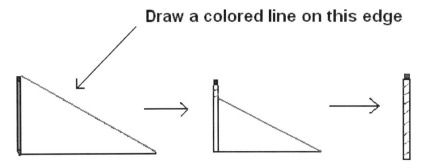

Show them how the threads on a screw are just like the lines the edge of the inclined plane makes as it is wrapped around the pencil. A screw is just a modified inclined plane!

Part 4: Simple Machine #3; The Wedge

Ask your students if they know what a ***wedge*** is. Show them a wedge-shaped door stop so they can see what a wedge looks like. Ask them if it reminds them of anything (an inclined plane). A wedge is a type of inclined plane that has many uses, one of which is to stop doors. Wedges are also used to split things apart, such as the wedge a woodcutter uses to split wood with. That type of wedge is two inclined planes put together. Demonstrate this by taping two door stops together to form a double-sided wedge and using it to push two books apart. The blade of an axe itself is actually a wedge, as are the blades on a pair of scissors (show them the inclined plane on a pair of scissors).

Activity:

Have your students go through their house and list all of the inclined planes that they can find.

Part 5: Simple Machine #4; The Lever

Show your students a stick and tell them that even a stick can be a simple machine!

Activity:

  *Have a student lay his or her pinky finger on a table palm side up and place a book on top of it. See if he or she can lift the book up with just a pinky finger. Keep adding books to the pile (gently!) until he or she can't lift the pile. Now show your students how you can raise the same amount of books using a lever by taking a metal butter knife (make sure that it is one that is not very flexible), placing a pencil under it, and inserting one end under the stack of books so that about two inches of the knife is under the books. It should look like a teeter-totter with one end under the books and one end up in the air. Now have one of your students press down on the end of the knife opposite the books with their pinky finger and slowly lift them up (remind them how hard it was to lift the books with a pinky finger without the lever). The knife is now being used as a **lever** to lift the books. Levers are very helpful when you need to lift something heavy.*

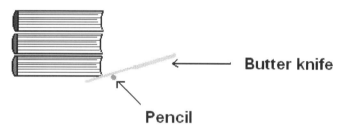

Butter knife

Pencil

  *Tell your students that a lever is a bar that is free to move, except at one point called the **fulcrum**. It is at this point that the lever pivots. In the picture above the fulcrum is where the pencil is.*

Activity:

  Using the same set-up as the previous experiment, try moving the fulcrum (where the pencil is) either closer to or farther away from the books. It should be easier to lift the books when the fulcrum is closer to them, but you can move the books higher when the fulcrum is farther from them.

Tell your students that there are three types of levers. The one we used in the above experiments, which works like a teeter-totter, is called a ***First Class Lever.***

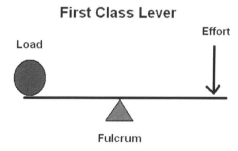

First Class Lever

Load

Effort

Fulcrum

The ***load*** is the item that you are lifting and the ***effort*** is where a person applies the force to get the lever to move. In a first class lever, the fulcrum is between the load and the effort.

A ***Second Class Lever*** is like a wheelbarrow, with the fulcrum (where the wheels are on the wheelbarrow) at one end, the load in the middle (where the bucket of the wheelbarrow is), and the effort on the other end (where the handles are). So, in a second class lever, the load is in the middle.

Second Class Lever

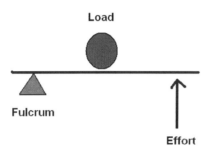

A ***Third Class Lever*** is like a fishing pole. The load is on one end, where the fish is caught. The fulcrum is on the other end, where a person holds the rod, and the effort is between the load and fulcrum, where the person applies force to lift the rod. In a third class lever, the effort is in the middle.

Third Class Lever

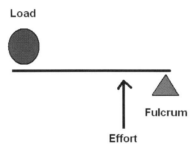

One way to help remember which lever is which is to remember "FLE" (you can say it like the word flee). Where the "F" stands for fulcrum in the middle for the first class lever, the "L" stands for load in the middle for second class, and the "E" stands for effort in the middle for third class.

> First Class   <u>F</u>ulcrum in the middle
> Second Class <u>L</u>oad in the middle
> Third Class   <u>E</u>ffort in the middle

Activity:
Have your students draw the three types of levers. Give them the following list and ask them to say which class of lever each item belongs to. If you have some of the items available, show the actual items to the students. First Class items: Teeter-totter, scissors, crowbar. Second Class items: Wheelbarrow, nutcracker. Third Class items: Tweezers, fishing pole, baseball bat.

Part 6: Simple Machine #5; The Pulley

Tell your students that a pulley is a simple machine that uses a wheel and a rope to raise, lower, or change the direction of objects. It can make lifting heavy loads easier.

Activity:
    Attach a pulley to a stationary object. Fill a beach bucket about ¼ - ½ full with sand or gravel and tie the pulley rope to one end of it. Before using the pulley, have your students feel how heavy the bucket is to lift by pulling it up using the rope without the pulley. Now use the pulley to help lift the bucket and compare the difference.

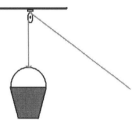

Activity:
    Give each of your students one or two pulleys and ask them to come up with a creative way to use them. For example, they could use it to move a bucket up and down in a Lego® set, or make an elevator for a doll to move from one place or another. If they have a tree house, they could use it to move things up and down from the tree house.

Part 7: Simple Machine #6; The Wheel and Axle

Tell your students that a wheel and axle is basically a large wheel attached to a small wheel. The small wheel is called the axle. A common example of a wheel and axle is the wheel on a car. Show your students the wheel and axle in a toy car.

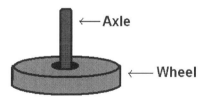

Activity:
    Wheels and axles can be used for many other things besides cars. One use for them is to raise and lower objects.
    Take a piece of foam board and using a compass, draw two circles about 6 inches in diameter and cut them out. Next cut out ten pieces of foam board that are 2 inches by 1 ½ inches. Now, take one of the circles and, using a pencil, place a mark at the top of the circle. Take a ruler and measure over from the mark 1 ¾ inches, like this:

Continue doing this until you have made ten marks around the circle. Using the ruler, draw lines 2 inches long on these marks from the outside of the circle toward the center. The lines should look like cuts into a pizza that didn't quite make it to the center.

Now, take some sewing pins and attach the rectangles you cut out of the foam board to the lines on the circle. Do this by placing the edges of the rectangles on the lines and poking the pins through the circle and into the edges of the rectangle. When you are finished, you should have ten rectangles standing up perpendicular to the circle in a "pizza" pattern. Put a line of glue on the side of each rectangle before you push the pins through it for extra strength. Take the other circle and place it on top of the rectangles and attach it to them with glue and pins in the same way as the first circle. Your finished wheel should look something like this:

1 1/2 inch x 2 inch foam rectangles

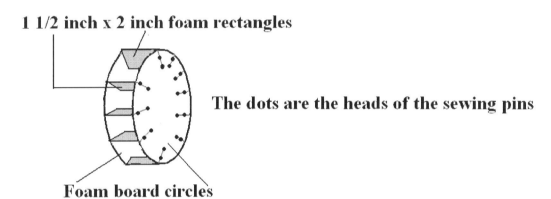

The dots are the heads of the sewing pins

Foam board circles

Next, punch a hole through the center of the wheel and push a ¼ inch dowel that is 12 inches long through it. The sides of the wheel should fit snugly against the dowel. If you accidentally cut the holes too large, you can cut small triangles out of the foam board and wedge them in the holes along side of the dowel to fill in the gap.

Now take two 1-quart milk cartons and cut the tops off. Make a V-shaped notch on the top of one side of each carton to rest the ends of the dowel on. Next, take a washer and tie it to one end of a string. Tape the other end of the string to the dowel between the wheel and one of the milk cartons.

Finally, take the whole apparatus to a bathtub and fill both milk cartons with water. This will help weigh them down and hold them in place. Arrange them so that the wheel is under the faucet where the water stream from the faucet will turn the wheel. As the wheel turns, the washer should get rolled up onto the dowel. In this model, the water wheel is the wheel and the dowel is the axle.

Dowel

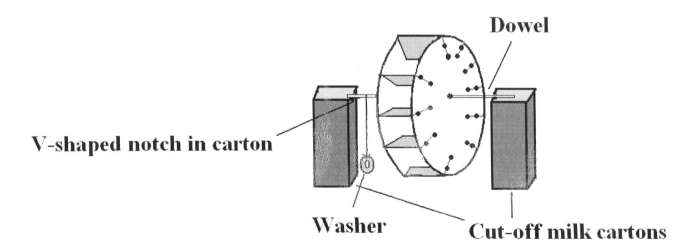

V-shaped notch in carton

Washer

Cut-off milk cartons

Test for Simple Machines

1) The <u>best</u> definition of a machine is:
    a. a device that moves
    b. a device that makes work easier
    c. a device that makes noise
    d. a device that dances

2) The <u>best</u> definition of work is:
    a. using a force to cause a change in motion
    b. using a force to make things easier for humans
    c. using a force to earn money
    d. using a force to make noise

3) The equation that scientists use to define the relationship between work, force, and distance is:
    a. Work = Force x Distance
    b. Distance = Force x Work
    c. Force = Distance x Work
    d. F = W x D

4) Name the six simple machines:
    a.
    b.
    c.
    d.
    e.
    f.

5) A bicycle is an example of a
    a. simple machine
    b. complex machine
    c. two-way machine
    d. three-way machine

6) A screw is actually a type of:
    a. wheel
    b. toy
    c. inclined plane
    d. pulley

7) A wedge is actually a type of:
    a. wheel
    b. toy
    c. inclined plane
    d. lever

8) The picture below is an example of what type of lever:

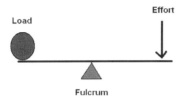

    a. First Class Lever
    b. Second Class Lever
    c. Third Class Lever
    d. Fourth Class Lever

9) The picture below is an example of what type of lever:

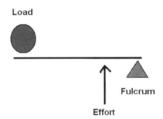

    a. First Class Lever
    b. Second Class Lever
    c. Third Class Lever
    d. Fourth Class Lever

10) The picture below is an example of what type of lever:

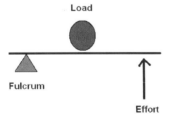

    a. First Class Lever
    b. Second Class Lever
    c. Third Class Lever
    d. Fourth Class Lever

Chapter 19: Light and Color
Ages 8-13

Materials Needed For This Unit

Hole punch
Three index cards
Modeling clay
Construction paper
Poster board
Two clear drinking glasses
Blue food coloring
Thermometer
Small mirror
Aluminum foil
Paper towel roll
Small mirror, see periscope activity for details
Clear tape
Colored construction paper
Drinking straw
Mirror
White poster board
Red cellophane
Green cellophane
Blue cellophane
Three rubber bands
Scissors
Cooking oil
A piece of white paper
Assorted items such as tissue paper, paper towel, fabrics, etc...(see part 2 for explanation)
Three flashlights, regular size that shine with about the same intensity

Part 1: Direction that Light Travels

Activity:

Set this up before you show it to your students; it can be a bit tricky to line up the index cards correctly and you don't want them to be sitting around waiting for you! Take two index cards and stack them together so that they are lined up exactly on top of each other. Punch a hole in them using a hole punch:

Next, take some modeling clay and use it to set the two index cards upright, lining the cards up so that their holes are in line with each other. You can take a bamboo skewer or other small, straight stick and poke it through the two holes to make sure that they are in a straight line from each other. Place a third card behind them.

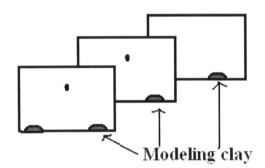

Now take a flashlight, and holding it fairly close to the first card, shine it through the holes in the first two cards. If they are lined up correctly, the light should shine through both of them to land on the card in the back. You may have to adjust the cards a bit to get the light to shine through both of the first two cards.

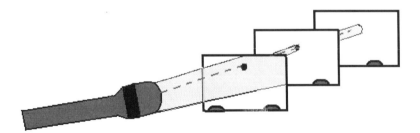

After you have shown this to your students, move the middle card out of line. The light won't be able to shine through to the third card, because light travels in a straight line from its source and it can't move sideways to get through to the next hole.

Part 2: What Can Light Travel Through?

Tell your students that light travels through some objects better than others. Clear objects like a window that light can travel through are called ***transparent.*** Objects that let some light through are called ***translucent,*** and objects that let no light through them at all are called ***opaque.***

Activity:

Gather together some assorted items for your students to test whether each item is transparent, translucent, or opaque. Examples of what you could collect for this are tissue paper, fabric, paper towel, something made of glass, a book, etc.... Have your students shine a flashlight through each item to see how much light it lets through. Classify each object by whether it is translucent, transparent, or opaque. Give them the following chart to fill out:

Object	Prediction	Result

A piece of paper looks opaque at first, but if light can shine though it, it is translucent. There are some colored substances that are transparent, even though when you look through them, everything is colored. If you come across something like this and you are not sure if it is transparent or opaque, look through it and if the objects behind it seem a bit blurry, than it is probably translucent, not transparent.

Activity:

Ask your students what happens when light hits an opaque object (the light is blocked and a shadow of the object is formed behind it). Have your students draw an outline of something on a piece of poster board and then have them cut it out. Now go outside and lay a piece of dark construction paper down somewhere in bright sunlight. Place the cut-out design on top of it. You may need to weigh the design down with small rocks if it is windy outside. Leave them outside for a few hours, until the construction paper on the bottom has faded a little. When you lift the cut-out design up, the bottom paper will have a "shadow" design underneath. Point out to your students that this happened because the piece of poster board on top of the construction paper was opaque, so the light could not go through it to fade the construction paper.

Part 3: Bouncing Light

Tell your students that there are two kinds of light; *reflected light* and *luminous light*. Objects like the sun, a fire, or fireflies are luminous; they make their own light. Other objects reflect light; it bounces off of them to move in a different direction. The moon is a good example of reflected light, it does not make its own light like the sun does, but reflects light from the sun.

When light hits an opaque object, it can't go through the object, but it has to go somewhere; it doesn't just disappear. Some of the light bounces off the opaque object and becomes *reflected light* and some of the light is absorbed by the object and converted into heat. Dark objects absorb more light and convert more heat than light objects.

Activity:

Fill two clear glasses with the exact same amount of water. Put enough drops of blue food-coloring in one glass to make it <u>very</u> dark-colored. Place both glasses outside on a flat surface in bright sunlight. Wait about one hour and measure the temperatures of the liquid in both glasses. The liquid in the glass with the dark blue water should be warmer than the water in the glass without the food coloring. This is because the darker water absorbed some of the light and it turned into heat.

Tell your students that a mirror reflects (bounces back) a lot of light, so much that it bounces back practically all of the light that hits it.

Activity:

*Take a small mirror and use it to reflect spots of light around the room. Point out to your students that the light is bouncing off the mirror and going toward where the spots of light are. Now place the mirror down on a flat surface, turn the lights off, and shine a small flashlight into the mirror. Notice where the reflection appears and what the angle of it is in comparison to the angle you are holding the flashlight at. Try holding the flashlight at different angles so that you can see that changing the angle of the flashlight changes the angle of the reflected light from the mirror. The angle between an imaginary line perpendicular to the reflective surface and the path of the beam of light is called the **Angle of Incidence**. The angle between the same imaginary line and the path of the reflected beam of light is called the **Angle of Reflection**. When the Angle of Incidence and the Angle of Reflection are equal, it means that the surface the light is hitting is very smooth and mirror-like.*

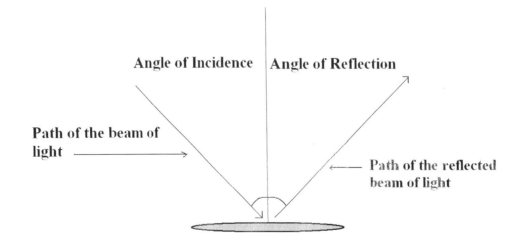

Tell your students that our eyes work by seeing reflected light--light that is bouncing off of the objects around us--which also gets bounced to our eyes. When we see an object our eyes are actually recording the light that is bouncing off of it. Everything we see is because of reflected light bouncing around.

Activity:

Now tell your students that periscopes use mirrors to bounce reflections from one mirror to another, enabling someone to see in the second mirror what is reflected in the first. They can use a periscope to peer around a door and see what is on the other side without going there themselves, or to look over something like a table while they are under it.

Take a paper towel roll and cut it so that if you are looking at it from the side, it looks like the diagram below. Please note how far the cuts go through the tube.

Now take some small mirrors and tape them into the openings like this:

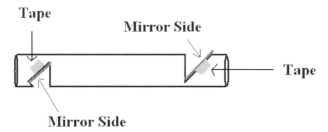

The more the mirrors fill the openings, the better the periscope will work. You can purchase small mirrors where crafts are sold. If you can't find any mirrors that are the correct size, use the largest ones that you can find that will fit, and place them in the <u>middle</u> of their respective slots. Make sure that the tape does not cover the mirror. Attach the tape to the edges of the mirrors and wrap it around the tube. Your students might want to decorate their periscopes when they are finished.

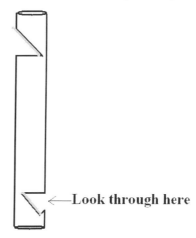

Part 4: The Speed of Light and Refraction

Remind your students that in the chapter titled "Force and Motion" they learned that the Italian scientist Galileo Galilei is sometimes called "The Father of Modern Science" because he used experiments to prove his theories. In one of his experiments Galileo tried to measure the speed of light by standing on a hilltop one mile away from a friend who was standing on another hilltop. He thought that if he flashed a lantern from the hill, his friend on the other hill could flash his lantern when he saw the light from Galileo's lantern, and that he could then measure the time it took between the flashes to come up with the speed of light. While this was a good idea, it unfortunately didn't work because light travels so fast through air (186,282 miles per second), that they just couldn't measure it. It wasn't until about three hundred years later that scientists were able to figure out how to measure the speed of light.

Activity:

Tell your students that the next time they are in a thunderstorm, count the seconds between when they see the lightning and hear the thunder. Since light appears almost instantaneously and sound travels at about 1 mile every 5 seconds, they will see the lightning first and hear the thunder later. They can calculate how far they are from the lightning by counting the seconds between the thunder and lightning and dividing them by 5. So, if they count 10 seconds between the thunder and lightning, they are only 10 divided by 5, or 2 miles away from where the lightning struck. If they want to see what the distance is in kilometers, they should divide by 3. This activity should not be done outdoors, because if there is thunder and lightning outside, they should be inside!

Tell your students that while light can travel very fast through air, it does not travel as quickly through other substances. When light that is traveling through air hits another substance, such as water, it changes direction, or bends. This bending of light is called ***refraction.***

Activity:

Take a jar or glass with straight sides and fill about one third of it with water. Now pour a layer of cooking oil in the glass that takes up about one third more of the glass. Let the oil settle a bit to form a separate layer. Place a straw into the glass. When you look at the glass straight on, you should see something like this:

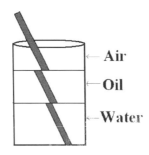

The straw looks like it is cut in three places because light travels at different speeds through the air, oil, and water. When the light traveling through the air hit the oil, it bent differently than when the light traveling through the air hit the water.

Part 5: Splitting Light

Activity:

Tell your students that what they see as white light is actually a mixture of different colors of light that when added together form white light.

Take a blank CD or DVD and shine a flashlight on it. You should be able to see a rainbow in the CD (you might have to move the flashlight around a little to see it). You have now split white light into some of its various colors! Ask your students if they know of anything else that splits light into its separate colors (rain or mist to make a rainbow). When white light from the sun hits raindrops in the air, the various colored rays of light within the white light are refracted at different angles, splitting them apart from each other.

Activity:

Another really neat way to show that white light is made up of colored light is to take three flashlights that shine with about the same brightness and, using a rubber band, cover the front of one with three pieces of green cellophane, cover the front of another with three pieces of blue cellophane, and cover the third with three pieces of red cellophane (if you have particularly dark cellophane, you might want to try two pieces). Explain to your students that mixing colored light is different from mixing colored paint. With paint, the primary colors are red, blue, and yellow. Using these colors you can mix them together to get all of the other colors. However with light, the primary colors needed to get all of the other colors are red, blue, and green.

Now go into a dark room with a white wall. If you don't have a white wall, use a large piece of white poster board. Point the red flashlight and the green flashlight at the white wall or poster board so that their beams overlap each other in the middle. The spot where the two beams of light overlap should be yellow.*

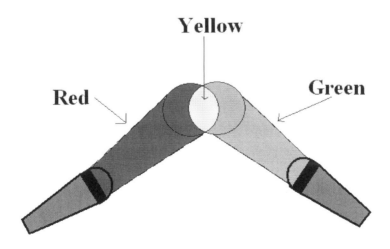

Sometimes the cellophane isn't exactly the correct shades of red, green, or blue to get the exact colors in this experiment. If you have that problem, the most important part of the experiment is the last part, where you show that all of the colors together make white, so make sure that the cellophane you have works for that part of the experiment. You can also try adding or subtracting layers of cellophane of the various colors to see if that helps.

Next do the same thing with the blue and green flashlight. In this case the place where the beams overlap should be cyan (a light blue):

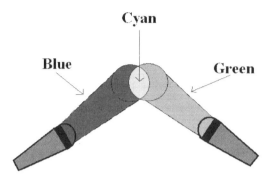

Now, do the same thing with the blue and red flashlight. The place where the beams overlap should be magenta:

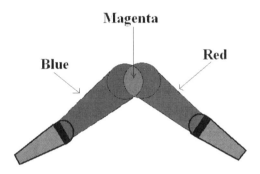

Finally, shine all three lights at the same spot. The place where the beams meet should be white, or very close to it. This is because, as we learned earlier, white light is actually beams of light of different colors mixed together.

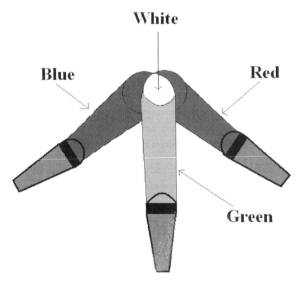

Part 6: How We See Color

Tell your students that the colored lights that make up white light are actually waves of light, somewhat like waves in an ocean. Each color of light has a different length between the tops of the waves. Red light is longer between the top of one wave to the next than blue light:

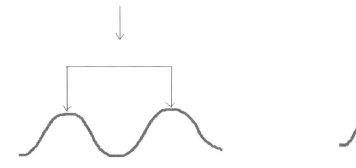

Distance from the top of one red light wave to the next

Distance from the top of one blue light wave to the next

Now tell your students that when white light hits an object, some of the light is absorbed by the object, and some of the light is reflected off (bounced off) of the object. The light that is reflected off of the object is the light that we see. If the light that is reflected off an object is blue, you will see the object as blue. If the light that is reflected off of an object is red, you will see that object as red, etc…. We cannot see the light that the object absorbs.

Test for Light and Color

1) How does light travel?
    a. 90 degrees from its point of origin
    b. 360 degrees from its point of origin
    c. In a straight line from its point of origin
    d. Backwards from its point of origin

2) An opaque object lets:
    a. no light through it
    b. all light through it
    c. some light through it

3) A translucent object lets:
    a. no light through it
    b. all light through it
    c. some light through it

4) When an object absorbs light it converts it into:
    a. cold air
    b. transparent light
    c. opaque light
    d. heat

5) When an object reflects light it is:
    a. bouncing it back
    b. absorbing it
    c. converting it to energy
    d. converting it to heat

6) The Angle of Reflection is equal to the….
    a. Angle of Refraction
    b. Angle of Incidence
    c. Right Angle
    d. Oblique Angle

7) Light travels:
     a. 186 miles per second
     b. 1862 miles per second
     c. 18,628 miles per second
     d. 186,282 miles per second

8) Refraction happens when:
     a. Light is traveling through the air and never stops.
     b. Light is traveling through the air and hits another substance.
     c. Light is traveling through the air and changes color.
     d. Light is traveling through the air and is absorbed by an opaque object.

9) White light is made up of:
     a. Only red and blue light
     b. All the colors of the rainbow
     c. Oxygen molecules
     d. Only green and purple light

10) The wavelengths of blue light are:
     a. Shorter than the wavelength of red light
     b. Longer than the wavelength of red light
     c. The same as the wavelength of red light
     d. Both a and c above

Chapter 20: Plants II
Ages 8-13

Materials Needed for this Unit

Two clear plastic bags
Masking tape
Eight identical small planting pots
Potting soil
Sponge
Scissors
Spray bottle
Paper
Markers or colored pencils
Carnivorous plant
Live flower; see Part 7 of this unit for more information.
Drawing paper
Spider plant with lots of runners
Contact paper
Clothesline or string
Celery
Red food coloring
Bean seeds
Two medium-sized planting pots
One or more houseplants from the list of plants in Part 8 of this unit
A glass jar to root a houseplant in
Duct tape
Access to a copy machine

Part 1: Stomata

Ask your students if they remember what plants are called in a food chain (primary producers). Ask them if they remember what primary producers do (get their energy from the sun rather than by eating something else). This is one of the really neat things about most plants; they are very self-sufficient and don't need animals as a source of energy. Another neat thing about plants is that during this process of making their own food, they give off oxygen, which we need to breathe. So while plants can survive perfectly well without humans, humans can't survive without plants. We call the process by which plants use carbon dioxide, water, and sunlight to make sugar *photosynthesis*.

Tell your students that plants take in the carbon dioxide that they need for photosynthesis through tiny holes in their leaves called **stomata.** These tiny holes are also where plants release the oxygen that they don't need back into the atmosphere.

Ask your students if they remember what the purpose of the stem of a plant is (structure and transport of nutrients). The transport system of the plant moves water from the ground and brings it to the leaves where photosynthesis takes place. However, this also presents a problem for the plants. The water that they need is now in the same leaves that have stomata in them to take in carbon dioxide. When the stomata are open to take in the carbon dioxide, they can also release water vapor, something that the plant needs for photosynthesis. This releasing of water vapor is called *transpiration,* and plants have some neat mechanisms for minimizing it, which we will talk about later in this unit.

Activity:
Take two pieces of celery with the leaves attached. Cut about ½ inch off the bottoms and place the stalks with the leaves attached in separate glasses with ½ cup of water in each glass. Add forty drops of red food coloring to one of the glasses. After awhile, you will be able to see that the leaves on the piece of celery in the glass with the food coloring have a red tint to them. A few hours later, the leaves will turn an even darker red. Point out to your students that the red water moved from the water in the glass, up the stems, and into the leaves. The leaves of the celery in the glass without the food coloring will remain green.

Activity:
Take two clear plastic bags and some masking tape outside and find a tree with leaves. Tape one of the bags over a clump of leaves on a branch with masking tape, so that the tape is wrapped <u>tightly</u> around the branch and the leaves are inside the bag. You want to make sure that you tape it so that no air can get out of the bag. Take the other bag and fill it with air (<u>not</u> by breathing in it) so that it is about the same size as the bag you tied over the leaves. Tape that bag to the tree in the same way, except without any leaves inside of it, making sure that the opening is taped tightly shut. Check the two bags periodically and compare them. The bag with the leaves should have more water in it than the bag without the leaves. Remind your children that this is because plants release water vapor and that is called transpiration. Tell your students that transpiration is responsible for about ten percent of all of the water vapor in the air and that an acre of corn can transpire 3000-4000 gallons of water in a day!

Part 2: Light and Photosynthesis

Point out to your students that you have now talked about two things that plants need for photosynthesis; carbon dioxide and water. Ask them if they remember what the third thing was (sunlight). Remind them how they learned in the chapter on Light and Color how light that is reflected is bounced off of an object and light that is absorbed turns into heat energy. Plants have special units in their cells called **chloroplasts** that capture this light energy and use it in photosynthesis. The pigment in chloroplasts that absorbs the light is called **chlorophyll.** Because chlorophyll absorbs the other colors in the light but bounces back the green light, chlorophyll is what gives plants their green color.

Activity:
Tell your students that they are going to do some more experiments dealing with plants, but that first they need to know something about doing proper scientific experiments. Most experiments should have something called a **control.** *A control is what a scientist compares his or her experimental subject to. For example, if you want to test what happens to a plant if you don't water it, you will need at least two plants; one that you water normally and one that you don't water. The one that you water normally is the control, and you would compare how it looks to the plant that you don't water. In this type of experiment, the two subjects need to be exactly the same except for the thing that you are testing. They will need to be exactly the same type of plant, the same size plant, in the same amount of soil, in the same type of pot, sitting in the same area of a room. That way, you know that the amount of water given to the plants is the <u>only</u> thing different about them. If, for example, you put one plant in the sun, and one in the shade, you wouldn't know for sure if it was the water difference affecting the plant or the sun difference.*
Take four bean seeds and plant them in four identical pots with the exact same amount of soil. Place two in a place where they will never see the sun (it is important that they are in a place where it is <u>completely</u> dark), and the other two in a place where they will. Water them with exactly the same amount of water. Observe the differences as they grow. The plants in the dark should be more yellow than the plants in the light. Their stems might be longer because they will be trying to reach a light source, but they should be less healthy-looking. Point out to your students how the plants in the dark are not growing as well as the plants in the light, because plants need sunlight for photosynthesis.

Tell your students that the chemical equation describing photosynthesis is as follows:

$$6CO_2 + 6H_2O + \text{light energy} = C_6H_{12}O_6 + 6O_2$$

CO_2 is carbon dioxide, H_2O is water, $C_6H_{12}O_6$ is a sugar molecule, and O_2 is oxygen. If you wrote this in words, it would read "6 carbon dioxide molecules, plus 6 water molecules, plus light energy equals one sugar molecule plus 6 oxygen molecules. Point to each part of the equation as you say to the students the following: "Using its stomata, the plant takes in six carbon dioxide molecules. Using its roots, the plant takes in six water molecules. Using the chlorophyll in its leaves, the plant absorbs light energy. When it puts all of these things together, the plant produces one sugar molecule and six oxygen molecules." Point out to your students that it's a fairly easy equation to memorize; there are six molecules of everything, except for the sugar molecule.

Part 3: Respiration

Ask your students if they knew that plants not only take in carbon dioxide and give off oxygen, they also take in oxygen and give off carbon dioxide! Most people know that plants give off oxygen, but lots of people don't know that they also give off carbon dioxide. Luckily for us, since we breathe oxygen, they give off more oxygen than carbon dioxide. Plants do this in a process called ***cellular respiration***, which is basically the opposite of photosynthesis. Here is the chemical equation for plant respiration using oxygen:

$$C_6H_{12}O_6 + 6O_2 = 6CO_2 + 6H_2O + energy$$

Notice that it uses the exact same molecules as photosynthesis; the molecules are just on the opposite sides of the equation. Using photosynthesis, plants take energy from the sun to make sugar molecules which they store for future use. When a plant needs energy to grow, it breaks down the sugar molecules using respiration which releases the energy it needs. Basically a sugar molecule is the way plants store energy from the sun. Another way to think of this is that photosynthesis is when the plants make the sugar and respiration is when plants "eat" the sugar.

One place that respiration happens in plants is in the roots. For a plant to grow, the roots need to grow, and growing takes energy. The roots get this energy by breaking down the sugar molecules that were produced using photosynthesis. Look again at the formula for respiration above. For the roots to release the energy in a sugar molecule, they need two things. Ask your students if they can tell from this formula what they are (a sugar molecule and oxygen). The roots get the oxygen from air trapped in the soil.

Activity:

You will need to prepare for this experiment about a week ahead of time by planting four bean seeds and giving them time to develop their first leaves. Place two of the bean plants in a bowl of water and place the other two next to them, but not in the bowl of water. The bowl should be about as tall as the pots that the plants are in. Completely fill the bowl with water, and purposefully over-water the plants that are in the bowl every day. Water the other plants a normal amount. Eventually, the plants in the bowl will start to die (you can keep them from completely dying by letting them dry out when the experiment is over). Explain to your students that this is because when you over-watered the plants in the bowl, it drove the oxygen from the soil so that their roots couldn't absorb it. The roots need oxygen for respiration. When they couldn't get it, the plants started to die.

Part 4: Plant Adaptations

Ask your students if they remember why the stomata cause a bit of a problem for plants (they release water vapor into the air that the plant needs for photosynthesis). Tell your students that there are usually more stomata on the undersides of leaves than on the tops. Ask them if they can figure out why that might be (the undersides of the leaves don't have direct sunlight on them, so the water won't evaporate out of the stomata as much).

Activity:

Take a sponge and get it wet. Find a tree or some other place outside where you can attach the sponge so that the topside is facing the sun and the bottom side faces away from the sun. You could try and stick the sponge onto a branch of the tree, or duct tape it flat onto the top of a railing so that about half of it hangs out into the air (be careful where you use the duct tape though, it tends to rip the paint off of things). Every five to ten minutes, check the sponge and compare the amount of moisture on the top of it to the amount of moisture on the bottom of it. The top should dry out faster than the bottom, because it is in the direct sun, while the bottom is protected from the sun by the top. Point out to your students that this is why plants tend to have more stomata on the underside of their leaves, to help keep the water inside them from evaporating out.

Tell your students that plants that live in the rainforest have different problems to deal with than plants that live in the desert. The rainforest is hot and wet, a perfect place for fungus to grow. Leaves in the rainforest need to be able to shed water off of them to keep fungus from growing on them. Also, the rainforest is very shady, so rainforest leaves need to be able to capture as much sunlight as they can. On the other hand, plants in the desert are exposed to lots of sunlight and need to keep their stomata from letting the water they've absorbed evaporate out. One way desert plants do this is by keeping their stomata closed during the day when it is hottest.

Activity:

On the following page are two shapes. Make a copy of the page and stick it between two sheets of contact paper. Cut out the shapes and fold the triangular-shaped one down the middle on the dotted line, and then open it slightly. Using masking tape, hang the shapes outside from a clothesline or string. Make sure that they are hanging straight up and down, not at an angle. Take a spray bottle and spray each leaf, one after the other with about the same amount of water. Do this more than once and observe what happens between each spraying. Notice which of them starts dripping water first and which keeps dripping water the most. Does one of them seem to have more water on it after the dripping stops? Point out to your students that leaf shapes affect how much water is shed off the leaf.

Now ask your students if they think small leaves or large leaves would work better in the desert. What about in the rainforest? In general, small leaves work well in the desert because they have less surface area for the leaves to lose water from. Large leaves are better in the rainforest because they have more surface area to absorb sunlight on.

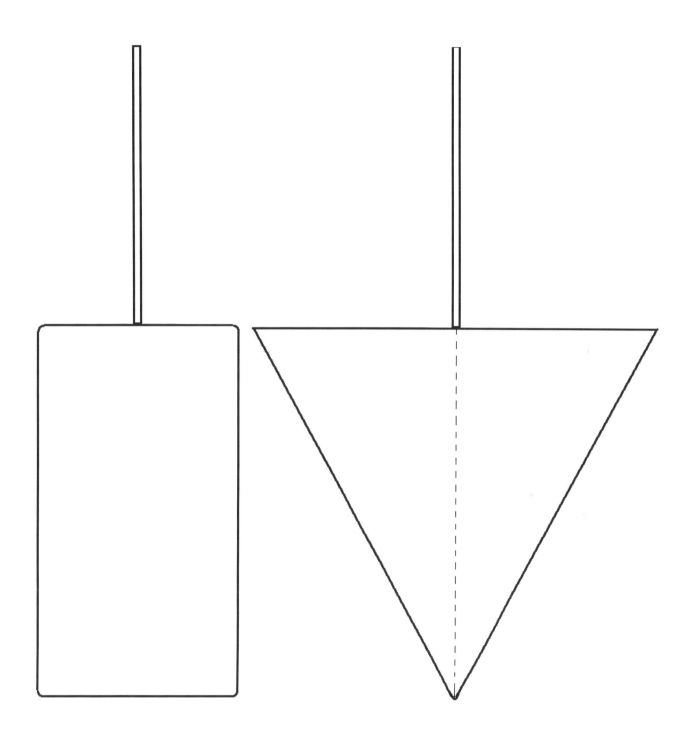

Activity:

Ask your students if they think they would be a healthy person if they ate <u>only</u> sugar. Tell your students that plants make the sugars they need for energy from photosynthesis, but just like us, they need other nutrients to grow and stay healthy. Some of these important nutrients for plants are nitrogen, potassium, and phosphorus. However, plants sometimes live in areas where the soil doesn't contain all of the nutrients they need. Carnivorous plants have found an interesting way to adapt to these types of soils. They get their nutrition by capturing small animals such as insects or protozoa.

If you can, show your students a live carnivorous plant. If it is a Venus flytrap, show them how it eats by gently placing a dead bug inside of one of its traps and watching it close up. You may need to wiggle the bug around a bit to get it to work. Tell your students that there are over 600 species of carnivorous plants and they have a variety of methods of catching prey. Some, like the Venus flytrap, snap shut. Others, like the Pitcher plant, are pitfall traps, where the insects fall in an open "container" formed of leaves. Inside the container, the plant secretes digestive enzymes that dissolve the insect so that it can be "eaten" by the plant. There are also plants like the sundew that act like flypaper, with sticky tentacles that insects get trapped on.

Give your students a piece of paper and have them design their own carnivorous plant. Tell them that it can eat whatever they choose, birds, fish, insects, even people, as-long-as it eats meat.

Part 5: Parts of a Flower

Activity:

Give each of your students a real flower and ask them to pretend that they are scientists who have discovered a new flower. They need to draw a detailed diagram of it to show the scientific world their new discovery. After they have drawn their flowers, show them the diagram on the following page and see if they included all of the parts of a flower listed in their diagram. Have them label their diagrams like the one on the following page (they won't be able to see the ovules inside the carpel). When choosing flowers for this project, choose simple ones where the parts below are easy to identify.

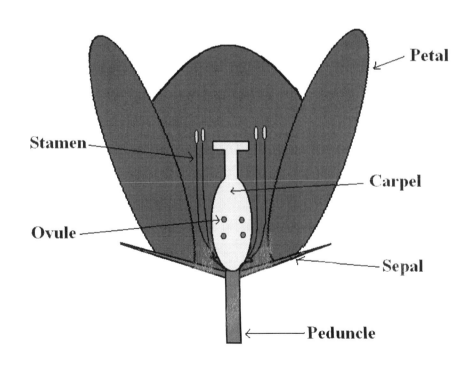

Have your students look closely at the stamen of their real flower. The little things on the top of each stamen are called anthers and they contain pollen. Tell your students that when honeybees come to a flower to collect nectar, they brush up against the anthers and the pollen sticks to them. When they move on to another flower the pollen goes with them. At the next flower, while the bee is moving around looking for nectar, some of the pollen it is carrying will fall off into the top of the carpel of the flower. Inside the carpel part of the pollen will join with the ovules and develop into seeds.

Part 6: Growing Plants without Seeds

Ask your students if they know what clones are (an exact copy of the parent). Sometimes, instead of having young that grow from seeds, plants will make clones of themselves. One way they do this is by sending out runners (like long stems) with baby plants on them. These baby plants will start growing away from the original plant and eventually the runner stem will wither away and the new plant will be separated from its parent plant.

Activity:

Show your students a spider plant with lots of runners. Have them cut one off with about two inches of the runner still attached and place it in a pot with dirt in it. Do not plant it so deep that the leaves are covered, just enough to hold it in the soil. Water the new spider plant regularly.

Tell your students that another way that plants can grow without seeds is from portions of their roots or stems.

Activity:

*You can grow clones of certain varieties of plants by placing a portion of them in water. Cut an end off of a plant that includes three points where the leaves come out of a branch. These points are called **nodes**. A node is the point on a plant stem where a branch, leaf, flower cluster, or root grows out from the stem.*

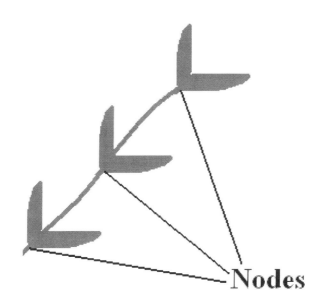

Trim the leaves off of the bottom two nodes and place the cutting in a glass jar with enough water in it to cover the two nodes that you trimmed, making sure that the leaf or leaves of the remaining node are not under water. Place the plant in an area where it gets some sunlight, but is not in direct sunlight. Every few days, pour out some of the water and add clean water. After a few weeks, little roots will form from the nodes that are underwater. Once there are a number of roots that are at least one inch long, transfer the cutting into a pot with soil in it. Some good plants to try this with are listed below; you can try growing more than one of them to see which work the best. Be patient, it can take a few weeks for the roots to form.

Cane-type Begonias	*Cissus (Grape Ivy)*
Coleus	*Ti Plant*
Creeping Fig	*Christmas Cactus*
Baby's Tears	*Impatiens*
Heart Leaf	*Swedish Ivy*
Wandering Jew	*Ivy Philodendrum*

The Christmas Cactus mentioned above will not need any of the leaves cut off. The nodes of the Christmas Cactus are where the joints are between the sections. Cut an end off of the cactus that has at least three nodes and place the bottom two under water.

Be sure to point out to your students that these plants were rooted from the stem of the original plant!

Test For Plants

1) What are plants called in a food chain?
   a) primary producers
   b) secondary producers
   c) tertiary producers
   d) predators

2) Photosynthesis is the process where plants….
   a) make protein
   b) make nitrogen
   c) make sugar
   d) make vitamins

3) For photosynthesis, plants need…..
   a) oxygen
   b) sugar
   c) all of the above
   d) carbon dioxide

4) Transpiration is when…
   a) plants use energy from the sun to make sugar
   b) plants release water vapor through their stomata
   c) plants convert sugar to energy
   d) the water transport system of the plant

5) Respiration is…..
   a) when plants take energy from the sun to make sugar
   b) when plants take water from the ground to make sugar
   c) when plants convert sugar to energy
   d) when plants give off oxygen

6)) A control is important to have in an experiment because…
   a. If you don't have control, everything goes haywire.
   b. It helps keep the experiment tidy.
   c. Nothing would happen in the experiment without it.
   d. You need it to compare your results with to see what is different.

7) Plants need the following to survive…
   a) carbon dioxide
   b) sunlight
   c) water
   d) all of the above

8) Stomata are…
   a) where plants take in water from the ground
   b) tiny hairs on leaves that sense light
   c) where plants take in carbon dioxide
   d) tiny hairs on stems that sense light

9) In a flower, pollen is produced on the…
   a) petals
   b) stamen
   c) carpel
   d) ovule

10) In a flower, seeds are produced in the….
   a) petals
   b) stamen
   c) carpel
   d) peduncle

Answer Sheet for Tests

Chapter 11, Insects: 1-c, 2-d, 3-a, 4-d, 5-b, 6-c, 7-c, 8-a, 9-c, 10-b

Chapter 12, Microscopes and Invisible Creatures: 1-b, 2-a, 3-d, 4-c, 5-d, 6-d, 7-c, 8-a, 9-b, 10-c

Chapter 13, Atoms and Molecules: 1-c, 2-a, 3-b, 4-d, 5-a, 6-c, 7-b, 8-d, 9-b, 10-c

Chapter 14, Matter: 1-c, 2-b, 3-d, 4-a, 5-c, 6-b, 7-a, 8-b, 9-d, 10-c

Chapter 15, Chemistry Fun: 1-b, 2-c, 3-a, 4-c, 5-d, 6-a, 7-b, 8-d, 9-c, 10-a

Chapter 16, Weather: 1-a, 2-c, 3-b, 4-d, 5-c, 6-b, 7-a, 8-c, 9-b, 10-d

Chapter 17, Force and Motion: 1-d, 2-a, 3-b, 4-c, 5-c, 6-a, 7-d, 8-b, 9-d, 10-b

Chapter 18, Simple Machines: 1-b, 2-a, 3-a, 4-Inclined plane, wedge, screw, lever, pulley, wheel and axle, 5-b, 6-c, 7-c, 8-a, 9-c, 10-b

Chapter 19, Light and Color: 1-c, 2-a, 3-c, 4-d, 5-a, 6-b, 7)-d, 8-b, 9-b, 10-a

Chapter 20, Plants II: 1-a, 2-c, 3-d, 4-b, 5-c, 6-d, 7-d, 8-c, 9-b, 10-c

Answers to Camouflage Worksheet

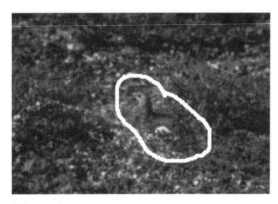

Ptarmigan

Nighthawk or Nightjar

Frogfish

Crab

Francolin with Chicks

Green Anole

Answer Sheet for the Electron Shell Worksheet

Draw in the electrons for the following atoms. Start with the shell closest to the nucleus. Fill up each shell completely before moving on to the next.

Shell one is called **K** and has no more than 2 electrons
Shell two is called **L** and has no more than 8 electrons
Shell three is called **M** and has no more than 18 electrons
Shell four is called **N** and has no more than 32 electrons

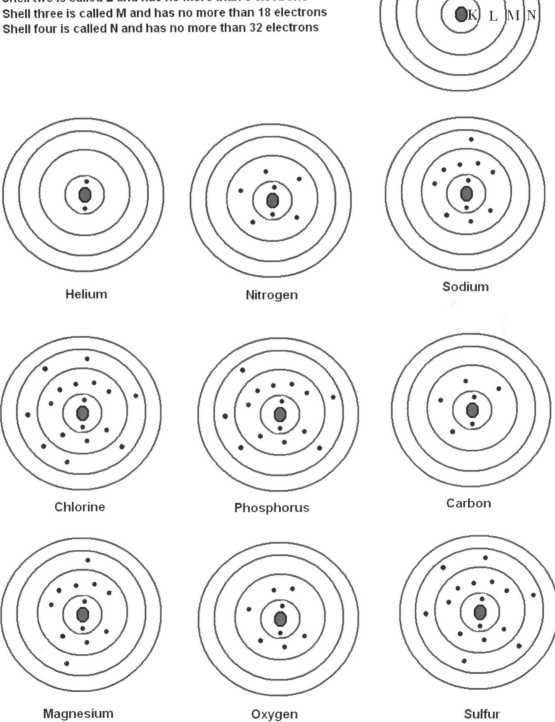

Helium   Nitrogen   Sodium

Chlorine   Phosphorus   Carbon

Magnesium   Oxygen   Sulfur

Made in the USA
Lexington, KY
31 December 2014